We're from Jazz
Festschrift in Honor of Nicholas V. Galichenko

Also by New Academia Publishing

RUSSIAN FUTURISM: A History, by Vladimir Markov

WORDS IN REVOLUTION: Russian Futurist Manifestoes 1912-1928
A. Lawton and H. Eagle, eds., trs.

IMAGING RUSSIA 2000: Film and Facts, by Anna Lawton

BEFORE THE FALL: Soviet Cinema in the Gorbachev Years, by Anna Lawton

NEW PERSPECTIVES ON SOVIETIZATION IN CENTRAL AND EASTERN EUROPE AFTER WORLD WAR II, Balázs Apor, Péter Apor and E. A. Rees, eds.

THE INNER ADVERSARY: The Struggle against Philistinism as the Moral Mission of the Russian Intelligentsia, by Timo Vihavainen

RED ATTACK WHITE RESISTANCE, by Peter Kenez

RED ADVANCE WHITE DEFEAT, by Peter Kenez

ASPECTS OF BALKAN CULTURE: Social, Political, and Literary Perceptions
by Jelena Milojković-Djurić

SLAVIC THINKERS OR THE CREATION OF POLITIES: Intellectual History and Political Thought in Central Europe and the Balkans in the 19th Century
by Josette Baer

Fiction

ON THE WAY TO RED SQUARE, by Julieta Almeida Rodrigues

Memoirs

THROUGH DARK DAYS AND WHITE NIGHTS, by Naomi F. Collins

JOURNEYS THROUGH VANISHING WORLDS, by Abraham Brumberg

www.newacademia.com

We're from Jazz
Festschrift in Honor of Nicholas V. Galichenko

edited by
Megan Swift and Serhy Yekelchyk

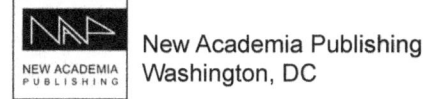

New Academia Publishing
Washington, DC

Copyright © 2010 by Megan Swift and Serhy Yekelchyk

New Academia Publishing, 2010

All rights reserved. No part of this book may be reproduced or transmitted in any form or by any means, electronic or mechanical, including photocopying, recording, or by any information storage and retrieval system.

Printed in the United States of America

Library of Congress Control Number: 2010922202
ISBN 978-0-9823867-7-4 paperback (alk. paper)

New Academia Publishing, LLC
P.O. Box 27420
Washington, DC 20038-7420
www.newacademia.com - info@newacademia.com

Contents

Introduction
Megan Swift and Serhy Yekelchyk   1

1. Bricolage in Bronze: The Bronze Horseman and the Petersburg Text
Megan Swift   5

2. Going to the Movies under Stalin: A Glimpse into Cultural Practices and Societal Attitudes in Prewar Soviet Ukraine
Serhy Yekelchyk   15

3. Confronting Antisemitism and Antifeminism in Turn-of-the-Century Vienna: Grete Meisel-Hess and the Modernist Discourses on Hysteria
Helga Thorson   51

4. Goethe and Schubert: An Eclectic Affinity. The Motif of the Wanderer in Schubert's Songs to Texts by Goethe
Angelika Arend   73

5. Полифункциональные лексемы как новое явление в грамматике русского языка
Julia Rochtchina   87

6. A Culture of Suffering: Isaak Babel and *How It Was Done in Odessa*
Regan Treewater   103

7. Intertextualität und Vampirismus bei Patrick Süskind und Adolf Muschg
Peter Gölz 121

8. Vancouver Island Croatians in the Coal Strike of 1912-1914, and the Internment Operations of 1914–1918 in Canada
Želimir B. Juričić 133

9. Evtushenko and the Legacy of "Babii Iar"
Amy Safarik 161

10. Converging Lines in Learning Languages Literacies and Learner Theory—Renewed Perspective, or Still a Vanishing Point?
Peter Liddell 179

11. Драматическое присутствие в повести Л.Н. Толстого «Смерть Ивана Ильича»
Andrew A. Donskov 193

About the Authors 204

Introduction

Megan Swift and Serhy Yekelchyk

Specialist in Russian literature and film, talented jazz musician, beloved teacher, community pillar, respected colleague, bon vivant—Nicholas V. Galichenko is, in the true sense of the Russian phrase, a "wide soul" (*shirokaia dusha*). The present collection of essays reflects the multi-dimensionality of the man it is intended to honour in various ways. Firstly, it covers the broad range of interests to be found at the University of Victoria's Department of Germanic and Slavic Studies, where Nick retired from a successful 37-year career in 2008. These interests extend over several centuries and large portions of Europe and Russia, from Stalinist culture to Austrian feminism, St. Petersburg monumental sculpture to vampire imagery. Secondly, this Festschrift reflects the wide network of colleagues and students with whom Nick associated. Contributors to this collection include former UVic colleagues like Andrew Donskov, who has gone on to a distinguished career at the University of Ottawa, current colleagues Julia Rochtchina, Megan Swift and Serhy Yekelchyk, all of whom began their careers under Nick's tutelage, and a selection of students (Amy Safarik and Regan Treewater) who have gone on to pursue academic careers in Russian literature after being inspired by Nick's courses on nineteenth and twentieth-century literature. Other contributors include Peter Gölz, Helga Thorson, Peter Liddell, Angelika Arend and Želimir B. Juričić.

The title of this collection, which refers to the 1983 film *We're From Jazz (My iz dzhaza)*, expresses themes from Nick's life both inside and outside of the university—his talent as a jazz musician, and his love of Russian and Soviet cinema. Like jazz music itself, this collection of essays is eclectic and broad-based, with something that will appeal to readers of diverse scholarly interests. It is fitting that the film's sequel, *We're from Jazz 2*, will arrive at the same moment that Nick is enjoying a new chapter in his life, and just as this Festschrift in his honour is published.

Nicholas Galichenko was born in Shanghai, China, but grew up in Vancouver, Canada. His parents, Vladimir and Lidia, ensured that both Nick and his sister, Tania, honoured the Russian philological tradition by learning fluent Russian and receiving an excellent education. Russian poetry and prose were respected and loved in the Galichenko family, and in fact Vladimir Galichenko emigrated from China with the library of the largest Russian bookstore in Shanghai. In the family tradition, Nick has carried Russian literature with him throughout his life as well. Nick studied at the University of British Columbia and at McGill University (where he completed a dissertation on the work of Mikhail Bulgakov) and then accepted a faculty position at the University of Victoria in 1971. Russian Studies, part of the university since the days of Victoria College, existed first as part of a Modern Languages department, then Slavonic and Oriental Studies, then independently, and most recently as part of Germanic and Slavic Studies. Throughout all these name changes, Nick maintained an unchanging commitment to students and to Russian language and literature.

When Nick joined the department in 1971, his teaching load consisted of four full-year courses, the equivalent of eight courses under the current system. Yet he rose to the challenge, completing his Ph.D. dissertation in 1976 and publishing a series of articles on Bulgakov's early prose and plays. By the early 1980s, the teaching load decreased slightly, but the very existence of the Russian program came under threat because of low enrolments at the time when the University was considering cuts. In order to boost student numbers, Nick developed a new, high-enrolment course on the Soviet cinema, Russian 304. No fewer than 123 students took it the first time it was offered in the spring of 1981; this number rose to 146 the following year. The introduction of this course, now divided into two and complemented by other popular offerings on Russian cinema, determined the profile of our program for decades to come. In making this change, Nick was guided by his lifelong love of Russian film, as well as his past experience of dubbing Russian documentaries for a New York film distributor. But as it happens so often in academia, the new course also inspired its creator to branch into a new field of scholarship. Thus began Nick's next major research project, which in 1991 resulted in the publication of his pioneering book, *Glasnost: Soviet Cinema Responds* (University of Texas Press).

The Russian program that exists at UVic today, including British Columbia's only fully fledged Russian language program, a wide range of courses in Russian literature, culture and cinema, and an active travel abroad program, has very much been shaped by Nick. In 2005 the Department paid tribute to Nick's many contributions by naming a prestigious travel abroad scholarship in his honour. This scholarship originated from a fundraising drive in the late 1980s to establish an earlier student exchange program with the Soviet republic of Georgia. Nick, who at the time was researching Georgian cinema, was the heart and soul of the campaign. Now named after him, the travel-abroad scholarship supports UVic students, who travel to the former Soviet Union to study Russian. In addition to this award, Nick's retirement in 2008 was marked by the inauguration of the Vladimir and Lidia Galichenko Scholarship established in honour of Nick's parents. This time, Megan Swift coordinated the fundraising campaign to which a number of Nick's colleagues, students, friends, and relatives contributed. By far the largest contributions, however, came from Nick and his partner Ellen Pollard, and from his sister and brother-in-law, Tania and Bill Little. The two families continue making very generous annual gifts to the Galichenko Endowment, which will support student scholarships as well as the Galichenko memorial lectures in Russian Studies. The Galichenko family legacy has thus become a part of our Russian program in perpetuity.

Alongside his academic career, Nick found time to nurture another love: music. True to his generous nature, Nick devoted himself not only to his own pursuit of music, but also made possible the enjoyment of countless others in the community. He purchased an entire suite of balalaikas at Expo '67 in Montreal and then donated them all to the Victoria Balalaika Orchestra so that generations of students could learn to play this beautiful instrument. At the same time, a talented jazz musician in his own right, Nick became a familiar face at jazz venues on the east and west coast, playing with many groups over the years. In retirement, Nick's talents as a jazz keyboardist have become even more in demand.

Although his booming voice is now rarely heard in UVic's corridors, Nick remains a notable presence in the lives of his younger colleagues and students. A great mentor, generous friend, and formidable host, his and Ellen's home on Belmont Avenue is an unofficial center of Russian community life in Victoria. We all wish Nick many years of happy and fulfilling life in retirement.

1
Bricolage in Bronze:
The Bronze Horseman Monument and the Petersburg Text

Megan Swift

From Tsar to Avatar

A recent monograph on the Bronze Horseman likens the monument, with its rupturing duality, to a giant question mark.[1] In fact, the Bronze Horesman may be better conceived as a quotation mark, open but not closed. Commissioned by Catherine the Great, sculpted by Etienne-Maurice Falconet and erected in one of the central squares of St. Petersburg in 1782, the massive metallic tribute to Peter the Great took on its famous name following the publication of Alexander Pushkin's *poema The Bronze Horseman*. Recently, however, scholars have argued that the crucial moment for the Bronze Horseman was not Pushkin's 1833 publication, which both 'named' and mythologized the monument according to the poet's image of a crushing bronze hoof extended over Russia. Rather, new research has placed the true 'birth' of the Bronze Horseman in the early twentieth century, when symbolist poetics began to sift through the "rather motley" [*dovol'no pestroe*] collection of nineteenth-century texts written on the Petersburg theme and selected those works that would become canonical to what has become known as the Petersburg text of Russian literature.[2] It was at this time that the Bronze Horseman monument and *poema* were re-sculpted to become part of a specific modernist construct, both quotations from a self-citing master text.[3] In this way the Bronze Horseman was appointed its central role as the "hieroglyph of the Petersburg text".[4]

Re-imagining the Bronze Horseman

Pushkin scholar Andrew Kahn has also argued that, in fact, Pushkin's *The Bronze Horseman* did not make its full impact until the twentieth century.[5] This claim is based on the fact that a text fully faithful to Pushkin did not become available until the 1930s, when scholars finally replaced the Zhukovsky edition of *Mednyi vsadnik* [*The Bronze Horseman*] that had been significantly altered by the "*mednaia glava*" [bronze head], Pushkin's personal censor, Nicholas I.[6] One of the major changes perpetrated by Tsar Nicholas was the censorship of the word *kumir* [idol] in relation to the animated monument of Peter the Great. In 1836, in an effort to publish the work, Pushkin changed *kumir* to *sedok* [rider/horseman], which became *gigant* [giant] for the first full publication of the *poema* in the Zhukovsky edition of 1841.[7] Peter as *kumir na bronzevom kone* [an idol on a bronze mount] of course evokes images of pagan idolatry—of Peter as anti-Christ and iconoclast—since the monument itself affronted the Orthodox ban on human statues, considered to be graven images and therefore forbidden by the First Commandment.[8] Thanks to this Orthodox prohibition, the genre of equestrian monument, a popular European tribute to great rulers, was unknown in pre-Petrine Russia.[9] Pushkin's depiction of the animation of the Bronze Horesman connects to folk superstitions about the entrapment of the human spirit in icons and images.[10] The Russian myth theorist Antsiferov revived this theme of Peter as a "*kumir narozhdaiuschegosia novogo obschestva*" [an idol giving birth to a new society], a titan not bound by human laws, in his early twentieth-century urban mythographies.[11] It was in Antsiferov's work, that is, in the 1920s, argues Kahn, that Pushkin's *Bronze Horseman* was "restored to its central place in the Petersburg theme".[12] The present essay is a study of how the Bronze Horseman as a monument, a literary representation, a 'sacred text', and a quotation in Andrei Bely's novel *Petersburg* (1916) and Andrei Bitov's novel *Pushkin House* (1971), has shaped, and in turn been shaped by, modernist and postmodernist poetics.

The Politics of Memory

The Bronze Horseman's complex role in the Soviet politics of memory has insured its survival through the cataclysms of twentieth-century Russian history. At the outset of the Soviet era a large number of Peter statues were taken down and destroyed in accordance with Lenin's 1918 "Decree on the Removal of Statues to the Tsars and Their Servants". This decree had the power of law and was executed in haste, piecemeal, and without a governing body.[13] While the decree stated that:

> …pamiatniki…ne predstavliaiuschie interesa ni s istoricheskoi ni khudozhestvennoi storon, podlezhat sniatiu s ploschadei i ulits…[statues that do not present either historical or artistic interest are subject to removal from the squares and streets],

in fact ideological concerns trumped artistic ones, an issue exacerbated by a lack of consultation with objective, qualified experts.[14] At least five well-known St. Petersburg statues and monuments of Peter the Great were melted down or hidden in warehouses at this time.[15] The Bronze Horseman's absence from this ambitious list can only be accounted for in terms of its perception, not as an equestrian tribute to imperial glory, but as a quotation in which Pushkin's theme of the little man crushed under the iron foot of superstructure looms large. The Bronze Horseman monument is not only conceived as a visual text with a semiotic code of its own by artists and scholars of the twentieth century, but was imagined as a "living book" even in the early nineteenth century.[16] Falconet's visual, physical text and Pushkin's literary Bronze Horseman have created a palimpsest of fact and fiction to which modernist and postmodernist poetics and Soviet and post-Soviet politics have continued to add layers.

Soviet Bricolage

For the political regimes of twentieth-century Russia, the Bronze Horseman represents the so-called "usable symbolic capital" through which events, images and ideas are self-consciously appropriated and re-shaped.[17] In 1918 Lenin was strategically selecting *which* monuments and events would enter the public space as figures co-opted by the Bolsheviks, and this process was repeated after 1991, when monuments, particularly of the Stalinist era, were removed in yet another re-shaping and manipulation of the national myth. This process represents what urban geographers have called a post-structuralist approach to the politics of monuments and memory, a focus not on issues of authorship or intention in the creation of visual texts, or the interpretation of those texts, but rather an attention to the question of readership.[18] Regimes exploit the semiotics of physical and represented landscapes to create a text for the viewing public through bricolage. Levi-Strauss first introduced the concept of bricolage, or the creation of a new system of mythic meaning through recombination, in his 1962 *Le pensée sauvage*. A recent article co-authored by a geographer and a political scientist argues that during periods of political opportunity, regimes "act like bricoleurs, taking a pastiche of materials at hand to create a coherent narrative of tradition, memory and history".[19] As we shall see, the Bronze Horseman was reconfigured in this way by its Soviet bricoleurs.

The Petersburg obsession with renaming streets, squares, buildings—and of course the city itself—attests to the importance that has been assigned to the symbolic control of city spaces and public landscapes.[20] The physical context and spatial framing of monuments is critical to this process. In the late eighteenth century, the Bronze Horseman was assigned a prominent role in imperial Petersburg by making its physical site integral to the five-square architectural ensemble of central Petersburg. This site had immediate connections with the sacred as a location left vacant by the demolition of the old stone Isaakievsky Cathedral, but was created as a 'square proper' in honour of Falconet's monument. The canals that crisscrossed the area were filled in and the space was rechristened—as Peter's Square. The monument's central position was enhanced at that time by the fact that the Isaakievsky pontoon bridge, connecting Vassilievsky Island to the center, gave off directly in front of the monument.[21] A subtle and provocative spatial decision was made by Catherine the Great in having the monument face north, symbolically turning its back on the ancient Russian empire and thus underlying Catherine's continuation of the great Petrine reforms.[22]

Over a century later the Bronze Horseman managed to maintain its central spatial position throughout the savage enthusiasms of Lenin's 1918 decree and its Stalinist aftermath. Many imperial monuments were purged at this time, or, like the Alexander III monument that had once stood prominently on Vosstaniia Square, moved to a space of tertiary importance, symbolically isolated from the public sphere inside the interior courtyard of the Russian Museum (by Stalin in 1937). Instead the Soviet regime attempted more subtle manipulations of cultural meaning. The Bronze Horseman monument was left untouched—but its context was changed. The square became Decembrist Square, its new nomenclature emphasizing the Pushkinian layers of the Bronze Horseman palimpsest thanks to Pushkin's links to Decembrist circles.[23] The Bolsheviks created a symbolically dense and layered landscape out of Peter's/Senate/Decembrist Square and the Bronze Horseman was now read as a Pushkinian symbol of conflicts between rebels and authority.[24] In this new spatial and symbolic context the monument re-interpreted past defeats (the Decembrist Uprising of 1825, the Russian Revolution of 1905) in light of the victory of 1917. Pushkin's 1830 comment that Peter the Great represented "la revolution incarnée, toute a la fois Robespierre et Napoleon" [revolution incarnate, both Robespierre and Napoleon], now inscribed the monument more forcefully than Catherine the Great's well-calculated "To Peter the First from Catherine the Second".[25]

Another fascinating readjustment of spatial context came when the Soviets, as an alternative to taking the Bronze Horseman out of the old imperial centre of the city, attempted to create a new 'Bolshevik centre' of Leningrad. While this would have put the Bronze Horseman on the periphery of the renamed city, the edge of empire, the monument instead came to emblematize the 'museum centre' of collective dream and memory depicted by Bitov in his novel *Pushkinskii dom* [*Pushkin House*]. In *Images of Space—St. Petersburg in the Visual and Verbal Arts* (1997) Kaganov likens this "*muzei-gorod*" [museum city] to Yaroslav Krestovsky's oil painting "Large Old House", in which old Petersburg is imagined as a childhood home, full of secrets and memories.[26] The Leningrad suburbs continued to encircle the old "museum centre" in the 1960s and 70s, and its status as a dream space at the mythological centre of the collective psyche was ensured by the fact that although four-fifths of the population now lived in suburban neighbourhoods, fully one-half had grown up within the boundaries of the old city.[27]

Another Bolshevik attempt to recontextualize the Bronze Horseman was the April 1926 unveiling of the monument to Lenin arriving at the Finland Station which was conceived and promoted as the 'new Bronze Horseman', its construction in bronze with a large, unusually-shaped granite pedestal an obvious borrowing, or quotation, from Falconet, and the famous armoured car a twentieth-century re-imagination of Peter's steed.

Representations of the Soviet penchant for symbolic manipulation of spatial landscapes can be seen in such artistic works as Vsevolod Pudovkin's 1927 film *The End of St. Petersburg*. This film, prepared for the tenth anniversary of the October Revolution, treats the Bronze Horseman unambivalently as a negative image from the city of tsars. Pudovkin montages the Bronze Horseman with two other pieces of equestrian imperial statuary: the heavy, corpulent Alexander III monument (which, as we have already mentioned, was moved from Vosstaniia Square in 1937) and the militaristic Nicholas I monument. Pudovkin emphasizes the Bronze Horseman's physical proximity to the new Isaakievskii Cathedral, repeatedly cutting between shots of the monument and the inscription above the doors of the cathedral, in order to link the oppression of Peter as a tsarist ruler to the oppressions of the church. Pudovkin employs images of imperial monuments strongly throughout the first third of the film, at an average of once every two minutes. As we approach the end of St. Petersburg announced in the film's title and the birth of Leningrad, however, these equestrian tributes symbolically disappear from the landscape. The imperial monuments are replaced by Soviet symbols of industry, by swinging cranes and ship masts in dockyards. This film uses few explanatory intertitles, relying upon visual images to tell the story. By the end of *The End of St. Petersburg*, the glorious message proclaiming *Net Sankt-Peterburga*, and in giant lettering, *Da zdravstvuet gorod Lenina* [Petersburg is no more. Welcome to the city of Lenin] has already been achieved visually as the monuments to the 'city of tsars' are symbolically purged. In this cinematic text Pudovkin's iconoclasm exceeds even Lenin's 1918 decree on the removal of statues. And yet Pudovkin is also quoting from the Petersburg text, relying upon the very cultural mythology—of the Bronze Horseman as a symbol and guardian of St. Petersburg—which he sought to destroy.

Text and the City

Literary works from the modernist and postmodernist canon share in this aesthetic tradition. Andrei Bely in his 1916 *Petersburg* and Andrei Bitov in his 1971 *Pushkin House* treat the Bronze Horseman as a giant quotation. Bitov's chapter headings, which mix the canonical Petersburg texts *Bednye liudi* [*Poor Folk*] and *Mednyi vsadnik* [*The Bronze Horseman*], echo Bely's mixture of images from *Mednyi vsadnik* and *Kamennyi gost'* [*The Stone Guest*]. Bitov also 'misquotes' Pushkin by having his hero Lyova reproduce Evgeny's characteristic stance, but upon the wrong lions.[28] In *Petersburg* Bely quotes from another 'sacred text', The Book of Revelation, as Peter becomes a Horseman of the Apocalypse in that eminently Symbolist theme of Petersburg as the "culmination of urban civilization" and its "final stage before the catastrophic end".[29] Bely represents Petersburg not only in its traditional role as mausoleum-city and necropolis, but as a city that murders its inhabitants, a killer that torments and hunts them, desiring their death. Moreover, the other murderer of Bely's novel, the revolutionalry Dudkin, turns out to be a particularly suitable addition to the Petersburg text, having chosen a very literary tool—scissors—for his murder weapon. Bitov portrays Petersburg as a giant quotation in his fiction and essayistic writing, describing the hero of *Pushkin House*, Lyova, as a textual product, with a childhood "from a book...in quotations".[30] Bitov calls Petersburg, in a 1986 article, a city that transforms its citizens and visitors into the literary heroes of an authorless text.[31] In an essay from one year later, Bitov formulates a definition of writing as a kind of memory game in which texts are endlessly recalled and quoted. In the same work, Bitov likens the text to a matrioshka doll, "where one layer connotes and 'remembers' the previous one."[32]

The politics of memory figure prominently in Bitov's writing, and he specifically links his biography and art to important dates in Petersburg's history. He notes in "Articles from a Novel" (1986) that his May 27 birthday corresponds to the founding of the city and that he graduated from high school in 1953, the same year as the only Soviet-era Petersburg anniversary. Thanks to a Stalinist distortion of chronometry, this anniversary, Petersburg's 250th, was not celebrated until 1957.[33] Bitov's American literary biographer, Ellen Chances, notes that Bitov hurried to finish *Pushkin House* in time for the 100th anniversary of the publication of Dostoevsky's *Besy* [*The Devils*] in 1971.³⁴ In this way he paid tribute to the writer who has been called the "principle architect of the Petersburg text",³⁵ who, in *Notes from Underground*, coined the phrase "the most abstract and intentional city in the world" and whose novel *The Devils* invokes the 'fathers and sons' theme with which Bitov opens *Pushkin House*.

Bitov's concept of Petersburg as a fake theatre decoration is consonant with the city's elaborate history of artifice since, in order to mark the first anniversary celebrations for St. Petersburg (the 50th anniversary in 1753), the Empress Elizabeth put the set designer for the Imperial Theatre in charge of creating a map of the city.³⁶ Bitov's hero Lyova, whom he portrays as his own contemporary, would have experienced the anomalous 250th anniversary, which was celebrated not only in the wrong year (1957) but also in the wrong month (June). It is strange that the anniversary was celebrated at all, since the occasion in effect marked the continuing imperial history of the city. Indeed, two contradictory holidays were marked in 1957, the 250th anniversary of St. Petersburg, and the 40th anniversary of the October Revolution. By that time several more layers had been added to the matrioshka-city and its palimpsestic emblem, the Bronze Horseman. Beginning in the 1930s Stalin began to embrace heroic nationalism and Peter the Great, along with Ivan the Terrible and Alexander Nevsky, was enjoying rehabilitation. Two conventions of the Petersburg text were emphasized by Soviet celebrants of the 250th anniversary: Leningrad was improving its status as necropolis (the writers claimed that pre-Soviet Petrograd had the highest mortality rate in Europe) and continuing its affiliation with texts and quotation (Leningrad had been declared the first fully literate city of Russia in 1931).³⁷

The Bronze Horseman has come to stand at the center of the Petersburg text as a palimpsest of political, cultural and literary meaning. This essay has ranged widely through examples from modernist and postmodernist texts, Soviet film and Petersburg architecture, monumental sculpture and public celebrations, in order to demonstrate how the Bronze Horseman has been brilliantly and endlessly reconceived by the twentieth century through a process of open-ended quotation and recombination.

Notes

[1] Alexander Schenker, *The Bronze Horseman, Falconet's Monument to Peter the Great* (New Haven: Yale University Press, 2003) 291.

[2] Z.G. Mints, M.V. Bezrodnyi, A.A. Danilevskii, " 'Peterburgskii tekst' i russkii simvolizm" in *Semiotika goroda i gorodskoi kul'tury: Peterburg*, ed Iu. M. Lotman (Tartu, 1984), 78–81. All translations from Russian are mine unless otherwise noted.

[3] Mints, Bezrodnyi and Danilevskii 82.

[4] Schenker 297.

[5] Andrew Kahn, *Pushkin's The Bronze Horseman* (London: Bristol Classical Press, 1998) 3.

[6] Kahn 8.

[7] Kahn 7–8.

[8] Xenia Gasiorowska, *The Image of Peter the Great in Russian Fiction* (Madison, Wisconsin: University of Wisconsin Press, 1979) 67.

[9] Schenker 75.

[10] Waclaw Lednicki, *Pushkin's Bronze Horseman, The Story of a Masterpiece* (Berkeley: University of California Press, 1955) 17.

[11] N.P. Antisiferov, *Byl' i mif Sankt Peterburga* (Peterburg: Izdatel'stvo Brokgauz-Efron, 1924) 54.

[12] Kahn 22.

[13] N.N. Efremova, "Sniatye i utrachennye monumenty Sankt-Peterburga" in *Peterburgskie chteniia 96*. S-Peterburg: Russko-Baltiiskii informatsionnyi tsentr BLITS, 1996, 158.

[14] Efremova 158.

[15] Among them: the monument to Peter in the dress of the Preobrazhensky Regiment in front of Samsonievskii Cathedral; the monument to Peter the Great as founder of the arsenal in front of the New Arsenal building; the statue depicting Peter visiting the newly-built Liteinii dvor; Peter saving the drowning sailors in Lakhta in 1724 and the so-called "tsar-plotnik" [tsar-carpenter], which showed a young Peter learning shipbuilding in Holland. See Efremova 160.

[16] Kahn 113.

[17] Benjamin Forest and Juliet Johnson, "Unraveling the Threads of History: Soviet Era Monuments and Post-Soviet National Identity in Moscow" (Revised for the Annals of the Association of American Geographers, August 2001) 4.

[18] Forest and Johnson 36.

[19] Forest and Johnson 48.

[20] St. Petersburg was renamed Petrograd in 1914 and Leningrad in 1924.

[21] Schenker 272.

[22] Schenker 78.

[23] In December 1825 a group of noblemen eager for liberal political reform staged an uprising on Senate (formerly Peter's and later Decembrist) Square that was swiftly put down by the regime. A number of the Decembrist leaders were hanged and others sent to exile in Siberia.

[24] Lubomir Dolezel, "The Visible and Invisible Petersburg", *Russian Literature* VII (1979) 485.

[25] Catherine's inscription was intended to legitimize her right of succession (she was not a native Russian and had married into the Romanov dynasty). See Schenker 30.

[26] Grigory Kaganov, *Images of Space. St. Petersburg and the Visual Arts*, trans. Sidney Monas (Stanford: Stanford UP, 1997) 170.

[27] Kaganov 171.

[28] Andrei Bitov, *Pushkin House*, trans. Susan Brownsberger (Illinois State University: Dalkey Archive Press, 1987) 333.

[29] Mints, Bezrodnyi and Danilevskii 87.

[30] Andrei Bitov, *Pushkinskii dom*. (Ann Arbor: Ardis, 1978) 315–16.

[31] Andrei Bitov, *Stat'i iz romana*. (Moskva: Sovietskii pisatel', 1986) 98.

[32] Andrei Bitov, "Novyi Robinson". (K 125-letiu vykhoda v svet "Zapisok iz mertvogo doma", *Znamia* 12 (1987) 223.

[33] Stalin died in 1953, throwing the country into uncertainty and making the timely marking of St.Petersburg's anniversary impossible. See Bitov 1986, 17.

[34] Ellen Chances, *Andrei Bitov: An Ecology of Inspiration* (Cambridge: Cambridge University Press, 1993) 230.

[35] M. Amusin, "Roman A. Bitova 'Pushkinskii dom' i peterburgskii tekst", *Russian Literature* XLIII-IV (1998) 417.

[36] Kaganov 19.

[37] B.G. Ananev and A. I. Markushevich, eds. *Materialy nauchnoi sessii posviaschennoi 250-letiiu Leningrada*. (Moskva: Izdatel'stvo Akademii pedagogicheskikh nauk RSFSR, 1959) 6.

2
Going to the Movies under Stalin:
A Glimpse into Cultural Practices and Societal Attitudes in Prewar Soviet Ukraine

Serhy Yekelchyk

The literature on Soviet cinema during the Stalin era is considerable and continues to grow, yet most of it focuses on film techniques, movie plots, and the state's control over the film industry. In contrast, very little is known about the popular reception of films. There was no objective polling of viewers and no "target groups" selected for previews. Indeed, at the time modern sociological research was in its infancy even in the West, not to mention the Soviet Union. Attendance figures are sometimes available—we know, for example, that the total number of movie tickets sold stood at 900 million in 1940, and statistics for individual films can be unearthed in the archives. But unlike in the West, the amount of money a film made was not a reliable indicator of its popularity. Soviet citizens could be forced to attend certain films or they could have no choice because all cinemas screened the same recent Soviet film.[1]

In any case, statistical data reveal little about the motives and impressions of ordinary people. What did they think about the movies they saw? Did these films have a desired educational impact or did they simply serve as escapist entertainment? Did the public prefer Soviet or foreign films, and why?

Partial answers to such questions can be found in an underutilized source on Stalinist culture, the interview collection of the

Harvard Project on the Soviet Social System (HPSSS). The four-year project began in 1950, when Harvard University's Russian Research Center was contracted by the Human Resource Research Institute, the US Air Force intelligence agency, to conduct a comprehensive study of Soviet society. The military's interest was in gauging Soviet social stability, the extent of the party's political control, and the Soviet Union's defense capabilities. However, the young sociologists and political scientists working on the project devised a questionnaire covering a range of other issues, including health care, family life, and anti-Soviet jokes. During 1950–51, the team of researchers conducted 764 extensive interviews with refugees from the Soviet Union then residing in West Germany and the US: 329 were general "life-story" interviews known as Series A and the rest, targeted anthropological interviews called Series B. The section on "Communication" in Series A included questions about the books Soviet citizens read and the movies they saw.[2]

During the 1950s and early 1960s, American social scientists summarized the project's findings in several major books and dozens of articles, but almost all of them marginalized cultural topics or viewed them from a narrow "social communications" perspective. One notable exception was the work of the literary scholar Maurice Friedberg, who published two articles on the popular reception in the USSR of foreign and Soviet literature, respectively.[3] Interest in the interview collection has waned somewhat since the 1970s both because of the cumbersome transcript cataloguing system and because social historians working on the Stalin period were slowly obtaining access to Soviet archives. However, this corpus of sources received a new lease on life in 2007, when funding from the Harvard University Library Digital Initiative and expert advice from the Soviet historians David Brandenberger (University of Richmond) and Terry Martin (Harvard) allowed for the digitization of the interview transcripts. They are now full-text searchable from the HPSSS Online home page (http://hcl.harvard.edu/collections/hpsss/index.html).

Cultural historians of Stalinism are already rediscovering the HPSSS interviews as an underutilized source on their topic, as evidenced by Brandenberger's collection of unofficial jokes of Stalin's time.[4] There is more valuable material in the Harvard Project interviews, which awaits subtle interpretation by contemporary social and cultural historians.

Western Assumptions

The questions about cinema are found within the "Communications" section of Schedule A, between the questions on newspapers and political information meetings. Such a pairing already reveals the narrow social-science approach of the project designers. In the subsection on newspapers, they wanted to find out which ones the interviewees read, how frequently, which pages, and how reliable they considered the information found there. Regarding meetings, the American sociologists had a similar set of queries: which meetings people had to attend, how many in a month, what subjects were discussed, and whether they saw the information obtained as reliable. The questions on films are phrased in the same way, suggesting that the cinema mattered primarily as a source of information—which could be true or false, Soviet or foreign:

> C. (Movies) Did you attend any movies? (If "Yes," ask the following:)
> 1. What sort of movies did you attend? (Domestic or foreign).
> 2. How many in a month?
> 3. Did you think they showed things in a true light?[5]

Such an approach was typical of the rigid social-science theories of the early 1950s, in which cinema figured primarily as a communication medium playing an important role in the global processes of modernization and mass mobilization. One of the Harvard Project's leaders, the sociologist Alex Inkeles, expressed just such an understanding of film in his book that was published immediately before the commencement of the project, *Public Opinion in Soviet Russia: A Study in Mass Persuasion*. Aside from the misleading title—Inkeles wrote about the state's efforts to shape public opinion rather than about their results—the book also contained a chapter on the Soviet film industry, which opens with the statement, "Of all the arts, the film is most clearly also a means of mass communication."[6] Inkeles is correct in saying that the Soviet authorities saw film "as an instrument for spreading communist ideology and mobilizing the masses in support of the party and the government," but his own approach is likewise one-dimensional and, ironically, very similar to that of Soviet ideologues.[7]

For some reason, however, the information on movie attendance and reception collected during the interviews was not used in the project's final report, *How the Soviet System Works*, co-authored by Raymond A. Bauer, Alex Inkeles, and Clyde Kluckhohn. The authors do say that all forms of mass communication were the direct monopoly of the Soviet regime: "The system is as comprehensive as possible and includes the fine arts, literature, and music."[8] Curiously, though, there is no mention of film anywhere in the book.

A partial explanation for this can be found in the bulky follow-up volume that is usually considered the most important result of the Harvard Project, *The Soviet Citizen*, by Alex Inkeles and Raymond A. Bauer. The authors placed their cursory discussion of movie attendance (but not reception) in the chapter entitled "Keeping Up with the News." This chapter is devoted to Soviet official media defined in the following way: "The official media include not only the pointed sources (newspapers, magazines, and journals), and the radio and a developing television network, but also the theater, movies, the arts, and a system of oral agitation."[9] Yet on the very next page the authors qualify their statement by saying, "The theater and movies are only partially media of information and will not be considered systematically here."[10]

The rest of the chapter contains the occasional reference to film and overall summarizes the findings reported in an earlier article by Raymond Bauer and Peter H. Rossi on "Soviet Communications Behavior."[11] These Western social scientists concluded that Stalinist society was highly stratified in this respect, with exposure to communication media being the highest among the urban intelligentsia and the lowest among the peasantry. They also argued that the use of communications media by Soviet citizens tended to be "patterned," usually focusing on one of the four clusters of media exposure: "mass official" (newspapers, magazines, books, and Soviet radio), "aesthetic official" (movies and theatre), "personalized official" (lectures and agitation meetings), and "covert" (discussion with friends, rumors, and foreign radio). That is, a person that frequently read Soviet newspapers was likely also to listen regularly to the radio, but not necessarily go to the movies; while the moviegoer was likely also to be a theater patron, but not necessarily an avid reader of official newspapers.[12] This division seems somewhat problematic given that the urban intelligentsia, which had the highest exposure to theater and film, quite obviously had no way of avoiding political information lectures—in fact, most lecturers probably came from within its ranks. Preparing for such lectures, of course, included the regular reading of Soviet newspapers. Perhaps, the interviewees' disingenuous denials of participation in Soviet public life proved somewhat misleading for the project collaborators.[13]

In analyzing specifically the data on movie attendance, the project authors conclude that it is at its highest in cities and among those with higher education, and at its lowest among collective farmers with little education.[14] This point, of course, is not new and could have been gleaned from Soviet newspapers. Moreover, it is not clear just how meaningful such an analysis is. Because films were not shown or shown only very rarely in the countryside during the 1930s, attendance was not a matter of choice for the peasants and thus not a reliable indicator of their interest in the official media. The urban intelligentsia and white-collar employees, too, probably had more free time on their hands and more disposable income than ordinary workers, and thus went to the movies more often. Overall, Inkeles and Bauer's general argument in this chapter, that "communications behavior is independently influenced by the degree of individual's involvement in the system,"[15] seems problematic when applied to film attendance. It assumes that an anti-Soviet person would not go to see Soviet films even if they were musical comedies or patriotic historical films about Russia's greatness. It also leaves unexplained the authors' interesting conclusion that movie attendance in the Soviet Union, just like movie attendance in the US, peaked at the age 20 and then declined steadily.[16] It appears that Soviet citizens went to the movies not just (or at all) to demonstrate their support of the party line.

Indeed, one wonders why the sociologists working with the Harvard Project interviews used the data on film attendance but not the information that had been gathered on movie reception. Could it be because their question, based on a rigid "communications" formula, elicited rather unexpected answers?

Movie Attendance

For the purposes of this article, I searched the HPSSS interview transcripts to identify interviewees from the Ukrainian Soviet Socialist Republic in its pre-1939 borders. The HPSSS team went to great lengths to protect the identities of their collaborators, but the A Series of interviews typically include information about age, gender, occupation, and ethnicity (although the latter is sometimes missing). This enabled me to search for ethnic Ukrainians, who answered the question about movies in reasonable detail. In order to identify people of other ethnicities who had lived in Ukraine before the war, I also searched for references to Ukrainian cities and regions in the texts of interviews. This added to my sample a dozen ethnic Russians, Poles, and Armenians from Ukraine, who had answered the cinema question. The corpus of sources for this paper is comprised of 48 interviews conducted in Munich and New York in 1950 and 1951.

As mentioned earlier, the Harvard Project team was primarily interested in quantifiable data on cinema attendance and its correlation with the interviewees' education and place of residence. American sociologists and political scientists found few surprises there. My sample fully confirms their conclusion that young and educated urbanites were the most frequent cinemagoers and semi-literate peasants, the least frequent. The average movie attendance for the entire group of Harvard Project interviewees, calculated by the HPSSS team at 3.5 times per month (the mean) and 2.3 times per month (the median), also seems about right.[17] Those reporting that they went "rarely" usually specified "once a month" when pressed for a more exact answer, but overall in my sample "once a week" or "two or three times a month" was a more common answer. Extremes are represented by a female student from Kharkiv, who went to the movies "every day after school" and a middle-aged male collective farmer, who was the only one of 48 interviewees to answer "no" to the question if he attended any movies while he lived in the USSR.[18] However, a close reading of the texts reveals a host of economic, social, cultural, and economic factors influencing movie attendance, which sometimes cannot be reduced to the general categories of education and place of residence.

This diversity becomes apparent already in the opinions on the affordability of movies. The urbanites, who had been in their teens or twenties before the war, tend to agree that tickets were quite affordable: "Tickets were comparatively cheap—from 1.20 rubles to 3.00, and I went to the movies about four or five times a month"; "Tickets were inexpensive, this was the cheapest entertainment in the Soviet Union."[19] Things were even better for high school and college students: "Films were very, very cheap. Students could get in for reduced prices. Also, there were special showings for students."[20] Older working-class interviewees, who likely had families at the time, saw things differently: "Well, movies are not expensive. But still, I think I had to economize, I could not afford them too often"; "You had to have money to go to the movies." Both workers reported patronizing the cinema once or twice a month, the first also volunteering the information that his salary was 350 rubles per month.[21] Even a nurse from Kyiv, who was in her early twenties at the time, reported that she could afford going to the movies perhaps once a week, although she actually went more often: "Often I went to the movies 4 or 5 times a week. But with friends. On my own money I do not know whether I could have gone more than once."[22] Thus, income, family status, and entitlement to student discounts emerge in these examples as the main factors influencing the frequency of film attendance in the cities.

In the countryside the shortage of film projectors limited the extent of Soviet "cinefication" drive. In 1940, which was the year that the Harvard Project team was asking the respondents about, in the entire Soviet countryside there were 17,571 film projectors, 11,171 of them mobile and only 9,676 suitable for screening sound films.[23] Even those interviewees who were willing to see all films and able to afford the cost could only go to the movies once a month, whenever a mobile projector arrived in their village. More likely than not the traveling projector had no capability to show sound films—a notorious problem and the reason why the Soviet Union continued making silent versions of sound films well into the 1940s.²⁴ According to the interviews in my sample, the semi-literate peasants often could not read the subtitle before the scene changed.²⁵ Moreover, the lack of electricity in some villages required that mobile projectors have hand-powered generators: "Well, four fellows would get free admission and take turns cranking a dynamo in pairs to make electrical current for the machine."²⁶

On collective farms with stationary projectors, films could be shown as often as twice a week, but the harvesting season dictated the exact schedule—for example, there could be a movie every Saturday in the winter and less regularly in the summer.²⁷ Yet, just like in the city, a person's income was also an important factor. Older males in particular stressed this point: "I did not have either the time or the money to go to the movies"; "In the district or at work at the MTS the director would bring tickets, and money was deducted from your pay. So we had to go to the movies. Otherwise I had no money to go on my own desire."²⁸

The last example introduces an important political dimension. Indeed, during the Stalin era local authorities could make movie attendance obligatory for certain categories of workers, either for reasons of political education or as a means of raising ticket sales in the district. In the case of the tractor driver mentioned above, it was likely the latter. In another case, that of a student at a military school who reported "compulsory" movie attendance, it was probably the former. Soviet soldiers too were shown two or three films a week.²⁹ A big-city school teacher felt obliged to see all new films as part of her professional development: "I had to go to the movies because all of them had ideological significance. I had to tell my pupils about the films and I had to tell them why they should go see a particular film." As a result, she went to the cinema twice a week on average.³⁰

If she went because she worked with children (or so she claimed), others might have avoided cinemas precisely because they were seen as places for children. "Movies were attended mostly by children," said a middle-aged driver by way of explaining his lack of interest. Social stereotypes could be supplemented by cultural divisions, as in the case of an agricultural mechanic, who claimed liking the (Ukrainian-language) theater better than (Russian-language) films and therefore going to the movies only five or six times a year.[31] In cases involving pre-teens and teens, their movie attendance could be controlled by parents—for example, until the age 13 in the case of one respondent. Adults sometimes claimed being "too tired to go to the movies in the evening" because "we had to work so much and so hard," but societal norms could also be at play here—the interviewee in question was actually a housewife before the war, and she was probably speaking on behalf of her generation rather than as an individual. In any case, Saturdays and Sundays are mentioned as the days when adults could and would go to the movies.[32]

Other factors, ranging from the availability of tickets to the public's willingness to see films more than once, also influenced attendance patterns. A young girl from Kharkiv could go to the cinema "every day, after school" because she used a free pass issued to her artist father. This meant, of course, that she saw the same films repeatedly. For another urban youth, a turner by occupation, money was no object, but because he would rarely see the same movie twice, his habits reflected Soviet film distribution patterns: "Each film plays three days if it is bad and seven days if it is good; thus, on average, I went to the movies five times a month." For a female artist from Odessa, going to the movies was dependent on getting a ticket before the end of the work day: "It was difficult to get tickets for a movie, so one person in our place of employment was designated to get them. If you went for a ticket yourself, you had to stand in line, and you stood a good chance of not getting one because the house would be sold out by the time your turn came."[33]

Soviet notions of what kind of behavior was acceptable inside the cinema also differed from Western models. Two interviewees, who had been in their early twenties before the war, made an interesting comparison between public behavior at the movies in the Soviet Union and in the West (represented in their cases by postwar West Germany and the US, respectively). One felt that public conduct was better in the West: "For instance, in the Soviet Union if the film breaks there is terrible shouting, whereas people here just sit quietly until it is repaired." Another, on the contrary, praised the modesty and discretion of young Soviet people: "We did kiss in the movies, but we kissed in the last row, or way [in] the side seats, where we hoped nobody would see us. But over here, boys and girls kiss in the movies and they don't care if somebody sees them or doesn't." There was also a telling afterthought from another respondent, "You know that in the Soviet Union the movie houses are magnificent? They are not as dingy as here."[34]

Finally, some respondents in my sample had experience with the movies, which went beyond that of an average Soviet person. Two had worked as movie projectionists. One of them was arrested in 1938, when the film of Stalin's speech caught fire from a cigarette his friend had dropped on the floor of the projectionist booth. Originally accused of "wrecking," the projectionist escaped with a milder sentence of eight months in prison and an 800-ruble fine only because he was drunk at the time of the accident. The other projectionist operated a portable film projector that traveled from one village to another. He claimed that all his colleagues were anti-Soviet, as were the peasants: "The movie projectionists knew very well what the regime did because we went around to all the different villages and saw how the people lived there and how they felt. I understood why the people did not come to see the propaganda films, and I could also see the attitude of the chairman of the village Soviet [to] the people."[35]

Another interviewee had a projectionist friend at a Kyiv cinema theater, who had once let him in to see a preview of a movie for party and state officials. The film, which depicted Ukrainian kulaks, was apparently never released. A respondent from Odesa described the security procedures that were employed whenever a local party boss went to the cinema: police at every entrance, a search of the government box, the announcement that everyone should remain in their seats for the duration of the film, and all the doors locked until the chief's departure.[36]

Overall, the Harvard Project interviews leave the impression that in the 1930s cinema played a large role in the lives of Soviet people whether or not they identified with the system. Seen by the state as a component of political education, it was also the most affordable mass entertainment—widely available in Ukrainian cities and less so in the countryside.

Soviets Watching Foreign Films

Of course, if Soviet films were aimed at educating the public in the spirit of socialism, exposure to foreign films could undermine this propagandist effect. The Harvard Project interviewers, who treated cinema as a potential source of political information, wanted to find out if the Soviet public watched foreign films. After establishing that the respondent went to the movies while in the Soviet Union, this was the first thing they asked: "What sort of movies did you attend (domestic or foreign)?" If the interviewee proceeded to talk about Soviet films, the interviewer would typically interrupt with another question, such as "Did you ever see foreign movies?" or "Did you see foreign movies or only Soviet movies?"[37]

In so doing, the interviewers were also signaling to the respondents that this point was of particular importance to them. This resulted in some curious answers from those interviewees who, consciously or subconsciously, were trying to "please" the American social scientists. For example, when asked if he saw any foreign films, a former school principal answered, "Yes, I saw a number of them. But I cannot recall any titles at the moment." Another person, a mechanic by occupation, also painted himself into a corner with his answer, "Of course, I mostly went to see non-propaganda films. For example, foreign romantic films (respondent tried to think of some titles, but was unable)."[38] Even the respondents who said correctly that very few foreign films were available during the 1930s, and who could remember almost all the titles, still showed a tendency to express their admiration for "American" films when asked about "foreign" ones, no doubt because of their interviewers' identity. The "American" films they named included British, Czech, and Austrian movies.[39]

Some interviewees gave knowledgeable answers about the evolution of Soviet policy towards foreign films. Two people noted that foreign films were shown widely and freely during the NEP period, although they were not old enough to remember the 1920s.[40] Various respondents also said that foreign films, although they were very rare, remained available in the Soviet Union until 1936 or 1937—Charlie Chaplin's films were particularly memorable. According to one interviewee, she could watch old foreign silent films even after 1937 at a small Odesa movie theater that did not have a sound projector.⁴¹ This information is confirmed by present-day scholars. There were three foreign films released in the Soviet Union in 1936—*Peter* (Hungary, 1934), *Under the Roofs of Paris* (France, 1930), and *Cabin in the Cotton* (US, 1932)—but none in 1937.⁴²

However, foreign cinema truly received a new lease on life in the Soviet Union with the mass release of "trophy" film prints captured during the annexation of Eastern Poland in 1939. By far the most popular of them was the American musical *The Great Waltz* (1938), a fictionalized biography of the Austrian composer Johann Strauss II, which the Soviet public saw in 1940.⁴³ Ukrainian youngsters were so impressed with this film that its release is even mentioned in some memoirs written sixty years later. One also learns from this source that Kyivites felt a special connection to the star of this movie, the singer Miliza Korjus, who had lived in Kyiv during 1918–28 and underwent her initial musical training there.⁴⁴

Two interviewees in my sample defected to the West in the late 1940s and could attest to the wide availability and impressive popularity of "trophy" films captured in Nazi Germany. Maya Turovskaya's research proves that by far the most popular of these was the German film *The Girl of My Dreams* (1944), which was released in the Soviet Union in 1947 and far exceeded any Soviet competition that year in terms of turnover per copy.⁴⁵ Yet the respondent who gave some movie titles referred to American films from the same war booty trove: *The Roaring Twenties* (1939), *The Little Foxes* (1941), and *His Butler's Sister* (1943).⁴⁶ Most of the interviews, however, cover the period just before the war, when foreign films were extremely rare and therefore played a different role in the structure of Soviet cultural consumption.

In fact, respondents from cities often indicated that they saw foreign films "seldom" or "very seldom."⁴⁷ Those from small towns and villages typically said that no foreign movies were shown, but they sometimes assumed (possibly, inferring from the question itself) that the situation was different in big cities: "I don't remember that foreign films were shown in our area"; "No foreign films were ever shown even in [the district city of] Artemivsk"; "We did not have any in our city, which had a population of about 20,000 in the Donbas."⁴⁸ In one case, a foreman of a collective farm reported seeing one foreign film, *The Great Waltz*, but qualified this as an anomaly: "Well, foreign films we never could see, except this film I mentioned, which was an exception."⁴⁹

Those who did see foreign films—the large majority of respondents—usually added that they liked them.[50] As we will see below, however, for the greater part of interviewees this did not imply a total rejection of Soviet films, which they also liked. Some apparently sensed larger societal reasons for the success of foreign movies and phrased this statement differently, not simply as their personal preference: "They were always successful"; "The American films were always popular"; "People in the Soviet Union were most interested in going to foreign films."[51] One individual who defected to the West in the late 1940s, when foreign movies comprised a large share of new releases, reported that people could get same-day tickets for a Soviet film, but they had to buy them three days in advance for a foreign movie.[52]

In order to sort out the reasons for such popularity, let us first look at the list of foreign films the interviewees remembered seeing. In the case of the Stalinist 1930s, it is dangerous to assume that the films people could recall ten years after the event were those that impressed them most. Because of the distribution patterns described above, some respondents saw only a couple of foreign movies and, naturally, remembered the titles well. Yet, interviewees often made evaluative comments, which allow us to reconstruct their attitude to foreign films.

When a respondent remembered—or had seen—only one or two foreign movies, they were inevitably the films of Charlie Chaplin (usually referred to simply as "Charlie Chaplin") and/or *The Great Waltz*.[53] These films apparently received the greatest distribution, but were also genuinely liked. Of Chaplin's works, the interviewees who mentioned film titles usually named two, *City Lights* (1931) and *Modern Times* (1936). Only one individual, who had left the Soviet Union in the late 1940s, also mentioned *The Great Dictator* (1940), which was apparently released there during the war but not seen in Ukraine until after the war.[54]

Not far behind Chaplin's films and *The Great Waltz* in terms of citation frequency were the two films with Franciska Gaal that were released in the USSR during the late 1930s, the musical *Peter* (1934) and the comedy *Little Mother* (*Kleine Mutti*, 1935), both co-productions of Austria, Hungary, and the US. *One Hundred Men and a Girl* (1937), an American musical comedy starring Deanna Durbin and

Leopold Stokowski, which, like *The Great Waltz*, was part of the 1939 war booty, was also fondly remembered.[55] Coincidentally, Henry Koster (Hermann Kosterlitz) directed all three films.

Foreign films mentioned only once in my sample included silent films with Douglas Fairbanks and Mary Pickford, which were seen decades before the war; Soviet releases from the 1930s, such as *Under the Roofs of Paris* (France, 1930) and *The Invisible Man* (US, 1933); more "trophy" films from 1939, such as *Catherine the Last* (*Katharina, die Letzte*, Austria/Hungary/USA, 1936, another Koster comedy starring Gaal) and an unidentified Polish musical starring Jan Kiepura; and foreign films released in the Soviet Union during the war (*Lady Hamilton*, Great Britain, 1941; known in the US as *That Hamilton Woman*).[56]

Soviet citizens apparently could see through the authorities' motives in the selection of foreign movies. The individual who saw only two foreign films, namely the Chaplin films, said, "I immediately realized why we could see them, because they described unemployment in America, the assembly line, and also because the film was silent and there was nothing bad for the Soviet Union and you could propagandize with that."[57] Another interviewee, who saw *Modern Times* at a military school, reported that the screening was preceded by a lecture by one of their political officers:

> He said that the American workers, due to their working system, [had] ceased to be normal human beings. Because of their monotonous work their mentality got abnormal. They are unable to think about anything other than their screws or hammers with which they work. 'Chaplin's film,' he said, 'is a true reflection of that horrible life.' Naturally the majority of the students did not take his words seriously. Most of us noticed that Charlie Chaplin was good comedy and not a satire.[58]

The last sentence is somewhat questionable—was it possible not to see the satirical edge of *Modern Times*? Perhaps, this interviewee was either shamelessly trying to please the American sociologists or, on the contrary, was giving tongue-in-cheek answers. Since the questionnaire featured numerous questions about whether Soviet newspapers, radio, novels, and films "showed things in a true light," one could make fun of the interviewers by applying this notion to an American film and denying any truth to it.

In any case, we know that Ukrainian moviegoers could both decipher the authorities' motives in allowing a certain foreign film and notice things in this film that did not fit the official interpretation. The school teacher, who went often to the movies so that she could advise her students about them, gave two excellent examples of this:

> I saw *One Hundred Men and a Girl*, a[n] American film. And one reason [why] I think why they permitted it to be shown in the Soviet Union is that there was an unemployed musician in the movie. And yet what struck me was that even though he was unemployed, he had three rooms and was living well, and he was well dressed. And even though he was unemployed, he lived in much better circumstances than people who were employed, lived in the Soviet Union. Then I remember seeing another foreign film called *Little Mother*. I think it was an Austrian film, but it dealt with life in the United States and I saw it three times in 1936 and each time that I saw it, they had cut more out of it. That was very obvious[;] for instance, they cut the long scenes which took place in the children's home. Because it showed that conditions were much better outside of the Soviet Union.[59]

This interpretation was, of course, based on the viewer's assumption that foreign films showed life abroad in a true light—either a naïve or very sly position aimed to please the interviewers. The latter were not supposed to ask about the truthful depiction of life in foreign films—this question was reserved for Soviet movies—but occasionally the respondents gave an answer to it in relation to foreign films, usually as a result of a misunderstanding or the interviewer's mistake. The three answers available in my sample are all different. One person felt that foreign movies gave a true depiction of life abroad: "We know that they did. Foreign films had an effect upon us, because it was through these foreign films that we saw how people in other countries and other societies had lived." Another person, who saw only one foreign movie, *The Great Waltz*, answered noncommittally, "I cannot say that." The third respondent, who had just explained to the interviewer that the Soviet cultural product was not intended to portray real life, answered, "I could not say, of course, either that foreign films give a truthful picture of life. But this is not the task of the film."[60]

The last answer, finally, exposed the fallacy of the narrow sociological approach to cinema as simply one of "communications media." Yet the questionnaire used by the Harvard Project team did not include any questions about why Soviet people liked certain novels or films and disliked others. The interview scheme literally imposed on the respondents a constricted understanding of cinema as a source of information and a propaganda weapon. There are only occasional hints in the transcripts as to why the Ukrainian moviegoers *liked* foreign films as opposed to being simply *interested* in them as an information medium.

One reason was the beautiful music. No prewar Soviet film incorporated classical hits the way it was done in *The Great Waltz* and *A Hundred Men and a Girl*. A respondent who was in his teens before the war testified:

> I remember, for example, before *The Great Waltz* was shown in the Soviet Union, very few people ever went about whistling or humming some of the Strauss waltzes. But the minute *The Great Waltz* began to be shown, almost everybody wherever you went on the streets or in the trolley-cars or at work, everybody was whistling one of the Strauss waltzes from the film. This same thing was true of the Deanna Durbin film *A Hundred Men and a Girl*. Before that nobody whistled or hummed anything from it. But afterwards everybody went around with this Second Hungarian Rhapsody on their lips.[61]

Another, weightier, reason was good entertainment. A young working-class interviewee put it this way: "When they showed such American films of Charlie Chaplin as *City Lights* or *The Great Dictator*, people held their stomach, so much did they laugh. Also there was a film called *Viennese Waltz* [*The Great Waltz*], which people enjoyed very much. People do not like sad films."[62] Even educated respondents, who were able to name many film titles, claimed that Western movies, Chaplin's included, were "without political tendencies."[63] This is as puzzling as the opinion discussed above about Chaplin's films being pure comedy and not satire. Perhaps Soviet audiences really wanted to "read" foreign films this way, as pure entertainment and comedy? Perhaps they applied to foreign movies the same viewing technique as to Soviet films—skipping through the political message to enjoy the slapstick and romance aspects. One would argue that such a separation of form and content was not truly possible, but Soviet moviegoers could be deceiving themselves too, not just the American sociologists, in looking for escapist entertainment.

Soviet Films and How to Enjoy Them

In answering the question about "what sort of movies" they saw, a number of respondents explained to the interviewers that they really had no choice. The similarity of the language they use is remarkable: "But you had no choice. You could either see these ones or not go to the movies"; "But in general, there was no choice"; "I never deliberately chose which movie I would see. Most people in the Soviet Union just go and see one. The choice of films in a small town is very narrow."[64] Scholars have discussed this phenomenon—at a time of the growing demand for movies, the number of films released in the Soviet Union during the 1930s actually went down, leaving audiences with no choice. From the peak of production in 1930, when 111 pictures were made, the Soviet film industry slowed down to 35 movies in 1937, 38 in 1938, 54 in 1939, and 40 in 1940.[65] The number of foreign films released in the country also went down dramatically during the same period. As a result, active moviegoers, especially young urbanites, ended up seeing each and every film ever shown in the country, some of them repeatedly: "I went to see all the Soviet films and if I liked them I would go many times"; "Look, I saw all the films in all the theaters"; "I saw almost all of the films."[66]

Likely prompted by a series of questions about the truthfulness of the Soviet media, including the cinema, a large number of respondents tried to impress upon the interviewers a single point, that all Soviet movies were propaganda. Again, they use remarkably similar language: "The Soviet films were all propaganda films"; "There were no films in the Soviet Union without propaganda"; "All Soviet films are of the same character—pure Party line propaganda"; "There was always a political tendency"; "Basically the Soviet films have an agitational character, regardless of their artistic merit"; "There is no such thing as pure entertainment. Every film contains propaganda, exactly the same propaganda as you find in newspapers. That's what movies are made for!"[67] One interviewee even explained Lenin's concept of cinema as the most important of the arts, because it was best for propaganda purposes, and argued that "the Soviets carried Lenin's concept of film into full bloom."[68] Yet, as we shall see below, such unanimous protestations of Soviet films' objectivity and value as an information medium did not mean that they were not liked.

Many respondents attempted to make generalizations about Soviet films in order to give the interviewees an idea of what they were about. Since they were asked to think back to the year 1940, the general picture they paint reflected the immediate prewar years rather than the entire decade. Some people gave descriptions applicable to Stalinist cinema in general. One said that Soviet films "had as their subject matter the struggle between the rich and the poor or the history of the Revolution," while another named two types of films: "Pictures about Soviet patriotism. Or there might be propaganda films about foreign countries." Yet another respondent referred to films "mainly about industrialization, or when new plants were built, then the military film [and] historical."[69] The increased militaristic spirit of Soviet cinema in the immediate prewar years skewed other responses: "Most of them were military films or about Soviet life"; "From among the Soviet films I saw mostly military films"; "Maybe seventy or eighty percent were spy stories and the rest, twenty percent, were in a military spirit, about the army or some general propaganda. There was propaganda everywhere. The other fifteen percent were historical films, old films."[70] Following this stereotype, one interviewee reported seeing "[m]ostly military films like *Chapaev*," even though this 1934 blockbuster belonged to the historical-revolutionary genre, if not adventure.[71] It is also notable that respondents did not include the popular genre of musical comedy, although they named most of its exemplars in the subsequent discussion.

What titles did the interviewees name? One junior member of the Harvard Project team subsequently calculated that in their entire sample of approximately 250 interviews, altogether there were some 350 mentions of 125 Soviet films. *Chapaev* (1934), *Peter the Great* (Part One, 1937), *Alexander Nevsky* (1938), and *Lenin in October* (1937) led the way in terms of citation frequency. *Chapaev* was well ahead of the competition, having been named by one in every seven respondents. This sociologist also argued that the "recall" method (asking people what movies they remembered seeing) highlighted the films that left the strongest and, in most cases, positive impression on the viewers.[72] My sample of Ukrainian interviews generally confirms this analysis, albeit with some Ukrainian specifics. *Chapaev* and *Lenin in October* shared the top spot with six mentions each, although one of the references to the latter film was explicitly negative. *Alexander Nevsky* trailed slightly behind with five mentions. Next in line, however, was the Ukrainian production, the republic's answer to *Chapaev*, Alexander Dovzhenko's *Shchors* (1938), with three mentions, which surpassed *Peter the First* (two mentions).

There were at least two people among the interviewees with a significant knowledge of the Ukrainian film industry, who could elaborate on its history and name numerous titles of Ukrainian-made movies. The two respondents in question described the creation of the Kyiv and Odesa film studios in the mid-1920s, the supervisory functions of the All-Ukrainian Photo and Cinema Administration (VUFKU), the switch to Ukrainian subtitles in the late 1920s, beginning with such films as *Taras Shevchenko* (1926), the finer details of Dovzhenko's career, and the switch to Russian with the advent of sound films. One of them emphasized that even such award-winning Ukrainian films as *Shchors* and *Bohdan Khmelnytsky* (1941) were made in Russian and only later dubbed into Ukrainian. Only film versions of Ukrainian operas, such as *Natalka Poltavka* (1936) could be filmed in Ukrainian.[73] This treasure trove of information, however, is found in the B Series interviews, where a series of problems, including the nationalities issue, received closer attention. I was unable to link any A Series interviews with these two individuals; it is conceivable that they were not even selected for general "life story" interviews. Thus, my sample from the A Series does not include any interviewees with specialist knowledge of the Ukrainian film industry. The responses and reactions I analyze are those of the mass viewer and are very similar to those of ordinary people from other parts of the Soviet Union.

Like Soviet citizens from other republics, respondents from Ukraine liked some things about Soviet movies and disliked others.[74] One popular complaint was the spy hysteria in Soviet films released on the eve of the war, a point also noted in specialist literature. According to Peter Kenez, the unmasking of the hidden internal enemy was a common trope in Soviet films of the 1930s, but not a single movie from 1940 features the hunt for traitors. The main adversary is now a foreign agent smuggled across the border.[75] Moviegoers noticed the change too: "In 1940 there were many films about spies. Mainly these ones in this year"; "[P]articularly in the last years before the war, it was only films about espionage and spies, spies, spies. You must be vigilant and things like that."[76] All interviewees who mentioned the predominance of spy movies either implied or said directly that they disliked this. Yet, there are signals in the transcripts that the spy mania in the movies was having some effect on Soviet society. One respondent, who was a young girl at the time, confessed that she also wanted to catch a spy. Another interviewee phrased his objection to spy films in the following way: "I was not willing to attend films about vigilance and spies. When people saw these films, they began to think that there were spies everywhere and they began distrusting everyone; a brother was afraid of his brother and discord arose in every family."[77] Although this respondent is probably talking about the cumulative effect of the hunt for both internal enemies and foreign agents during the 1930s, his strong wording is still significant. Indeed, the research and memoirs on everyday life in Kyiv during the first weeks of the war confirm the gravity of this problem. A veritable witch hunt was underway in the streets, where crowds of people detained individuals as suspected German spies, usually because they were wearing some unusual garment or hairstyle, had asked for directions, or were "German-looking." Young Kyivites, those active moviegoers of the prewar years, led the way in "exposing" alleged enemy agents.[78]

Ten years later, sitting in front of American interviewers in Munich, people who had been teenagers in prewar Soviet Ukraine could be very reluctant in offering answers to the question, "What kind of movies did you prefer to see?" Soviet movies being inescapably political, an answer could be interpreted as an expression of socialist sympathies and thus prevent immigration to North America.[79] In one case, after this question is recorded, the interviewer adds a parenthetical note, "Respondent thought an unusually long time before answering this relatively simple question." The respondent in question, an ethnic Ukrainian worker, who was in his early teens before the war, finally chose his strategy. He began by saying, "I liked the films about Soviet youth because I was in a position to compare what they said with what I knew existed," and then gave the example of *The Road to Life* (1931), the first Soviet sound film and a huge success with audiences mainly because of its topic, the gangs of homeless children that roamed Soviet cities for much of the 1920s. The film's main message was the reeducation of street children into good citizens, but the interviewee claimed that, in his experience, "such children were not treated that way, but rather they were oppressed and they lived in misery and hunger, and they did not become such fine people as the film said."[80] Thus, the respondent managed to turn the question about the Soviet films that he liked into an answer about their falsehood.

The majority of interviewees, however, answered in a different vein, trying to salvage a significant part of Soviet movie production as non-political and therefore likeable. The most popular answer by far was, in fact, Soviet historical films.[81] As one interviewee put it, "I liked the films that were non-political in character, i.e., historical films." To the interviewer's surprise, the respondent gave the example of *Alexander Nevsky* (1938), Sergei Eisenstein's great film about the thirteenth-century Russian prince, but also a nationalistic historical tale approved by Stalin. An interesting exchange followed:

(Did you not think that these films—even though historical—had a political context?) Take that film about Alexander Nevsky. It had a patriotic tinge, a Great Russian patriotic tinge and not a communist aspect. Take the film about Bogdan Xkhmelistky [Bohdan Khmelnytsky], who liberated the Ukraine from the Poles and made union with the Russians. These films did not have a communist line in them. From 1938 they started films with an ideology of patriotism, of Great Russian patriotism, which reached its climax in 1943, when they re-established shoulder boards [epaulets] for the officers.[82]

Classifying such Russian and Ukrainian patriotic historical films as *Alexander Nevsky* and *Bohdan Khmelnytsky* as "non-political" meant limiting the political sphere to pure Marxist ideology—a curious contradiction of the popular suggestion that *all* Soviet films contained propaganda. Perhaps, the meaning of "propaganda" was also limited to that of communist propaganda? This would explain another respondent's statement, "All Soviet films are of the same character—pure Party line propaganda. Only in the late thirties did we receive some historical films portraying Peter the Great and Ivan the Terrible as great Russian patriots who made Russia great."[83] Another Ukrainian interviewee also defied the conventional Western reading of *Alexander Nevsky* as a Stalinist film about a Stalin-like great leader, which was made in preparation for the war against Germany. He said that this film "was very popular because it was historical, it had nothing to do with Stalin and no connection was made between the war against the Germans depicted in this movie and the future war. People simply felt that this was a patriotic picture, describing the national sentiment and [they] enjoyed it very much."[84]

At this point it becomes clear that the interviewees were rewriting their memories—they surely saw all the connections they now denied, but were unwilling to acknowledge that the films they liked contained political propaganda. By doing so, they were trying to erase their own Soviet identity: if they liked a Soviet film, it must have been un-Soviet. In terms of ethnic identity, one can also conclude that a large proportion of Ukrainian moviegoers during the 1930s still found it easy to identify with the Russian national past as represented in *Alexander Nevsky*.

The respondents used a similar strategy with other Soviet films. They readily acknowledged liking films based on literary classics and thus presumably free of Soviet ideology.[85] They also felt safe about the film versions of Ukrainian classical operas.[86] However, Soviet musical comedies—one of the most popular movie genres during the 1930s—presented a problem. The transcripts contain examples of interviewees opposing them to "propaganda" films: "[T]here is a film I saw ten times. This film was called *Circus*. I also saw another good Soviet film called *Happy Children* [*Jolly Fellows*]. Another one called *Wolga, Wolga* [*Volga, Volga*]. I liked very much musical films and I did not like propaganda films."[87] In answering the question about the truthfulness of Soviet films, another interviewee stated, "If it was a comical movie devoid of propaganda, then there was no use looking in it for some hidden meaning."[88] Yet another respondent also named *Circus* as her favorite, yet she had doubts about its non-political character, which she still ascribed to two other musical comedies. When asked which film made the greatest impression on her, she replied, "*Circus* with Orlova, this was a very popular film without any spies or war, but there was still propaganda about America. Then there was also one, *Happy Kids* [*Jolly Fellows*]. This was the only one completely without propaganda. There was another non-propaganda film, *A Musical Story*."[89]

There could, of course, be another explanation for such an approach, in addition to rewriting one's identity in new circumstances and in front of American interviewers. Perhaps the same perception mechanism as with Charlie Chaplin's movies was at work, with Soviet people *wanting* to enjoy them simply as comedies with no social message. Here is how one respondent explained his love of Soviet comedies: "The comical stories were usually about the kolkhoz or the Soviet factory. They tried to place the Soviet Union in a good light, naturally. But we enjoyed them for their humor and never looked at them critically. We never discussed whether they gave a fair picture of Soviet life or not. To us the important things w[ere] the acting or the humor involved."[90]

At the same time, and perhaps the greatest surprise to the American social scientists working on the Harvard Project, some interviewees openly acknowledged liking even those Soviet films where the political message was central and dominant. The respondent who just expressed his preference for musical films over propaganda movies went on to say, "But Soviet films, even propaganda films were much better th[a]n Western films because they had to make propaganda interesting. There were no cheap type movies, no cowboy movies, no detective films. The Soviet public is more serious[,] it has higher demands than the American or the German public. The Soviet public wanted to see real real [sic] films and no cowboy films. Such Western films would fall [fail] miserably in the Soviet Union."[91] Along the same lines, another interviewee explained that "[f]or instance, *Lenin in October* was a work of art. Soviet films caught your attention and attracted you."[92] Yet another respondent, a middle-aged Ukrainian tractor driver, in addition to the artistic qualities of Soviet films, emphasized their moral message:

> Oh, Russian films! Did you ever see Soviet pictures? You would have liked them. Very beautiful. There are no such films like Russian films. If you look at an American film, what do you see? Presentation of loose morals, shootings, and so on. Over there it's well done. It's very smartly done by the Soviets. Over there, if in a film [there] were shootings, children would not be allowed, not children under 18. I saw different films, the German films, I don't like them. I saw French films, I don't like them either. About English, I don't know. Look at German films. What do you see? They kiss each other, and they kiss each other. Over there it would not be shown for people under 18 years. Have you ever seen Soviet films? Well you must like them if you see them. (What kind of films did you see?) Oh, mainly about industrialization, or when new plants were built, then the military films, historical, the film *Boris Godunov*, the Soviet picture *Cha[p]aev*. All this, of course, was made as an agitation and propaganda for the Soviet power, but it was beautifully made.[93]

Overall, although the majority of respondents agreed that most Soviet films contained propaganda, many also said openly that, in general, Soviet movies were good: "Our films—the Soviet films in general—were good films"; "we had good movies," "there were good Russian films"; "anyhow, we used to love them."[94] Some were aware of this contradiction. One respondent noted about Soviet films, "I enjoyed them very much, but I knew they were portraying a certain situation with a definite goal in mind and from a definite viewpoint."[95] Another interviewee clarified the perceptional strategy allowing moviegoers to enjoy most Soviet movies irrespective of the genre: "Most of the contemporary films were of a political nature, and this had to be discounted." He went on to explain, "Of course, we knew that life in Soviet films did not represent real life. We did not go to movies to see real life; we were tired of it. If propaganda did not distort the plot too much, if the story was interesting and the acting good, we enjoyed the film."[96]

Yet, it would be a mistake to overemphasize the escapist aspect of going to the movies under Stalin. In my sample there are no easy, thoughtless films among those mentioned most often by respondents. Rather, one might suggest that the Soviet Ukrainian viewers fulfilled their escapist dreams by consuming the cinematic dream world as prescribed by Socialist Realism, Soviet life as it ought to be. As one interviewee tried to explain, Soviet books and films "were not meant to show people what life was like, but how it should be."[97] This is perhaps what another respondent attempted to express rather awkwardly when he was talking about his preference for Soviet "romantic films which had less propaganda than war films": "In romantic films you see a young romantic hero, living like a capitalist. He has all the modern conveniences, eats chicken for dinner, etc."[98] This way, Ukrainian moviegoers could enjoy Stalinist cinema even though they knew it was a world of socialist illusion: "If life in the Soviet Union was actually that which was portrayed in the film, life would be good, the Soviet people would be satisfied, there would be no refugees from the Soviet Union, and I would be sitting at home or I would be going home now."[99]

Socialist Dream World

Such answers, of course, preempted and made irrelevant the last and most important question that the American sociologists wanted to ask about Soviet films, "Did you think that they showed things in a true light?" The social scientists on the Harvard Project team wanted to find out whether Soviet audiences trusted films as a source of information, but the answers they received often subverted the question.

To be sure, the majority of respondents in my sample characterized Soviet films as untruthful.[100] Even those individuals who had just praised Soviet movies on the previous page of the interview transcript answered in the negative.[101] Yet, there was also a substantial number of respondents who felt that only some things in Soviet films were embellished. This position is represented by answers, such as "Not always [true to life]"; "Sometimes true, sometimes not"; and "Yes, but I did not believe everything." In the last case, the interviewer interjected an additional question, "Why didn't you believe everything?" The respondent replied, "Because I knew that some of that was untrue. I saw how dirty the Russian cities were and how the people lived in the Soviet Union."[102]

The interviewees giving such conditional answers possibly tried to express the same sentiment as those who were denying the truthfulness of Soviet movies yet liking them—that they *wanted* to believe in the socialist dream world, although they knew it did not (yet) exist in reality. Other, less common, types of answers could also reflect this same position—from the statement that it was "interesting" to watch Soviet movies, regardless of their truthfulness, to the refusal to answer ("I don't know"). In the latter case, the interviewer also tried to clarify, "I am particularly asking about any political films." Again, the answer was, "I don't know whether they gave correct information or not."[103] In his answer, one interviewee combined all three approaches described above, with the addition of a hint that other moviegoers may have believed everything: "Every person knows there was coloring. I knew that it was not all as they described it. But I did not know about how others felt. Say that in the picture *On the Border* a spy is caught. Well, maybe that is so, I don't know."[104]

In some cases, respondents argued that some categories of Soviet films were more truthful than others, particularly in relation to the (notoriously disingenuous) movies about the Red Army. In the three cases where the interviewees praised the military movies, they had not served in the army at the time. Tellingly, one of the respondents dismissed as untruthful the portrayal of village life, which he knew best, but believed in the idealistic image of the military: "Military films appeared to me to be correct, why, I do not know. I had not seen military life at that time and so they looked correct to me. However, I did not believe the films on collective farm life were true. They were false."¹⁰⁵

Finally, other respondents tried to explain to the interviewers the fallacy of their social-science approach. They made it clear that the Soviet people did not go to the movies to receive information, but to enjoy them as art or to be entertained: "I went to the movies not to obtain factual information but to appreciate art"; "These were no[t] films of information but rather entertainment films"; "I just went to the movies to rest"; "[I] regarded films as a way of escape from unpleasant reality."¹⁰⁶ In one revealing case, the interviewer decided not to ask the question about the truthfulness of Soviet films because s/he felt that it would be futile, given the respondent's clear preference for "escapist entertainment."¹⁰⁷ This, of course, skewed the statistical sample, but the interviewer's decision is telling as a reflection of the American social scientists' frustration with the answers they were getting.

This was probably the reason why the final report and the other main publications resulting from the Harvard Project did not include materials on film reception in the Soviet Union. While most other aspects of everyday life under Stalin covered in the interviews soon became the subject of numerous books and articles, the film preferences of the Soviet people were given short shrift. In 1959, one of the interviewers, John David Rimberg, defended his Ph.D. thesis in Sociology on Soviet cinema from 1918 to 1952, which incorporated the analysis of the project's findings. His dissertation, however, remained unpublished until 1973, when it finally appeared (unrevised, as a photocopy of the original text) in the Arno Press "Dissertations on Film" series. In his work, Rimberg explains the numerous favorable comments about Soviet films by their "uncritical acceptance" by the audience.¹⁰⁸ The most important question for him as a sociologist is "whether Soviet audiences were satisfied or dissatisfied with the degree of propaganda content in Soviet films." In order to answer it, Rimberg compares, "in terms of propaganda content," the films named by the respondents with all the Soviet films that were released between 1934 and 1940, to conclude that there is virtually no difference. From this it follows that "the average Soviet film-goer was generally satisfied with the film fare produced in Soviet studios during the period 1934–1940."[109]

Such conclusions likely would not fit well into the final report of the project that was conducted at the height of the Cold War and funded by the US military. More importantly, however, the American social scientists probably realized that their questions were misguided. The Soviet people did not view films as an information medium. They liked Soviet movies and wanted to identify with the world of socialist illusion presented in films, even if they knew that the reality was different and claimed to dislike propaganda. In that respect, moviegoers in Soviet Ukraine and the Soviet Union in general were not much different from cinema audiences elsewhere.

Notes

The author thanks David Brandenberger for his comments and Marta D. Olynyk for her editorial assistance.

[1] The total number of admissions for 1940 is in Peter Kenez, *Cinema and Soviet Society from the Revolution to the Death of Stalin* (London: I. B. Tauris, 2001), 119. The Russian film scholar Maya Turovskaya has proposed an interesting technique for estimating the real extent of a film's popularity in Stalin's time — calculating the turnover per copy of a film. This, however, is a time-consuming task and also dependent on the availability of complete data. Her team was able to establish that in 1937 an Armenian adventure film for youth, *Karo*, far outstripped the official favorite, *Lenin in October*. In 1938, however, the official and the popular choice coincided in *Alexander Nevsky*. See Maya Turovskaya, "The 1930s and 1940s: Cinema in Context," in Richard Taylor and Derek Spring, eds., *Stalinism and Soviet Cinema* (London: Routledge, 1993), 50 and idem, "The Tastes of Soviet Moviegoers during the 1930s," in Thomas Lahusen and Gene Kuperman, eds., *Late Soviet Culture: From Perestroika to Novostroika* (Durham: Duke University Press, 1993), 103.

[2] For the history of the Harvard Project, see David Brandenberger, "A Background Guide to Working with the HPSSS Online," http://hcl.harvard.edu/collections/hpsss/working_with_hpsss.pdf; Raymond Bauer, Alex Inkeles, and Clyde Kluckhohn, *How the Soviet System Works: Cultural, Psychological, and Social Themes* (Cambridge, MA: Harvard University Press, 1959), 3-15; Alex Inkeles and Raymond Bauer, *The Soviet Citizen: Daily Life in a Totalitarian Society* (Cambridge, MA: Harvard University Press, 1959): 3–64.

³ See Maurice Friedberg, "Foreign Authors and Soviet Readers," *Russian Review* 13, no. 4 (October 1954): 266–75; idem, "Russian Writers and Soviet Readers," *American Slavic and East European Review* 14, no. 1 (February 1955): 108–21.
⁴ David Brandenberger, ed., *Political Humor under Stalin: An Anthology of Unofficial Jokes and Anecdotes* (Bloomington: Slavica, forthcoming in 2008).
⁵ "HPSSS. Qualitative File Manual of A-Schedule Materials. Second-Run Edition," 3 (http://pds.lib.harvard.edu/pds/view/5646842?n=128).
⁶ Alex Inkeles, *Public Opinion in Soviet Russia: A Study in Mass Persuasion* (Cambridge, MA: Harvard University Press, 1950), 289.
⁷ The quote is from Inkeles, *Public Opinion*, 310.
⁸ Raymond A. Bauer, Alex Inkeles, and Clyde Kluckhohn, *How the Soviet System Works: Cultural, Psychological, and Social Themes* (Cambridge, MA: Harvard University Press, 1959), 25–26.
⁹ Alex Inkeles and Raymond A. Bauer, with the assistance of David Gleicher and Irving Rosow, *The Soviet Citizen: Daily Life in a Totalitarian Society* (Cambridge, MA: Harvard University Press, 1961), 159.
¹⁰ Ibid., 160.
¹¹ Peter H. Rossi and Raymond A. Bauer, "Some Patterns of Soviet Communications Behavior," *Public Opinion Quarterly* 16, no. 4 (Winter 1952–53): 653–66.
¹² Rossi and Bauer, "Some Patterns," 655; Inkeles and Bauer, *The Soviet Citizen*, 166–67.
¹³ The project team attempted to identify the most biased interviewees through a sophisticated "distortion index." However, they did not account for the considerable difference between the interviews conducted with people in Germany, most of whom were waiting for immigration clearance to leave for North America or Australia, and those done in New York—the interviewees already in the United States expressed a more positive view of Soviet achievements. The authors explain this change by the difficult transition period in the US rather than greater freedom of expression after passing the immigration purgatory, although both factors probably were at work. See Inkeles and Bauer, *The Soviet Citizen*, 41–64.
¹⁴ Rossi and Bauer, "Some Patterns," 660; Inkeles and Bauer, *The Soviet Citizen*, 169.
¹⁵ Inkeles and Bauer, *The Soviet Citizen*, 170.
¹⁶ Rossi and Bauer, "Some Patterns," 663.
¹⁷ John David Rimberg, *The Motion Picture in the Soviet Union: 1918–1952: A Sociological Analysis* (New York: Arno Press, 1973), 134.
¹⁸ HPSSS, Schedule A, Vol. 15, Case 285, p. 32 ("rarely" as "once a month"); Schedule A, Vol. 7, Case 98 ("seldom" as "once a month");

Schedule A, Vol. 33, Case 454/(NY)1350, p. 29 ("seldom" as "not even once a month"); Vol. 14, Case 258, p. 80 (every day); Vol. 10, Case 129, p. 29 (never).

[19] HPSSS, Schedule A, Vol. 31, Case 102/(NY)1011, p. 56; Schedule A, Vol. 14, Case 266, p. 25. From this point onward, I am leaving unchanged the occasionally odd grammar and syntax of the interview transcripts. Although the interviews were conducted in Russian or Ukrainian, the transcripts were prepared in English only and never edited properly. I have corrected only the obvious typos.

[20] HPSSS, Schedule A, Vol. 10, Case 127, p. 38. Another person mentioned free movie showings for students and staff at the college where she worked (Schedule A, Vol. 37, Case 95/[NY]1720, p. 32.)

[21] HPSSS, Schedule A, Vol. 10, Case 129, p. 29; Vol. 6, Case 74, p. 7.

[22] HPSSS, Schedule A, Vol. 30, Case 642, p. 41.

[23] See Table 1 in Richard Taylor and Ian Cross, eds., *The Film Factory: Russian and Soviet Cinema in Documents, 1896–1939* (London: Routledge and Kegan Paul, 1988), 423.

[24] Kenez, *Cinema and Soviet Society*, 124.

[25] HPSSS, Schedule A, Vol. 20, Case 394, pp. 21-22.

[26] HPSSS, Schedule A, Vol. 20, Case 394, p. 22. See also Vol. 20, Case 399, p. 28.

[27] HPSSS, Schedule A, Vol. 34, Case 494, p. 31 (twice a week); Vol. 8, Case 103, p. 43 (seasonal difference).

[28] HPSSS, Schedule A, Vol. 10, Case 129, p. 29; Vol. 8, Case 103, p. 43. MTS is the abbreviation of Machine and Tractor Station, a technical centre serving several collective farms.

[29] HPSSS, Schedule A, Vol. 36, Case 333/(NY)1582, p. 33 (military school); Vol. 17, Case 332, p. 30 and Vol. 26, Case 514, p. 33 (soldiers).

[30] HPSSS, Schedule A, Vol. 7, Case 91, pp. 37–38.

[31] HPSSS, Schedule A, Vol. 32, Case 643/(NY)1215, p. 43 (driver); Vol. 36, Case 492/(NY)1654, pp. 29–30 (mechanic).

[32] HPSSS, Schedule A, Vol. 10, Case 127, p. 38 (until 13); Vol. 7, Case 98, p. 24 (housewife); Vol. 16, Case 323, p. 37 (every Saturday); Vol. 17, Case 332, p. 30 (Saturday and Sunday).

[33] HPSSS, Schedule A, Vol. 14, Case 258, p. 80 (free pass); Vol. 9, Case 121, p. 18 (3 and 7 days); Vol. 35, Case 97/(NY)1528, p. 47 (getting tickets).

[34] HPSSS, Schedule A, Vol. 23, Case 456, p. 24 (broken film); Vol. 33, Case 644, p. 51 (kissing); Vol. 22, Case 449, p. 18 (movie houses).

[35] HPSSS, Schedule A, Vol. 15, Case 284, pp. 19-20 (fire and arrest); Vol. 16, Case 314, pp. 10–11 (anti-Soviet). The second projectionist also claimed that his colleagues dispatched from Russia were often NKVD agents sent to study the attitudes in the Ukrainian countryside.

36 HPSSS, Schedule A, Vol. 31, Case 102/(NY)1011, p. 56 (preview); Vol. 35, Case 97/(NY)1528, pp. 47–48 (party boss).
37 HPSSS, Schedule A, Vol. 26, Case 520, p. 24; Vol. 33, Case 644, p. 56; Vol. 14, Case 266, p. 25; Vol. 22, Case 446, p. 59.
38 HPSSS, Schedule A, Vol. 5, Case 61, p. 37 (school principal); Vol. 25, Case 492, pp. 38–39 (mechanic).
39 HPSSS, Schedule A, Vol. 14, Case 258, p. 81 is a particularly telling example. See also Vol. 24, Case 479, p. 41 and Vol. 7, Case 98, p. 24.
40 HPSSS, Schedule A, Vol. 10, Case 127, p. 39; Vol. 35, Case 97/(NY)1528, p. 47.
41 HPSSS, Schedule A, Vol. 12, Case 148, p. 29 (until 1936); Vol. 22, Case 449, p. 18 (until 1937 and a movie house in Odesa).
42 See Kenez, *Cinema and Soviet Society*, 120 and Turovskaya, "The 1930s and 1940s," 42.
43 HPSSS, Schedule A, Vol. 18, Case 355, p. 22; Vol. 35, Case 97/(NY)1528, p. 47.
44 See Dmytro Malakov, *Oti dva roky...: U Kyievi pry nimtsiakh* (Kyiv: Amadei, 2002), 152 and http://en.wikipedia.org/wiki/Miliza_Korjus.
45 Turovskaya, "The 1930s and 1940s," 51; idem, "The Tastes of Soviet Moviegoers," 104
46 HPSSS, Schedule A, Vol. 17, Case 332, p. 30; Vol. 9, Case 121, p. 18.
47 HPSSS, Schedule A, Vol. 30, Case 644, p. 60; Vol. 28, Case 537, p. 23.
48 HPSSS, Schedule A, Vol. 20, Case 399, p. 28; Vol. 34, Case 147/(NY)1467, p. 37 (no foreign films); Vol. 36, Case 492/(NY)1654, p. 29 ("don't remember"); Vol. 34, Case 494, p. 31 (Artemivsk); Vol. 23, Case 456, p. 35 (town of 20,000).
49 HPSSS, Schedule A, Vol. 15, Case 285, p. 32.
50 HPSSS, Schedule A, Vol. 14, Case 266, p. 25; Vol. 25, Case 507, p. 37; Vol. 14, Case 258, p. 81; Vol. 24, Case 479, pp. 41–42.
51 HPSSS, Schedule A, Vol. 25, Case 507, p. 37; Vol. 37, Case 95/(NY)1720, p. 32; Vol. 22, Case 446, p. 60.
52 HPSSS, Schedule A, Vol. 9, Case 121, p. 18.
53 See, for example HPSSS, Schedule A, Vol. 26, Case 520, p. 24; Vol. 30, Case 642, p. 41; Vol. 34, Case 90/(NY)1441, p. 51; Vol. 34, Case 104/(NY)1492, p. 23; Vol. 12, Case 147, p. 74; Vol. 15, Case 285, p. 32; Vol. 22, Case 449, p. 18.
54 HPSSS, Schedule A, Vol. 16, Case 323, p. 37; Vol. 14, Case 258, p. 81; The only mention of *The Great Dictator* is in Vol. 9, Case 121, p. 19.
55 HPSSS, Schedule A, Vol. 33, Case 644, p. 56; Vol. 20, Case 398, p. 17; Vol. 14, Case 258, p. 81; Vol. 22, Case 446, p. 59; Vol. 16, Case 323, p. 37; Vol. 14, Case 266, p. 25 (*Peter* and/or *Little Mother*); Vol. 24, Case 479, p. 42;

Vol. 14, Case 266, p. 25 (*One Hundred Men and a Girl*).

[56] HPSSS, Schedule A, Vol. 16, Case 323, p. 37; Vol. 20, Case 398, p. 17; Vol. 14, Case 258, p. 81; Vol. 22, Case 446, p. 59.

[57] HPSSS, Schedule A, Vol. 26, Case 520, p. 24.

[58] HPSSS, Schedule A, Vol. 36, Case 333/(NY)1582, p. 34.

[59] HPSSS, Schedule A, Vol. 7, Case 91, p. 38.

[60] HPSSS, Schedule A, Vol. 10, Case 127, p. 39 (yes); Vol. 15, Case 285, p. 32 (cannot say); Vol. 25, Case 507, p. 37 (no).

[61] HPSSS, Schedule A, Vol. 10, case 127, p. 39.

[62] HPSSS, Schedule A, Vol. 9, Case 121, p. 19.

[63] HPSSS, Schedule A, Vol. 20, Case 398, p. 17.

[64] HPSSS, Schedule A, Vol. 25, p. 37; Vol. 7, Case 98, p. 24; Vol. 34, Case 104/(NY)1492, p. 23.

[65] Turovskaya, "The 1930s and 1940s," 42; the numbers are from Table 2 in Taylor and Cross, *The Film Factory*, 424.

[66] HPSSS, Schedule A, Vol. 20, case 398, p. 17; Vol. 14, Case 258, p. 80; Vol. 22, Case 446, p. 59.

[67] HPSSS, Schedule A, Vol. 34, Case 494, p. 32; Vol. 10, Case 127, p. 38; Vol. 35, Case 97/(NY)1528, p. 47; Vol. 14, Case 266, p. 25; Vol. 16, Case 323, p. 37; Vol. 33, Case 644, p. 56.

[68] HPSSS, Schedule A, Vol. 35, Case 97/(NY)1528, p. 47.

[69] HPSSS, Schedule A, Vol. 35, Case 97/(NY)1528, p. 47; Vol. 12, Case 147, p. 74; Vol. 8, Case 103, p. 43.

[70] HPSSS, Schedule A, Vol. 28, Case 537, p. 23; Vol. 36, Case 333/(NY)1582, p. 34; Vol. 14, Case 258, pp. 80–81.

[71] HPSSS, Schedule A, Vol. 23, Case 456, p. 35.

[72] Rimberg, *The Motion Picture in the Soviet Union*, 150.

[73] HPSSS, Schedule B, Vol. 7, Case 67, pp. 37–38; Vol. 9, Case 495, pp. 45–46. Some signs in the text point to the well-known literary historian and cultural figure Hryhorii Kostiuk as a possible interviewee in Case 495. Compare his memoirs, *Zustrichi i proshchannia* (Edmonton: Canadian Institute of Ukrainian Studies Press, 1987–98), 2 vols.

[74] I deal here with the opinions of those respondents who had reasonable exposure to Soviet movies and were willing to discuss their experiences. My sample of interviews from the Harvard Project also contains two rather dismissive and tendentious responses. One person claimed that he went to the movies only two or three times in his life because of his intense dislike for Soviet cinema: "I hated it. It was full of lies" (HPSSS, Schedule A, Vol. 32, Case 643/(NY)1215, p. 43). Another expressed the view that "irreligious and immoral movies and plays should be forbidden and religious tendencies should be encouraged" (Vol. 36, Case 492/(NY)1654, p. 42).

75 Kenez, *Cinema and Soviet Society*, 149.

76 HPSSS, Schedule A, Vol. 25, Case 507, p. 37; Vol. 15, Case 285, p. 32. See also Vol. 22, Case 449, p. 18 and Vol. 14, Case 258, p. 80.

77 HPSSS, Schedule A, Vol. 14, Case 258, p. 80 (wanted to catch a spy); Vol. 16, Case 323, p. 37 (quote).

78 See Karel C. Berkhoff, *Harvest of Despair: Life and Death in Ukraine under Nazi Rule* (Cambridge, MA: Belknap Press of Harvard University Press, 2004), 24–25; Malakov, *Oti dva roky*, 50; Fedir Pihido-Pravoberezhnyi, *"Velyka Vitchyzniana viina": Spohady ta rozdumy ochevydtsia* (Kyiv: Smoloskyp, 2002), 31–32.

79 One famous case of a Ukrainian DP in postwar Germany who was not allowed to immigrate to the US because of his socialist (although not pro-Soviet) views was that of Ivan Maistrenko, who quite possibly participated in the Harvard Project. See his memoirs, *Istoriia moho pokolinnia: Spohady uchasnyka revoliutsiinykh podii v Ukraini* (Edmonton: Canadian Institute of Ukrainian Studies Press, 1985).

80 HPSSS, Schedule A, Vol. 18, Case 349, pp. 48–49.

81 HPSSS, Schedule A, Vol. 14, Case 266, p. 25; Vol. 34, Case 147/(NY)1467, p. 37; Vol. 22, Case 446, p. 59; Vol. 16, Case 323, p. 37; Vol. 10, Case 127, p. 38; Vol. 24, Case 479, p. 42; Vol. 30, case 642, p. 41.

82 HPSSS, Schedule A, Vol. 10, Case 128, p. 16. On the change in the late 1930s from proletarian internationalism to a peculiar form of nationalism, often specific to the Soviet republic in question, see David Brandenberger, *National Bolshevism: Stalinist Mass Culture and the Formation of Modern Russian National Identity, 1931–1956* (Cambridge, MA: Harvard University Press, 2002) and Serhy Yekelchyk, *Stalin's Empire of Memory: Russian-Ukrainian Relations in the Soviet Historical Imagination* (Toronto: University of Toronto Press, 2004).

83 HPSSS, Schedule A, Vol. 35, Case 97/(NY)1528, p. 47.

84 HPSSS, Schedule A, Vol. 9, Case 118, p. 28.

85 HPSSS, Schedule A, Vol. 10, Case 128, p. 16; Vol. 18, Case 355, p. 23; Vol. 30, Case 642, p. 41; Vol. 30, Case 644, p. 60; Vol. 37, Case 95/(NY)1720, p. 32. Maurice Friedberg, who has analyzed the reading practices of the Harvard Project interviewees, notes, "It is curious that the indiscriminate belief in the truthfulness of the classics was also extended to the Soviet films based on the classics which quite frequently deviate to a significant extent from the original literary works" (Friedberg, "Russian Writers and Soviet Readers," 114, n. 16). Friedberg also comments on the respondents' tendency to emphasize their love for pre-revolutionary and foreign literature and to deny liking—or even reading—Soviet literature (Ibid, 113–114).

86 HPSSS, Schedule A, Vol. 16, Case 323, p. 37.

[87] HPSSS, Schedule A, Vol. 20, Case 398, p. 17. *Jolly Fellows* (1934), *Circus* (1936), and *Volga, Volga* (1938) were musical comedies directed by Grigorii Aleksandrov and starring his wife Liubov Orlova. All three contained an unmistakable ideological message about the opportunities that were opening up for ordinary people under socialism; *Circus* also features a critique of capitalism in general and American racism in particular.

[88] HPSSS, Schedule A, Vol. 34, Case 90/(NY)1441, p. 51.

[89] HPSSS, Schedule A, Vol. 14, case 258, p. 81. The main character of *Circus*, an American circus performer by the name of Marion Dixon, is almost lynched in her country for having a baby out of wedlock and with a black man. She finds happiness and new love in the Stalinist Soviet Union, where there is no racial discrimination. *A Musical Story* (1940) is a musical film with elements of comedy starring the great Soviet tenor Sergei Lemeshev. Of course, the movie was not free from a political message—it showed how a simple truck driver could develop his singing talent with the state's support for amateur performers and eventually become an opera star.

[90] HPSSS, Schedule A, Vol. 30, Case 642, pp. 41–42.

[91] HPSSS, Schedule A, Vol. 20, Case 398, pp. 17–18.

[92] HPSSS, Schedule A, Vol. 5, Case 61, p. 37.

[93] HPSSS, Schedule A, Vol. 8, Case 103, pp. 43–44.

[94] HPSSS, Schedule A, Vol. 22, Case 446, p. 59; Vol. 20, Case 399, p. 28; Vol. 9, Case 121, p. 18; Vol. 14, Case 258, p. 84.

[95] HPSSS, Schedule A, Vol. 31, Case 102/(NY)1011, p. 56.

[96] HPSSS, Schedule A, Vol. 37, Case 95/(NY)1720, p. 32.

[97] HPSSS, Schedule A, Vol. 30, Case 642, p. 42.

[98] HPSSS, Schedule A, Vol. 34, Case 147/(NY)1467, p. 37.

[99] HPSSS, Schedule A, Vol. 22, Case 446, p. 60.

[100] HPSSS, Schedule A, Vol. 12, Case 148, p. 29; Vol. 35, Case 97/(NY)1528, p. 47; Vol. 36, Case 333/(NY)1582, p. 34; Vol. 36, Case 492/(NY)1654, p. 30.

[101] HPSSS, Schedule A, Vol. 8, Case 103, p. 44; Vol. 20, Case 398, p. 18.

[102] HPSSS, Schedule A, Vol. 7, Case 91, p. 38 ("not always"); Vol. 20, Case 399, p. 28 ("sometimes"); Vol. 28, Case 537, p. 23 (exchange with the interviewer).

[103] HPSSS, Schedule A, Vol. 26, Case 520, p. 24 ("interesting"); Vol. 7, Case 98, p. 24 ("don't know").

[104] HPSSS, Schedule A, Vol. 17, Case 332, pp. 30–31. *On the Border* (1938) was a film about saboteurs, Russian White émigrés trying to cross the border from China. Reports of similar real incidents can be found in Soviet newspapers of the time.

[105] HPSSS, Schedule A, Vol. 23, Case 456, p. 35 (quote). See also Vol. 26, Case 514, p. 34 and Vol. 26, Case 520, p. 24.

[106] In the order in which the quotes are cited: HPSSS, Schedule A, Vol. 5, Case 61, p. 37; Vol. 10, Case 128, p. 17; Vol. 25, Case 492, p. 39; Vol. 34, Case 104/(NY)1492, p. 23.

[107] "Interviewer's note: It is readily apparent that the respondent's contacts with communications media were rather rare and whenever possible she chose escapist entertainment. Therefore probe c3 in the Speks was not pushed" (HPSSS, Schedule A, Vol. 24, Case 479, p. 42).

[108] Rimberg, *The Motion Picture in the Soviet Union*, 80–82.

[109] Ibid, 151–153

3
Confronting Antisemitism and Antifeminism in Turn-of-the-Century Vienna: Grete Meisel-Hess and the Modernist Discourses on Hysteria[1]

Helga Thorson

Turn-of-the-century Vienna was marked by increased anxieties about the changing relations between the sexes as well as the ethnic diversity of the dual monarchy. Within Viennese society, the boundaries between what was considered normal and healthy, on the one hand, and what was considered sick and degenerate, on the other, were constantly being negotiated. Those individuals who stepped outside of the realm of respectability—whether by transgressing appropriate gender roles or by exhibiting other forms of "difference" (e.g., linguistic, physiognomical, or physical)—were thought to be highly suspect and often constructed as a threat to the health of the nation.

Various strands of antifeminism and antisemitism permeated Viennese society at the end of the nineteenth and the beginning of the twentieth century and were interwoven in the nationalistic rhetoric of the time. It was argued that the emancipation of women, like the emancipation of the Jews, would endanger the social and moral fabric of the Habsburg monarchy. The popular images of the "masculinized" woman and the "feminized Jew" were used to illustrate that these social movements disrupted the natural order of things and were thus viewed as unnatural, perverse, and even hysterical.

Sex differentiation and sexuality lay at the heart of these matters. A clear differentiation between the sexes, for example, was equated with the health and vigor of a nation as well as the evolutionary superiority of its people. In his *Psychopathia Sexualis*, for example, the neuropsychologist Richard von Krafft-Ebing claimed: "The higher the anthropological development of a race, the more prominent these differentiations become. The lower the level of development, the less these differences between man and woman are apparent."[2] Within fin-de-siècle medical discourses, sex differentiation implied evolutionary perfection, thus separating (and simultaneously hierarchically ranking) people in terms of race, class, ethnicity, and gender role expectations. The Berlin sexologist Iwan Bloch maintained that it was the bourgeoisie of civilized nations that had reached the highest level of evolutionary progress:

> With increased refinement within a civilization the polarity of the sexes emerges more acutely and more individually, while under more primitive conditions, even among the peasantry and the proletariat, it is less pronounced and to some extent even blurred and equalized. One has only to bring to mind modern images of women from working-class circles who appear to us almost as men in disguise.[3]

Thus, within bourgeois German and Austrian society, the fear of the "Zwitter" (intersexual being) took on new meanings. This mixed-sexed body was thought to represent an evolutionary "Rückschritt" (regression) — a step backwards to more primitive times — as well as a threat to civilized society. The emancipated woman — the so-called "masculinized" woman — was often viewed by doctors as physically incapable of bearing children, a view which was thought to be reinforced by the declining birth rates. The male Jew also represented another dangerous "Zwitter." As scholars such as Sander Gilman and Klaus Hödl have shown, the "feminized" body of the male Jew was viewed as thoroughly diseased and contaminated[4] — thus further threatening the health of the Austro-Hungarian monarchy and impeding evolutionary progress.

Similarly, sexuality was viewed as another good measure of a nation's health and vitality. Hysteria and syphilis — the two most publicly profiled illnesses at the turn of the century—were afflictions that were popularly linked to women and Jews and their so-called deviant sexuality. Syphilis was thought to exist in the realm of abhorrent female sexuality (prostitution), and hysteria, a word etymologically linked to the female body, was historically viewed as a typical female malady. Furthermore, male Jews were thought to be linked to these illnesses because of the rumor that they were heavily involved in prostitution rings and white slavery and the belief that their so-called femininity and agitation were the results of a natural proclivity to hysteria. Modernism, with all its "nervousness," was thought to have led to the increased stimulation that manifested itself in hysteria. In both medical texts as well as images of popular culture, hysterics were depicted as either asexual or frigid (Anaesthesia Sexualis), as overly sexual (Hyperaesthesia Sexualis), or as possessing what was considered to be a perverse sexuality (Psychopathia Sexualis).

Antifeminist and antisemitic discourses were often constructed on similar grounds[5] and clearly intersected in the construction of the hysterical mixed-sexed body. How did feminists and Jews react to this construction of the dangerous "Zwitter" in turn-of-the-century Viennese society? The focus of this article is to highlight the response of one woman living in Vienna around the turn of the century—the writer Grete Meisel-Hess.[6] By analyzing the specific strategies that this feminist writer used to confront antifeminist and antisemitic discourses, I hope to illustrate the tensions that she felt both as a woman and as a Jew living in fin-de-siècle Viennese society. I begin by analyzing Meisel-Hess's response to Otto Weininger's book *Geschlecht und Charakter* (*Sex and Character*) in order to illustrate the strategies she used to confront Weininger's antisemitic and antifeminist rhetoric. I then focus on her reaction to Sigmund Freud and his theories on female sexuality and show how Meisel-Hess took Freud's strategy of de-centering the medical construction of the hysterical Jew one step further in her attempt to de-center the hysterical woman in early twentieth-century medical discourses.

Meisel-Hess's Response to Otto Weininger

One of the most obvious examples of a text that brings together antisemitic and antifeminist sentiments is Otto Weininger's

Geschlecht und Charakter,[7] a revised version of his doctoral dissertation in which he attempted to bring philosophical, psychological, and biological issues of sex differentiation together under one complete and comprehensive system. Every person, according to Weininger, possesses a combination of both male and female sex characteristics. Thus, sex differentiation was not to be viewed as a binary opposition, but rather as a spectrum of possibilities with the total male (M) at one extreme and the total female (W) at the other. According to Weininger: "We find, so to speak, never either a man or a woman, but only the male condition and the female condition."[8] In this way, Weininger's paradigm not only disrupted traditionally held notions on sex differentiation, but also suggested that the mixed-sexed body is the norm rather than the exception.

In addition, Weininger explained that in order for sexual attraction to occur, a total male (M) must come together with a total female (W). Thus, a man who is three-quarters M and one-quarter W would be attracted to a woman who is one-quarter M and three-quarters W. This theory of intermediary types drew on research by other turn-of-the-century medical doctors, most notably Magnus Hirschfeld whose *Jahrbuch für sexuelle Zwischenstufen* (*Yearbook for Sexual Intermediaries*) began publication in 1899 and Wilhelm Fliess who accused Weininger of plagiarizing his ideas on the inherent bisexuality of all individuals.[9] Yet, while the first several chapters of Weininger's text appear to revolutionize the way one views sex differentiation and sexual orientation by allowing for a range of possibilities, the latter half of the study brings out the misogynist nature of the text by describing the specific qualities represented by "M" and "W." Weininger's metaphysical construction of binary types reinforced and solidified traditional gender-based assumptions about the specific attributes and behavior of the sexes.

Weininger claimed that his era was not only the most "feminine" but also the most "Jewish" of all times,[10] and throughout his text he brought together notions of femininity, Judaism, and hysteria in his discussions of modernity. Just as Weininger insisted that all people exist on a spectrum somewhere between the total M and the total W, so too, he claimed, they vacillate between Judaism and Christianity. Individuals not only possess a mixture of masculine and feminine qualities, according to Weininger, but also a combination of both

Christian and Jewish qualities. Similar to his discussion of M and W, Weininger moved the discussion of Judaism away from the theories of racial science popular at the end of the nineteenth century to allow for a metaphysical possibility in which "race" was not a factor. He claimed: "There are Aryans who are more Jewish than Jews, and real Jews who are more Aryan than certain Aryans."[11]

At a time when medical discourses focused on the biological and physiological differences between the sexes as well as among various racial and ethnic groups, Weininger focused on the individual character of a person. An individual in Weininger's system was not confined to a static gender or racial destiny, but could fight against negative qualities that exist within. Thus, on the one hand, Weininger's paradigm is quite liberating in that it disrupts traditional binary oppositions and moves discussions of sex differentiation and ethnicity away from theories of biological determinism. Yet, on the other hand, it becomes clear that only one end of the spectrum (the male and the Christian) represents evolutionary progress. He concluded his chapter on Judaism as follows:

> The decision must be made between Judaism and Christianity, between business and culture, between male and female, between the race and the individual, between unworthiness and worth, between the earthly and the higher life, between negation and the God-like. Mankind has the choice to make. There are only two poles, and there is no middle way.[12]

For Weininger it was not the emancipation of women or the emancipation of the Jews that would lead to progress for humanity, but rather an individual's decision to rid himself of all "feminine" and "Jewish" qualities. In fact, Weininger's characterology conflated the female and the Jew to a large extent, thereby accentuating popular turn-of-the-century stereotypes of the effeminate Jewish male, who, like the female, lacked both an ego and a personality and who exhibited a natural proclivity to hysteria. As a Jewish male who had converted to Protestantism, Weininger made an appeal to reject the "Jewish" (and "feminine") side of human nature. Weininger's greatest concern seems to rest not with the emancipation of women, but rather with the feminization of men or what Misha Kavka has labeled "the collapse of manhood into the nothingness of femininity."[13]

Weininger called on men to embrace the masculine and Christian qualities found within themselves and to rid themselves of everything material and base (i.e., feminine and Jewish). However, he did not suggest that women should also embrace their masculine and Christian sides. In fact, he stated that the female (W) could never transcend her own limitations: "There are ... men who have become women or have remained women; but there is no woman who has surpassed certain circumscribed, not particularly elevated moral and intellectual limits. ...[T]he woman of the highest standard is immeasurably beneath the man of lowest standard."[14] Similarly, he stated that since females were amoral and lacked both an ego and a personality, there could be no such thing as a Christian woman.

Weininger's *Geschlecht und Charakter* illustrates the anxiety that existed in fin-de-siècle Vienna around issues of gender and ethnic identity. The book aroused a huge sensation, especially after the twenty-three-year-old Weininger's suicide, which occurred shortly after its publication. Whereas many individuals, including Karl Kraus and August Strindberg, rallied behind the book, others challenged its antifeminist and antisemitic tendencies. As a young Viennese author, Grete Meisel-Hess was the first and only woman to write a direct response to Weininger's text shortly after its publication and Weininger's suicide.[15] Her treatise, *Weiberhaß und Weiberverachtung. Eine Erwiderung auf die in Dr. Otto Weiningers Buche "Geschlecht und Charakter" geäußerten Anschauungen über "Die Frau und ihre Frage"* (*Misogyny and Contempt for Women. A Response to the Expressed Views in Dr. Otto Weininger's Book "Sex and Character" concerning "Woman and her Question"*), challenged Weininger's conclusions on female sex characteristics and women's emancipation.

It is not clear whether Meisel-Hess had ever met Weininger personally. It is quite possible since they both attended Vienna University at the same time. Meisel-Hess, who audited classes in philosophy, sociology and biology for five years, began her writing career in 1900 by writing articles and book reviews for various journals and by publishing monographs on important cultural issues.[16]

Her first novel, *Fanny Roth*, was published in 1902. According to Weininger's friend Emil Lucka, Otto Weininger was familiar with much contemporary literature by women, including the work of Meisel-Hess.[17]

Referring to Weininger's book as "an actual encyclopedia of contempt for women,"[18] Meisel-Hess critiqued Weininger's form of argumentation and reasoning—in particular, his use of words such as "richtig" (right, exact, true), "echt" (genuine, real), "absolut" (absolute) and "an sich" (in itself) to describe things that did not even exist: "He characterized the 'Jew in itself' and the 'Woman in itself' as *metaphysical concepts*, because, according to his own statements, they so genuinely (i.e., afflicted with astonishing defects and monstrosities)—do not even exist."[19] Furthermore, she claimed he reached conclusions through faulty logic and unlikely cause and effect reasoning. In fact, she suggested that his narrative was indeed hysterical itself, not only because it contained seeds of destruction, but also because of its gaps, inconsistencies, and faulty reasoning. Interestingly his "chattering, —clattering logic," which she described as "a logic with broken joints and jumbled shaken limbs,"[20] was not only similar to the way that Freud described the narratives of hysterical patients,[21] but also was a clear allusion to Weininger's epilepsy, a disease that was thought to be directly associated with hysteria and deviant sexuality at the turn of the century.

Weininger's narrative, like his physical state, was for Meisel-Hess a sign of sickness and degeneration. She maintained that it is not "female" or "Jewish" qualities that should be considered a threat to civilized societies, but rather strong feelings of antifeminism and antisemitism: "Misogyny and contempt for women are abnormal occurrences whose invalid assumptions are inherent in their very nature. The hatred of one sex towards the other and its degradation and debasement was always the sign of decline, degeneration, and decay—of the individual, if practiced by a few, or of whole nations, if rampant among the masses."[22] Weininger's pessimism and despair stood in stark contrast to Meisel-Hess's belief in evolutionary progress and optimistic hope for the future of humanity. As a follower of Darwin and Haeckel, Meisel-Hess believed that humanity was continuously evolving and perfecting itself. Furthermore, her monistic worldview was opposed to Weininger's "disgraceful dualism"[23] as she called it. Finally, Weininger's aversion to anything physical, material, or sexual conflicted with Meisel-Hess's hope for a healthy sexuality in both men and women—a sexuality that was neither characterized by frigidity nor perversity.

In her response to *Geschlecht und Charakter*, Meisel-Hess set out to deconstruct various types of borders that existed in Viennese society at the turn of the century. She maintained that it was impossible to compare the achievements of one group compared to another, as Weininger had attempted to do, and stated that comparisons can only be made on the individual level:

> An intellectual hierarchy is actually – so it appears to me – only applicable from individual to individual; not even among nations or tribes can a comparative judgment as a whole be made, let alone when it comprises one giant half of humanity; it is ludicrous and foolish to attempt to cordon women off within an artificially delimited domain with its own rules and values; for at any given time millions of individuals will be jumping out of the enforced gender sphere and transcend its boundaries.[24]

Besides highlighting the absurdity of attempts to define and rank the sexes or various ethnic groups, Meisel-Hess maintained that early twentieth-century women were already bursting through these constructed borders, thereby illustrating the very constructedness and fallibility of the definitions themselves. Throughout her text, Meisel-Hess claimed that such labeling and categorizing— even on the metaphysical level—was doomed to fail, because it neither accounted for existing individual differences nor the dynamic process of change constantly occurring both within individuals as well as within the entire species.

Meisel-Hess reminded her readers that Weininger's arguments may sound lofty and grand in theory, but that his arguments lose all ground when confronted with reality. She suggested that one has to look at the historical, economic, social, and psychological background—which, she maintained, was totally missing from Weininger's text. According to Meisel-Hess, it is impossible to compare the achievements of men and women or Jews and non-Jews not only because these groups are different from one another,[25] but also because they do not start out on equal footing. She explained that whereas a man is encouraged to achieve a significant position in society, women most often have to fight against their families, customs, tradition, and societal norms. Similarly, Jews have been persecuted and tormented for centuries, driven from their homes during various pogroms, and thus their achievements cannot be compared to other groups of people who were able to build roots in their homeland for several generations. Furthermore, Meisel-Hess maintained that one could no longer even talk about a Jewish people. Through their assimilation in various countries throughout the world, they were no longer a unified "Volk"—but were citizens of the nation in which they lived.

Throughout her text, Meisel-Hess critiqued Weininger's attempt to define and compare gender and ethnic characteristics. She wrote: "It is downright terroristic to characterize certain traits, characteristics, or predispositions as only "masculine" or "feminine." Often they are not one or the other, but rather simply *human*.[26] According to Meisel-Hess, evolutionary progress could only come about if one transcended gender, ethnic, class, and national limitations. She claimed: "Every individual who strives forward and upwards will seek to step out of the confinement of its mere national and gender-'type', in order to become more and more *human*, more and more culturally genuine."[27] She was not convinced that Zionism was the answer to the so-called "Jewish question," but rather that integration and assimilation were most beneficial for humanity. At the same time, however, she recognized the need for a territory that would accommodate the unassimilated Eastern European Jews, who she believed would otherwise be persecuted and tormented.

Meisel-Hess explained that variation was essential for the survival of the species. She called for the dynamic evolutionary development of humanity based on racial hygienic principles. Although she warned against miscegenation between blacks and whites in the German colonies,[28] she was convinced that the evolutionary ideal within "civilized societies" lay in what she referred to as a cultural cosmopolitanism. In a review of a lecture in 1911 by the political economist Werner Sombart, who discussed his ideas on the future of the Jews which he published a year later in his book *Die Zukunft der Juden* (*The Future of the Jews*), she critiqued his claim that it was of utmost importance to preserve the "type." Meisel-Hess claimed that progress could only be achieved by transcending culturally imposed constructions and limitations: "Only a cosmopolitan humanity that will learn to look and feel beyond national borders will finally bring about a bloodless opportunity for dialogue between people and will build the bridge, which torpedoes and grenades always tear down again."[29]

Whereas *Geschlecht und Charakter* could be viewed as quite revolutionary since it disrupted traditional notions of sex differentiation and moved Judaism from the realm of racial science that had become increasingly popular at the end of the nineteenth century, Weininger's text simultaneously reinforced and solidified traditional stereotypes such as the emancipated "Mannweib" (virago) and the feminized male Jew. Meisel-Hess's response to *Geschlecht and Charakter* focused on the fact that female emancipation was neither caused by nor the end result of a mixed-sexed body (the M in a female body that demanded it), but rather that female emancipation as well as the assimilation of the Jews would help society transcend traditional borders based on sex differentiation, gender role expectations, nationality, and ethnicity. According to Meisel-Hess, emancipation did not lead to an atavistic "Zwitter"—but rather to a new form of humanity that was breaking through the constructed barriers of sex and ethnic differentiation to form a cultural cosmopolitanism that existed beyond physical and psychological borders.[30]

Meisel-Hess attacked Weininger's antifeminism and antisemitism maintaining that they were the products of abnormality and illness and contained the seeds of destruction that would lead to degeneration and decay. She characterized Weininger's narrative as hysterical by illustrating its internal gaps, inconsistencies, its "chattering, —clattering logic," and its lack of adherence to reality. At one point in her monograph, Meisel-Hess accused Weininger of being totally unfamiliar with women—except for perhaps with prostitutes—and thus not in the position of being able to discuss the "woman's question" with any authority. This remark further highlighted Weininger's diseased state by suggesting that he had associated with prostitutes and, thus, that his diseased body was most likely also teaming with syphilis. His arguments, she claimed, were full of feverish delusions: "Born in delusion, they resemble spooky apparitions of phantoms that only exist for the one whose feverish brain conjured them up and that despite the tenacity of his hallucination do not become the slightest bit more real."[31] In this way, Meisel-Hess used the image of the diseased and hysterical body to discount Weininger's theories, claiming that they were the result of his illness. Although she claimed that Weininger's *Geschlecht und Charakter* was interesting and at times quite ingenious, she also insinuated that his narrative was completely and thoroughly hysterical.

Meisel-Hess's Response to Sigmund Freud

Whereas Meisel-Hess responded directly to Weininger's antisemitism and antifeminism through the publication of her monograph *Weiberhaß und Weiberverachtung* shortly after Weininger's suicide, her reaction to Freud's theories was much less direct and was diffused throughout her writings. On the one hand, Meisel-Hess was deeply influenced by Freud's work. She referred to Freud with great respect in her theoretical texts and clearly agreed with many of his theories—especially his notion that sexuality is an important force in the lives of both men and women. Similarly, her fictional works were clearly influenced by Freud. Her short stories are rich with dream sequences and stream of consciousness narratives that illustrate the inner-workings of the mind; she embraced topics that reflect the psychological and sexual forces affecting her individual protagonists; and she even introduced the character of the psychoanalyst to German fiction. In fact, her novel *Die Intellektuellen* (*The Intellectuals*) has been cited in Freud's *Zentralblatt für Psychoanalyse* (*Central Review of Psychoanalysis*) as the first work of fiction to provide a description of psychoanalytic treatment.[32]

While Meisel-Hess was clearly influenced by Freud, she also shifted the focus of some of his findings in order to highlight important issues facing women at the turn of the century. As a feminist fighting for the emancipation of women, Meisel-Hess was interested in many of the issues that Freud glossed over or even ignored in his work. In his studies on hysteria, for example, Freud focused on the hysterical bourgeois woman who was sexually frigid. Meisel-Hess, however, concentrated on the hysterical bourgeois male and issues of sexual violence, which were more or less absent in Freud's work. By analyzing Meisel-Hess's discussions of hysteria compared to Freud's, I will point out the strategies both authors used in order to confront the prevalent antisemitism found in turn-of-the-century medical discourses as well as the particular approaches Meisel-Hess used to challenge the phallocentric assumptions implicit in Freud's texts.

As assimilated Viennese Jews, both Freud and Meisel-Hess attempted to shift the discourses on hysteria away from the stereotypical image of the "hysterical" Jew by universalizing the illness, a strategy discussed by Sander L. Gilman in several of his books. Freud characterized modern nervousness as the result of the process of civilization—a process that mandated the repression of sexual instincts through the prevailing codes of sexual morality. As Gilman has explained, Freud discussed this harmful development in terms of "Kulturvölker" (civilized people) and "Schichten" (classes), rather than in terms of race or ethnicity—thus attempting to shift the medical discourses away from the image of the hysterical Jew.[33]

Similarly, Meisel-Hess attempted to move the discussions of hysteria away from that of race and ethnicity and claimed that all members of civilized societies were prone to hysteria—especially those who did not possess a healthy sexual outlet. Women, according to Meisel-Hess, were especially prone to hysteria—not because they had a natural proclivity to the illness, but because the prevailing double standards in the moral code made it more difficult for them to satisfy their natural sexual instincts. In addition, however, Meisel-Hess stressed that the prevailing sexual order was also harmful to men and led to their hysteria as well.

Although Freud did not view hysteria as an illness restricted to women—indeed he presented a paper to the Viennese Society of Physicians on male hysteria in 1886—the majority of his case studies focused on bourgeois Viennese women. In his *Drei Abhandlungen zur Sexualtheorie* (*Three Essays on the Theory of Sexuality*), Freud claimed that women were more prone to hysteria because they often remained trapped in an underdeveloped or "infantile" sexuality. For Freud, an important expression of hysteria in women was their apparent aversion to the male phallus. He stated: "[T]here is no doubt that the genitals of the opposite sex can in themselves be an object of disgust and that such an attitude is one of the characteristics of all hysterics, and especially of hysterical women."[34]

In what is perhaps the most famous case study of hysteria published in the twentieth century, Freud's *Bruchstück einer Hysterie-Analyse* (*Fragment of an Analysis of a Case of Hysteria*), Freud linked his female patient's hysteria to her arrested sexuality. Ida Bauer, whom Freud named Dora for the purposes of his study, began her treatment with Freud when she was eighteen years old. In his analysis, Freud maintained that Dora was "already entirely and completely hysterical" at the age of fourteen when she was disgusted by Herr K.'s sexual advances. Freud remarked: "I should without question consider a person hysterical in whom an occasion for sexual excitement elicited feelings that were preponderantly or exclusively unpleasurable...."[35] According to Freud, a "normal" woman would not be disgusted by the advances of a man who "was still quite young and of prepossessing appearance."[36] In fact, Freud claimed that Dora was merely repressing her own desire for Herr K.—a desire that he even believed Dora had displaced onto him.[37] Freud even goes so far as to suggest that Dora's second dream is a rape fantasy or, in Freud's words, "a fantasy of defloration, the fantasy of a man seeking to force an entrance into the female genitals."[38]

Whereas Freud constructed a problem around the image of the hysterical, frigid woman, Meisel-Hess concentrated on the sexually abusive, hysterical man. She problematized male sexual violence and thus disrupted the silence within the medical discourses on this issue. Freud did not see anything unusual in Herr K.'s behavior—his sexual advances towards the young Dora or his stalking her in public. It is Dora's "frigidity" that is problematic for Freud, not Herr K.'s aggressive behavior.

In her writings, Meisel-Hess attempted to de-center the image of the hysterical woman by focusing on the problems of male sexuality and sexual violence. Discussions of rape were curiously missing from medical discourses at the turn of the century and marital rape seems to be viewed as a contradiction in terms. Even Krafft-Ebing's influential book on deviant sexuality, which depicted everything from exhibitionism to nymphomania, included only isolated references to rape. Krafft-Ebing maintained: "It is unlikely that a morally-intact person would commit such a highly brutal crime.... In fact rape is in many cases an impulsive act of imbeciles in which according to circumstances even the bonds of blood relationship are not being respected. Cases involving raving madness, satyriasis, and epilepsy are conceivable and have occurred."[39]

Meisel-Hess's first novel *Fanny Roth* challenged the myth that "normal" bourgeois citizens could never be perpetrators of sexual violence. Within this novel, Meisel-Hess not only broke the silence surrounding issues of sexual violence, but also disrupted traditional literary conventions regarding the appropriate representation of rape. Fanny's wedding night, which represents the climax of Meisel-Hess's narrative, illustrates that rape can also occur in a respectable bourgeois marriage. Upon returning to their hotel room after dinner and a walk, Joseph proceeds to rape Fanny:

> She cried out, as she sat there in front of him.... But he grabbed her and covered her neck and arms and face with kisses and lifted her up and carried her to bed.
>
> She lost all awareness for pleasure and aversion; she only knew that everything in her was wild, despairing defense. And why—why?! Hadn't she waited fervently for this redemption? And now—instead of the exhilarating, blissful oblivion of which she had dreamt, —horror....
>
> Had they all lied, the poets, who spoke of the blissfulness of this night? Hadn't anybody, anybody been honest?
>
> And as he clasped her body, she knew that they had all lied.[40]

In the midst of Fanny's horror and fear, Meisel-Hess addressed the literary tradition that, according to Fanny, had lied to women in a double sense: (1) in their romantic depictions of the wedding night in novels and fairy tales and (2) in the silence surrounding the realities of sexual violence. Through her own detailed representation of rape in *Fanny Roth*, Meisel-Hess's narrative challenged traditional narratives in which sexual violence or rape occur outside the body of the text or in the absences (in the ellipses and in what Susan Winnett has labeled "the mad dash"[41]) of the narrative.

Meisel-Hess's narrative did not relegate the rape of Fanny to the margins of the text, but rather provided graphic details of the rape to her early twentieth-century audience.

> And it was a wild, horrendous struggle: the despairing exertion of a small childlike body against brazen male force. Her screams were smothered in bloody kisses, an iron strength restrained the struggling limbs, a merciless will forged the blazing revolt.... She did not capitulate, but she sank—groaning and helpless—in this power.[42]

These details depict the terror, the screams, and the physical pain Fanny experienced the next day in her entire body "which felt as if its limbs had been crushed."[43] Although filled with plenty of "mad dashes," Meisel-Hess's dashes heighten rather than suppress the representation of rape within her text.

Coming at the end of Part One of a two-part book, the rape scene stands at the exact center of Meisel-Hess's narrative. In this way, she placed Josef's deviant sexuality in the exact center of her text. Not only is Josef's deviant sexuality characterized by violence and brutality, but also by what Fanny calls "change in object"[44]—his need to jump from one woman to the next. Once his relationship with Fanny becomes strained, Josef begins to stay out half the night. This split in his personality—between a "day side" and a "night side"—is what characterized Josef's hysteria. Meisel-Hess expanded on this theory in the first volume of her trilogy, *Die sexuelle Krise* (*The Sexual Crisis*), a book that several of her contemporaries described as an encyclopedia of sexology similar to those by Iwan Bloch and August Forel.[45] Meisel-Hess claimed that men often live a double life: "The male leads a double life: one of these lives is passed in the daylight, by the side of the wife who shares his social existence; the other is spent in a region wherein he is freed from all those restraints which in the daylight are imposed upon his bourgeois personality."[46]

Following Freud's theories on hysteria, Meisel-Hess maintained that this split consciousness was an important characteristic of hysteria. She stated: "...a patient is hysterical when the sense of the unitary personality has been lost, and when consciousness becomes dissociated into two or more conflicting elements."⁴⁷ Meisel-Hess claimed that this fragmented and split personality was a common characteristic of the early twentieth-century European bourgeois male.

According to Meisel-Hess, the bourgeois male led a double life, which ultimately developed into a split consciousness. He possessed a day-side and a night-side to his personality. Meisel-Hess explained that occasionally bourgeois women would get a glimpse of this dangerous night side of the male personality. As an example, she described a situation to which she felt her female readers could relate. A woman, who is walking home after attending the theater, walks down an empty street close to her apartment where she is approached by a "respectable" bourgeois man who blocks her way and expresses his sexual wishes. Situations such as this, she maintained, reveal the often hidden and psychopathic side of the male. Meisel-Hess's analysis of the fragmented male self continued as follows:

> Not without punishment can a man lead this double existence—expending, on the one hand, all his available energies in the fierce competition of modern life, and squandering, on the other, his biological forces in the morass of prostitution. His powers being thus sapped in two contradictory types of existence, he will hardly attain a high degree of functional capacity, either biological or social, and he will rarely acquire that psychical unity which is essential to the proper formation of character.
>
> It is for this reason that most men exhibit an unmistakable pathological taint. As we get to know them intimately, on a sudden as by a flashlight some obscure horror is momentarily revealed to us, a dreadful reflex from the night-side of life.⁴⁸

In conclusion, although Meisel-Hess agreed with many of Freud's theories such as his belief that sexuality was an important force in the lives of both men and women and that there was a direct relationship between sexual abstinence and hysteria, Meisel-Hess shifted the focus of the discussion from the hysterical, frigid woman to the hysterical, psychopathic male. Throughout her analysis, Meisel-Hess used the same vocabulary found in medical discourses on female hysteria to describe the male hysteric. For example, she called him childlike, highly suggestible, and sexually perverse—terms that were commonly used to describe female hysterics—and also maintained that his body may be thoroughly diseased through his nightly adventures with prostitutes. She claimed that the double standard in sexual morality led to the fragmented personality of the male, which was also expressed in the realm of sexuality. The hysterical male vacillates between two extremes, between sexual excess on the one hand and erotic revulsion on the other.

Meisel-Hess appropriated the exact language used in medical discourses to describe female hysteria, but put these words in a new context. In this way, she de-centered the female hysteric and focused on other aspects of hysteria—particularly on issues of sexual violence, a topic noticeably absent in the medical discourses at that time. At the same time, her novel *Fanny Roth* disrupted traditional literary conventions regarding the appropriate representation of rape. The rape scene, in all its graphic detail, is located at the structural and literal center of her text.

Conclusion

In her responses to both Weininger and Freud, Meisel-Hess entered into modernist debates on hysteria in order to confront the prevalent antisemitism and antifeminism in Viennese society at the turn of the century. She made use of the fear surrounding hysteria and syphilis to imply that Weininger's narrative existed outside the realm of sound health and reason. Meisel-Hess maintained that both Weininger's aversion to anything material or sexual as well as his strong feelings of hatred, as evidenced in his vehement antisemitism and antifeminism, were true signs of illness and degeneration. Throughout her published response to Weininger's *Geschlecht und Charakter* (*Sex and Character*), Meisel-Hess discounted his theories as the hallucinations of a sick man and suggested that his narrative was completely hysterical and diseased.

In several of her theoretical and fictional texts, Meisel-Hess expanded on Freud's theories of hysteria to show that the prevailing sexual morality in Viennese society was dangerous to both men and women. The repression of sexual instincts resulted not only in the frigid, bourgeois woman, so thoroughly described in Freud's case studies, but also in the psychopathic, hysterical bourgeois male. Like Freud, Meisel-Hess moved the discussions of hysteria away from race and ethnicity by universalizing the illness—claiming that all members of the civilized world were disposed to the illness. Yet, compared to Freud, Meisel-Hess probed deeper into the realities of modern civilization to examine how the accepted gender roles and sexual morality affected both men and women. Whereas Freud associated Dora's second dream as a rape fantasy—a pleasurable experience of forced penetration—Meisel-Hess spoke of the frightening realities of rape. Through her novel, *Fanny Roth*, Meisel-Hess disrupted the accepted literary tradition on the appropriate representation of rape and broke the silence surrounding sexual violence. Furthermore, her depiction of the hysterical male, whose split personality was evidenced in his day-side and night-side, served to de-center the image of the hysterical woman in fin-de-siècle literary and medical discourses and brought the realities of sexual violence to the forefront.

Meisel-Hess reacted against the constructed threat of the "New Woman" as well as the fear surrounding the increased ethnic diversity in Viennese society by illustrating that these changes would not lead to an evolutionary step backwards (which was thought to be evidenced in the mixed-sexed body of those "hysterical" individuals demanding change), but rather that women's emancipation and the assimilation of the Jews were key factors in bringing about evolutionary progress. She explained that humanity would reach a higher form of evolutionary perfection by transcending traditional binary oppositions based on gender as well as by transgressing artificial borders separating people in terms of nationality, ethnicity, and class. Furthermore, she believed that the women's movement, combined with the movement for the protection of motherhood,[49] would help bring about a healthy sexuality in both men and women—a sexuality that was neither characterized by frigidity nor sexual violence—which would humanize as well as spiritualize the union between the sexes. In addition, Meisel-Hess believed that evolutionary progress would also be achieved through responsible procreation based on racial hygienic principles. In her writing, she highlighted the importance of natural selection and variation and thus illustrated the notable benefit of assimilating Jews and other ethnic minorities into Western European society. Meisel-Hess called for a cultural cosmopolitanism in which people would be treated as unique individuals rather than as members of artificially-defined groups. She stated: "In earlier times the individual represented, to a much greater extent than he does to-day, the type of his country, his race, his co-linguals, his profession, his guild or his class. All such distinctions give place more and more to a cosmopolitan individualism."[50] According to Meisel-Hess, the seeds of this cultural cosmopolitanism were already beginning to sprout in the soil of feminism and multiculturalism in Viennese society at the turn of the century.

Notes

[1] This chapter is a slightly abridged version of a chapter previously printed in Klaus Hödl, ed., *Jüdische Identitäten. Einblicke in die Bewußtseinslandschaft des österreichischen Judentums* (Innsbruck: Studien Verlag, 2000), 71–94. All of the original German sources have been translated into English for this version. I would like to extend a special thanks to Barbara Bowlus for her suggestions and insightful comments regarding my translations.

[2] Richard von Krafft-Ebing, *Psychopathia Sexualis, mit besonderer Berücksichtigung der konträren Sexualempfindung. Eine medizinisch-gerichtliche Studie für Ärzte und Juristen*, Dr. Alfred Fuchs, ed., 15th ed. (Stuttgart: F. Enke, 1918), 31. My translation.

[3] Iwan Bloch, *Das Sexualleben unserer Zeit in seinen Beziehungen zur modernen Kultur*, 10th-12th ed. (Berlin: Louis Marcus Verlagsbuchhandlung, 1919), 58–59. My translation.

[4] Sander L. Gilman, *Differences and Pathology. Stereotypes of Sexuality, Race, and Madness* (Ithaca: Cornell University Press, 1985) and Klaus Hödl, *Die Pathologisierung des jüdischen Körpers. Antisemitismus, Geschlecht und Medizin in Fin de Siècle* (Vienna: Picus Verlag, 1997).

[5] See, for example, Bernhard Frumer and Jennifer Merchant, "The Emancipation of Women and of the Jews. Parallels in Anti-Semitic and Anti-Feminist Discourse," *History of European Ideas*, Volume 19, Nos. 4–6 (1994): 723–731.

[6] Margarethe Meisel was born in 1879 to a wealthy Jewish family in Prague. After attending boarding school in Bohemia, she joined her family in 1893 in Vienna where her father had set up a successful business in oils

and essences. In Vienna she eventually took classes at the university and began her writing career, before moving to Berlin in 1908.

[7] Otto Weininger, *Geschlecht und Charakter. Eine prinzipielle Untersuchung* (Vienna, Leipzig: Braumüller, 1903).

[8] Otto Weininger, *Sex and Character*, authorized translation from the sixth German edition (New York: G. P. Putnam's Sons, 1906), 8.

[9] See, for example, Wilhelm Fließ, *In eigener Sache. Gegen Otto Weininger and Hermann Swoboda* (Berlin: Goldschmidt, 1906) and Hermann Swoboda, *Die gemeinnützige Forschung und der eigennützige Forscher. Antwort auf die von Wilhelm Fliess gegen Otto Weininger und mich erhobenen Beschuldigungen* (Vienna, Leipzig: Braumüller, 1906).

[10] Weininger, *Sex and Character*, 329.

[11] Weininger, *Sex and Character*, 305.

[12] Weininger, *Sex and Character*, 330.

[13] Misha Kavka, "The 'Alluring Abyss of Nothingness': Misogyny and (Male) Hysteria in Otto Weininger," *New German Critique*, Volume 66 (1995): 125.

[14] Weininger, *Sex and Character*, 302.

[15] Other writers discussed Weininger's theories in their works (see Rosa Mayreder, *Zur Kritik der Weiblichkeit* (Jena, Leipzig: Eugen Diederichs, 1905)) or reviewed Weininger's book (see Charlotte Perkins Gilman, "Review of Dr. Weininger's *Sex and Character*," *The Critic*, Volume 48, No. 1 (1906): 414–417) but Meisel-Hess was the only female writer to publish a direct response to the book.

[16] Grete Meisel-Hess, *Generationen und ihre Bildner* (Berlin: Dr. John Edelheim Verlag, 1901) and *In der modernen Weltanschauung* (Leipzig: Hermann Seemann Nachfolger, 1901).

[17] In the words of Lucka, who referred to Meisel-Hess's treatise as a "strange booklet of a modern female writer," Weininger was quite familiar with women's literature: "In addition, he was familiar with most of the writings of modern women, ranging from H. P. Blavatsky and Selma Lagerlöf all the way down to Grete Meisel-Heß." Emil Lucka, *Otto Weininger. Sein Werk und seine Persönlichkeit* (Vienna, Leipzig: Braumüller, 1905), 58 & 129.

[18] Grete Meisel-Hess, *Weiberhaß und Weiberverachtung. Eine Erwiderung auf die in Dr. Otto Weiningers Buche "Geschlecht und Charakter" geäußerten Anschauungen über "Die Frau und ihre Frage,"* 2nd edition (Vienna: Die Wage, 1904), 3. My translation.

[19] Meisel-Hess, *Weiberhaß und Weiberverachtung*, 8. My translation. Emphasis in the original.

[20] Meisel-Hess, *Weiberhaß und Weiberverachtung*, 30. My translation. The alliteration in the German original, "klappende, klappernde Logik,"

comes even closer to signifying an epileptic fit.

[21] In his "Fragment of an Analysis of a Case of Hysteria," for example, Freud maintained that hysterics were incapable of producing precise narratives. Their narratives were characterized by incoherence, inconsistencies, and a lack of logical order. See Sigmund Freud, "Fragment of an Analysis of a Case of Hysteria," in James Strachey, ed., *Standard Edition of the Complete Psychological Works of Freud* (London: Hogarth Press, 1953), Volume 7, 16.

[22] Meisel-Hess, *Weiberhaß und Weiberverachtung*, 69. My translation.

[23] Meisel-Hess, *Weiberhaß und Weiberverachtung*, 50. My translation.

[24] Meisel-Hess, *Weiberhaß und Weiberverachtung*, 35. My translation.

[25] Meisel-Hess's views on sex differentiation, like that of many turn-of-the-century feminists, were based on the belief that the sexes were equal, but different. She claimed that emancipated women were not interested in becoming like men and provided examples of various female writers, actresses, and philosophers who achieved greatness, while remaining completely "feminine." At the same time, however, she maintained that men and women possessed different (but not hierarchically comparable) qualities, which led to their own particular talents in different areas. In a statement that seems quite unusual to readers today, she remarked that women were not as competent in certain fields—such as the field of surgery—as men. Meisel-Hess, *Weiberhaß und Weiberverachtung*, 34.

[26] Meisel-Hess, *Weiberhaß und Weiberverachtung*, 8. My translation. Emphasis in the original.

[27] Meisel-Hess, *Weiberhaß und Weiberverachtung*, 9. My translation. Emphasis in the original.

[28] Meisel-Hess, "Die deutsche Frau in den Kolonien," *Arena*, Volume 7, No. 2 (1912/1913): 306.

[29] Meisel-Hess, "Die Judenfrage in romantischer Behandlung," *Der Weg*, Volume 3, No. 32 (1911): 802. My translation.

[30] Yet, although she hoped to transcend certain borders such as those based on gender and ethnicity, it quickly becomes clear that she did not want to break down all borders. Although interested in natural selection based on variation—she was clearly talking about variation among various ethnic and national groups, not racial groups as is apparent in her discussions of German colonialism. She also reacted against homosexuality. Although she maintained that homosexuals deserve basic human rights, her ideal lay in the heterosexual union between men and women. See, Meisel-Hess, *Weiberhaß und Weiberverachtung*, 11–12.

[31] Meisel-Hess, *Weiberhaß und Weiberverachtung*, 60.

[32] Alfred Bauer-Imhof, "Review of *Die Intellektuellen* by Grete Meisel-Hess," in Sigmund Freud, ed., *Zentralblatt für Psychoanalyse. Medizinische*

Monatschrift für Seelenkunde, Volume 2 (1912): 288.

[33] Sander L. Gilman, "Sigmund Freud and the Sexologists: A Second Reading," in Sander L. Gilman, Jutta Birmele, Jay Geller, and Valerie D. Greenberg, eds., *Reading Freud's Reading* (New York: New York University Press, 1994), 66; *The Case of Sigmund Freud: Medicine and Identity at the Fin de Siècle* (Baltimore: Johns Hopkins University Press, 1993), 5; *Freud, Race, and Gender* (Princeton: Princeton University Press, 1993), 99.

[34] Sigmund Freud, "Three Essays on the Theory of Sexuality," in James Strachey, ed., *Standard Edition of the Complete Psychological Works of Freud* (London: Hogarth Press, 1953), Volume 7, 152.

[35] Freud, "Fragment of an Analysis," 28.

[36] Freud, "Fragment of an Analysis," 29.

[37] After describing the process of transference, Freud wrote: "I came to the conclusion that the idea had probably occurred to her one day during a session that she would like to have a kiss from me." Freud, "Fragment of an Analysis," 74.

[38] Freud, "Fragment of an Analysis," 100.

[39] Krafft-Ebing, *Psychopathia Sexualis,* 370. My translation.

[40] Grete Meisel-Hess, *Fanny Roth. Eine Jung-Frauengeschichte* (Leipzig: Hermann Seemann Nachfolger, 1902), 55–56. My translation.

[41] Susan Winnett, "The Marquise's 'O' and the Mad Dash of Narrative," in Lynn A. Higgins and Brenda R. Silver, eds., *Rape and Representation* (New York: Columbia University Press, 1991), 67–86.

[42] Meisel-Hess, *Fanny Roth,* 56–57. My translation.

[43] Meisel-Hess, *Fanny Roth,* 57. My translation.

[44] Meisel-Hess, *Fanny Roth,* 100. My translation.

[45] See, for example, reviews of *Die sexuelle Krise. Eine sozialpsychologische Untersuchung* (Jena: Eugen Diederichs, 1909) by Irma Goeringer in *Das literarische Echo,* Volume 12, No. 10 (1909/1910): 742; by Koerber in *Der Monismus,* Volume 5, No. 53 (1910): 524; and by Frida Stéenhoff in *Die neue Generation,* Volume 6, No. 10 (1910): 419.

[46] Grete Meisel-Hess, *The Sexual Crisis. A Critique of our Sex Life,* Eden and Cedar Paul, trans., 2nd edition (New York: The Critic and Guide Company, 1917), 91.

[47] Meisel-Hess, *The Sexual Crisis,* 331.

[48] Meisel-Hess, *The Sexual Crisis,* 91–92.

[49] Meisel-Hess was an active member of the League for the Protection of Mothers and the Reform of Sexuality after her move to Berlin in 1908.

[50] Meisel-Hess, *The Sexual Crisis,* 24.

4
Goethe and Schubert: An Eclectic Affinity.
The Motif of the Wanderer in Schubert's Songs to Texts by Goethe[1]

Angelika Arend

I

"Ohne [Goethe] hätten wir keinen Schubert," Hermann Abert asserted in 1922.[2] One might be inclined to dismiss this claim as an early enthusiast's biased declaration of dependence. However, a scholar, connoisseur of poetry and practitioner of music such as the teacher, colleague and friend we are celebrating in this Festschrift will listen with a keener ear, and discern in Abert's provocative dictum reverberations of a singular creative constellation: the profound affinity of two apparently dissimilar minds which drew the younger musician to the older poet's uniquely musical word-compositions and moved him to create not only a new type of song, but also some of the finest among his own *Lied* compositions.

It is one of the most-often cited ironies in German art and letters that these two kindred spirits never met. In fact, the person immediately responsible for this was none other than Goethe himself, who returned a collection containing Schubert's first settings of some of Goethe's poems without a comment or answer to Joseph von Spaun, who had written on behalf of the nineteen-year-old composer and included in his covering letter a respectfully worded request that his young friend be permitted to dedicate this collection to the poet, "[...] dessen so herrlichen Dichtungen er nicht nur allein die Entstehung eines großen Teils derselben [zugesandten Sammlung], sondern wesentlich auch seine Ausbildung zum deutschen Sänger verdankt" (17 April 1817).[3]

Various explanations have been offered to account for Goethe's failure to recognize in Schubert his truly congenial composer and bard. It is, first of all, a consequence of Goethe's own views on the nature and function of a musical setting. These views, as we know, were largely influenced by his long-time musical mentor Carl Friedrich Zelter: deliberately simple and strictly strophic, the setting was to act as a servant to the text, whose fine points, shades and shifts were to be brought out by the art of the singer, not that of the composer. This, of course, is the very conception Schubert broke away from, and Goethe's decision to keep his distance seems understandable.[4] Wilhelm Bode drew attention to another roadblock. In his letter to Goethe, von Spaun had pointed out that Schubert's pieces required particular "Fertigkeit und Ausdruck" on the part of the pianist. Where was Goethe to find a musician who possessed not only the ability but also the goodwill to do justice to a "Tonsetzer neuer Art"? His musical friends, we are told, were interested in their own compositions and the kind of music they knew and liked.[5] Years later, upon hearing Schubert's "Erlkönig" sung by the young dramatic singer Wilhelmine Schröder-Devrient, the delighted Olympian thanked her profusely and admitted that he had heard this composition before, but that it had not "reached" him; however, rendered this way ("so vorgetragen"), it came across as something that "gestalte sich 'zu einem sichtbaren Bild'."[6] May we infer from this that sensitive artistic interpretation might have helped Goethe to develop an appreciation of Schubert's music? Certainly, his reaction in 1785 to Mozart's "Entführung" is a noteworthy reminder of his openness to what was new to him. As Abert assures us, Goethe was never a doctrinaire.[7] Unable at first to understand what the audience around him saw and heard in the said opera, he soon learned to appreciate the novelty of its music and, bowing to the superior genius, he abandoned his own ideas and practical aspirations to establish something like a German *Singspiel* tradition with his and Kayser's "Scherz, List und Rache."[8] Some thirty years later he explained: "Alles unser Bemühen daher, uns im Einfachen und Beschränkten abzuschließen, ging verloren, als Mozart auftrat. Die ‚Entführung aus dem Serail' schlug alles nieder, und es ist auf dem Theater von unserm so sorgsam gearbeiteten Stück niemals die Rede gewesen."[9] And while he preferred not to mention his admiration of Mozart to Zelter, he expressed it freely to Eckermann as late as 11 March 1828: "Was ist Genie anders als jene productive Kraft, wodurch Taten entstehen, die vor Gott und der Natur sich zeigen können und die eben deswegen Folge haben und von Dauer sind. Alle Werke Mozarts sind von dieser Art."[10]

We would surely not hesitate to borrow Goethe's words and say that all of Schubert's songs are of this kind. Why did Goethe not see it? Why did he open his mind to Mozart and close it to Schubert? This was Bode's answer:

> Der achtundsechzigjährige Dichter hatte längst Grund, von den jungen Neuerern in der Literatur, Malerei und Musik mehr Verdrießliches als Erfreuliches zu erwarten: er hatte keinen Anlaß, sich um zukünftige Musik Gedanken zu machen; er hatte auch keine Zeit für den jungen Menschen in Wien, der wie so viele das Patronat seines berühmten Namens verlangte.[11]

An argument convincing as far as it goes. But the poet's Schubert-block may have been anchored more deeply in his own mind and psyche. Willy Tappolet points in a direction that seems worth exploring. A significant reason for Goethe to reject Schubert's settings may well have been the fact that he heard in them the voice of the very "demon" which he had worked so hard to silence within himself:

> Wenn Goethe Schuberts Lieder über seine Gedichte ablehnte, so geschah es vermutlich nicht nur aus dem Grunde, weil ihm die Fülle der Musik Abbruch zu tun schien, sondern weil er den Dämon in ihnen fühlte, und selber viel zu viel von diesem Dämonischen, Abgründigen in sich hatte, um es durch Musik in sich aufrühren lassen zu wollen.[12]

Involving his own poetry, Schubert's Lieder may have touched some sensitive chords and thereby precluded sufficient detachment.

The issue, then, was not only Schubert's music but also his selection from Goethe's by then extensive and diverse body of poetry. When he received the young composer's missive, the "classical" poet had dissociated himself emphatically from all things "romantic": "Klassisch ist das Gesunde, romantisch das Kranke. [...] Das Romantische ist schon in seinen Abgrund verlaufen; das Gräßlichste der neuen Produktionen ist kaum noch gesunkener zu denken."[13] Finding in the collection sent to him his own ostensibly non-"classical," some might argue "romantic," creations—among them "An Schwager Kronos," "Rastlose Liebe," "Gretchen am Spinnrade"—he can hardly have felt inclined to welcome with joy the young genius whose musical re-creations promised to bring into the lime-light what he must have preferred to see mercifully dimmed by the shade of history, or appropriately illumined by the specifics of poetic context. It seems fair to conclude that Goethe's silence *vis-à-vis* Schubert was in large measure a sensitive (and equally insensitive) reaction of a celebrated poet and educator who found that his praise was sung not only in over-elaborate tones but also with the wrong words.

The motif of the wanderer as employed and developed in Goethe's poetry and as selected therefrom by Schubert for musical rendering affords useful insight into the workings of the eclectic affinity which gave birth to the immortal body of Schubert's Goethe *Lieder* and at the same time kept apart its two progenitors.

II

Goethe lived his long productive life towering over the entire era of German Idealism—from the stirring years of *Sturm und Drang* to Weimar Classicism and the Romantic Movement. Among his friends and close associates he was known as "the wanderer," and he, too, spoke of himself as "wanderer" throughout his life. As Elizabeth M. Wilkinson and L.A. Willoughby have pointed out,

> [...] no German poet has written more about wandering than Goethe. [...] Early and late this image is a symbol for expressing every conceivable manner and mode of his wandering from the simple impulse to roam in space, through the urge to dalliance and philandering, or the limitless aspiration of individual striving, to every variation of self-fulfilment, including that soaring of the human mind which we call poetic vision.[14]

There was, of course, nothing original about the idea of man as "wanderer." We recall great "fugitives in the earth" and vagabonds such as Cain and the Wandering Jew; Ulysses; Don Quixote and those whom he emulated: the knights errant of the Arthurian epic; the pilgrims of Dante's *Divine Comedy*; Bunyan's Pilgrim; or, in the German context, Grimmelshausen's Simplicissimus—to mention only a few. However, to Goethe and his contemporaries, the symbol of the wanderer took on especial significance in their attempts to understand and re-define man's place in the world at a time of rapidly changing intellectual-historical and social realities. The earlier vagrants in literature had for the most part been sent on their journeys to demonstrate—through their actions and reactions, failures and successes—certain ideas and convictions about human life which, in spite of the wanderers' trials and tribulations, was held to be ultimately ordered and therefore meaningful. At the threshold of the modern era, when the foundations of the old intellectual, cultural and social structures began to crumble, such security of a universally shared world-view could no longer be enjoyed.

The literature of the time responded to these developments in various ways, promoting them on the one hand and attempting to counteract observed or anticipated loss and destruction on the other: the *Sturm und Drang*, revolting mainly against the rigidity of the German class-structure and the Frenchified culture of the aristocracy, inaugurated a new type of thinking which judged everything against the measure of personal life and inner need and experience. Weimar Classicism, looking back to the cradle of European civilization, developed aesthetic and ethical norms to salvage the humanistic heritage. Romanticism turned to medieval history, Christianity, myth, and nature with its manifold subterranean realms; it strove to halt man's growing alienation from the world and from himself by reconnecting him with his true inner origins.

The fictional wanderers created during those stirring decades reflect these concerns. Most of them are artists, that is, human beings possessing a heightened awareness and sensitivity, who cannot find contentment in their world of political despotism, dogmatic intolerance, aristocratic superficiality and bourgeois small-mindedness. The *Sturm and Drang* wanderer, driven by a burning consciousness of being a vital, sentient being, took, whatever he pursued or claimed, quite literally: by storm. The

Classical mind that rose from the ashes of such youthful fire created an ideal vision of an integrated union of nature, art and man. The Classical wanderer, after a due process of self-search, reflection and learning, comes to understand that, like Aaron's staff, which will blossom, without taking roots, wherever it is placed, he too will be "at home" wherever he places himself at the service of his fellow humans. Romantic thought, on the other hand, embraced the notion of alienation as a poetic principle. As Novalis put it: "Die Kunst, auf eine angenehme Art zu befremden, einen Gegenstand fremd zu machen und doch bekannt und anziehend, das ist die romantische Poetik."[15] The intention behind this, of course, is to point up the existence of realities beyond the reality perceived and experienced as alien to the human mind and spirit. The Romantic wanderer, therefore, is impelled by an inner knowledge, "Ahnung," to seek out and explore those other realities; he remains homeless in all corners of the social world. His art, however, which grows from these experiences, is an important testimony rendered on behalf of the human spirit.

All three types of wanderer are found in Goethe's poetry. The hot-blooded and high-flying rebel was to speak for the young Goethe only; he soon began to metamorphose into a more reflective man whose motto was "Gedenke zu wandern!"—remember to wander, be mindful of wandering. The homeless soul was given voice to render evidence of a mode of being essentially unfit to survive in the modern era of enlightened bourgeois culture. Schubert's selection from Goethe's poetry, as I shall attempt to show, was clearly an eclectic one, informed by his Romantic disposition.

Goethe's earliest explicit wanderer poem is "Wanderers Sturmlied",[16] written in 1772 at the age of twenty-three. Years later, in his autobiographical reflections *Dichtung und Wahrheit*, Goethe described it as "Halb-Unsinn" which he sang to himself passionately when hit by a storm on one of his many hikes. This desperate outpouring, which could be the envy of any Expressionist, was welcomed and celebrated by some Goethe exegetes as one of his "great hymns."[17] Others saw in it a wanderer poem with another kind of difference: a poem that treats this essentially Romantic subject with a humour and self-irony rarely found in German poetry.[18] In the intoxication of his own genius, the wanderer defies rain and storm.

With the Muses and the Graces for his companions he surges onward, soars upward, rising to godlike heights. But his exaltation ebbs away; he sees a peasant, weary and begrimed, but resolutely pressing homeward, encouraged by the warmth and food which await him there—while he, the poet and darling of the Muses, wanders without strength, despairing. In pessimistic mood he affirms the rule of Bromius, god of materialistic joys. What *he* needs, however, is the favour of Phoebus Apollo, which can only be won through self-reliance and fervour of soul. In a last effort to muster such fire he turns to Jupiter Pluvius in whom he celebrates the source, the substance and the purpose of his song. Such soaring exuberance, however, abandons him as abruptly as it was generated. His physical situation gets the upper hand, and the once inspired genius finds himself reduced to a sorry figure praying for sufficient strength to wade through the mud in order to reach his hut.

The same year (1772) saw the composition of the poem "Der Wanderer"[19]—a remarkably unidentical twin of the "Sturmlied." Three decades later, in 1815, Goethe placed it in second position within the section "Kunst" of his collected poetry, thereby affirming its significance as an expression of his conception of art. The poem renders an encounter in southern Italy of a sentimental art-seeking wanderer and a simple native woman with her child. On their way up a rocky path to the woman's humble dwelling, where she is to give him a drink of water, he detects, wherever he looks, ruins of an ancient temple, decaying and overgrown by ivy, moss, thistles and other agents of nature's destruction. He is dismayed and upset. However, at the sight of the child, his regret gives way to a recognition that from death and decay will spring life and growth. Seeing before him the peaceful life and humble human happiness, symbolized by the "Hütte, Weib und Kind," he comes to appreciate the simplicity of mind, which in the midst of the ruins of antiquity, does not admit of a distinction between life and art. There is a note of benevolent envy in the wanderer's farewell because all he can do is ask nature to guide his further wanderings, that is his artistic endeavors, towards this kind of balanced integration of life and art.

Goethe's treatment of the "Wanderer" motif culminates in a vision of wandering which is no longer a seeking prompted by a sense of absence or imperfection. Wandering is embraced as a way of living out, here and now, active humanity. Wilhelm Meister, on completion of his wandering years through various spheres of art and life, first as an apprentice and then as a journeyman, continues his "Wanderschaft" as a surgeon who is to stay at any one place only for a specified period of time and then goes on to widen the orbit of his usefulness. He gains a first understanding of this kind of life of the wanderer from a group of men about to emigrate to the New World. Their "Wanderlied" explains:

> Bleibe nicht am Boden heften,
> Frisch gewagt und frisch hinaus!
> Kopf und Arm mit heitern Kräften,
> Überall sind sie zu Haus;
> [...]
> Und dein Streben, sei's in Liebe,
> Und dein Leben sei die Tat.[20]

„Frisch gewagt und frisch hinaus!" clearly recalls the spirit of „Rasch ins Leben hinein!"—a line found in the poem „An Schwager Kronos," which was written fifty years earlier in those heady *Sturm-und-Drang* days. For all the quiet refinement of his ethical idealism, the mature Goethe never lost his inner spark. Nor was he the man to hold up an ideal vision insufficiently aware of, or unwilling to recognize, the darker sides of man. His prime witness in this regard, of course, is Faust. He was first conceived at about the same time as the gentle "Wanderer" in Italy and represents his counter-type: single-minded, self-seeking, demonic. Faust's wandering, though born of a profoundly human inquisitiveness and striving, is set on a path of destruction. His first (and probably best known) victims are Gretchen and her "kleine Welt," his last victims the friendly old couple Philemon and Baucis and their hospitable "Hütte." Faust knows very well that he is "der Flüchtling [...] Unbehauste/Der Unmensch ohne Zweck und Ruh"[21]—a man who has lost his humanness.

III

Except for two passages in *Faust*, none of the Goethe-texts I have commented on were selected by Schubert for musical setting. In the case of the emigrants' "Wanderlied" I can only speculate that, if Schubert read it at all, its heavy didacticism might not have been very attractive to him. In similar fashion, the poem "Der Wanderer" is too philosophical, too abstract to inspire the imagination of a composer of song. The "Sturmlied" might well have fired up Schubert's *Sturm-and-Drang* instincts, as did "Prometheus" and "An Schwager Kronos." But it is in large part obscure, cluttered with reference and allusion, and therefore quite unsuitable for a conversion into song.

Schubert's first setting of a Goethe text in October 1814, was none other than "Gretchen am Spinnrade".[22] This "Goethe Lied" is relevant to our topic of the wanderer in that it is a deeply moving rendering of the agony suffered by this innocent soul as a result of its attraction to that most pernicious of Romantic wanderers. She herself becomes a wanderer in the sense that she is made to err through the darkest chambers of despair in utter isolation—even in the midst of a crowd of people, as in that haunting church scene where she is tormented by the evil spirit of her desperate deed. Not surprisingly, Schubert, with a sure Romantic hand, picked this scene, too, in December of the same year.[23]

Chronologically, the next "wanderer" to be considered here is "Der Sänger" (February 1815).[24] This is the song sung by the Harper on his first appearance in Goethe's novel *Wilhelm Meisters Lehrjahre* (date of poem: 1783). Composed in the style of the popular ballad, it advocates the poet's freedom from worldly restraints. In a medieval setting, the wandering singer is called into the castle to enhance the festive scene with his song. He rejects the golden chain offered to him as a reward, likening himself to the bird whose only possession and reward can be its song. As the bird flies in full freedom, giving pleasure to those who hear it, so does the singer-wanderer give pleasure wherever he is heard. Needless to point out, all of the features mentioned are truly Romantic.

The idea of the wandering artist delighting his audience is taken one step further in "Musensohn" (December 1822).[25] This "son of the Muses" does not, as did the medieval singer, merely warm the hearts of his listeners and whet their respective virtues:

boldness in the men and pudency in the fair ones. He excites them to such a degree that they cannot help trying to break out of the confines of their limited capabilities: the oafish boy puffs himself up, the awkward girl wheels and turns around to his music. This mercurial giver of joy, however, has his own longing, too: it is for the warmth of that deliciously unidentified "bosom"—this poem's charming version of the "hut," place of rest from, and refreshment for, his wanderings. Goethe's Classical touch blends well with the native rural scene of "Feld und Wald und Höhn" in both summer and winter. The Romantic element clearly predominates.

The third of these sons of Orpheus, I suggest, is "Der Rattenfänger" (August 1815),[26] that old German favourite known to the English as the Pied Piper of Hamlin. Not only does his music exhilarate and stir up emotions, he is a master magician who uses the magic power of music to entrance and lure into submission nature's creatures: animals, children, women. In light-hearted fashion, we are here confronted with a phenomenon that reaches deep into the human psyche. It exercised many minds, particularly Romantic ones, well before the invention of Psychology; E.T.A. Hoffmann's "Ritter Gluck"(1807–8) and "Kreisleriana"(1810) spring immediately to mind, as do Heinrich von Kleist's "Heilige Cäcilie"(1810), and also Mörike's Mozart-novella (1855).

Probing even deeper into man's soul are the three "Gesänge des Harfners"(1816). Thematically they form a sequence that travels, as it were, from classical antiquity to Romantic modernity: from the idea of God-induced failing and consequent guilt ("Wer nie sein Brod mit Thränen aß"[27]) to that of resulting solitude ("Wer sich der Einsamkeit ergibt"[28]) and ultimate insanity ("An die Thüren will ich schleichen"[29]). Having been trapped unwittingly into the crime of incest, the Harper finds himself faced with the consequences: exclusion from human company, driving him into inexorable loneliness which only death can relieve and, until such time, into grinding derangement. In the context of Goethe's novel, the Harper's passage through suffering into darkness serves, among other things, to provide an example of the direction Wilhelm is *not* to follow. As I have indicated earlier, Wilhelm's path is to take him away from self-absorption to self-transcending usefulness to others.

While the Harper, for all the heavenly injustice, remains the victim of his own actions, Mignon is entirely innocent of her fate of being different, estranged and alone. She is a Romantic wanderer "homeless on earth" par excellence. Every one of her four songs points up one significant feature of such "homelessness": her longing for her "home" Italy ("Kennst du das Land," October 1815[30]); her longing for human company and love ("Nur wer die Sehnsucht kennt,"[31]); the mystery surrounding her origin and being ("Heiss mich nicht reden"[32]); her closeness, in spite of her youth, to death ("So lasst mich scheinen"[33]). The figure of Mignon is best understood as an allegory of poetry and, by extension, of art, illustrating the impossibility of their existence in the progressively rational and utilitarian world of the burgher.[34]

It remains open to speculation how Goethe would have reacted had he come to know the extent of Schubert's preoccupation with these two sympathetically drawn, yet clearly doomed figures. We are here touching upon the sensitive nerve that connects Goethe's thought with that of his Romantic contemporaries. They shared the sad conviction that within the ascending bourgeois society and culture there was no "home" for the true artist and his art. The Romantics embraced this sorry fact creatively, dwelling on "Sehnsucht" and "Ahnung" and the lure of other realities. Goethe, in a more worldly-wise manner, decided to face the given realities and look for a viable way to harmonize social and aesthetic needs. While he saw to it that his deep regret of the loss was clearly imprinted on his two "homeless" figures, he could have mustered no patience with the self-indulgent outpourings of "wanderers" such as those created by Schmidt von Lübeck or Wilhelm Müller. To see his Harper and his Mignon, rightly or wrongly, flung onto the same romantic band-waggon might have prompted a reaction more hurtful to Schubert than the silence Goethe chose to maintain.

His approval, on the other hand, would surely not have been withheld for the settings of "Wanderers Nachtlied," both I (July 1815) and II (by July 1824),[35] in which Schubert managed so masterfully "[sich] im Einfachen und Beschränkten abzuschließen." The sentiments expressed by these two short pieces transcend all differences between the Classical and the Romantic mind. In fact, "Ruhe," stillness, has long been a privileged concept in German letters and continued to hold its sway well into the 20th century. Universally shared human experience seems involved here: if the impulse to wander is one fundamental human drive, then the desire for rest and peace is seen to act as its complementary opposite. And Goethe, as Wilkinson and Willoughby point out, has explored more sensitively and more completely than any other German, poet or thinker, the relation of these two.[36]

Its complementary nature is brought into sharp relief by a brief comparative look at "Wanderers Nachtlied I" ("Der du von dem Himmel bist," written by Goethe at the slope of the Ettersberg near Darmstadt on 12 February 1776, and "An Schwager Kronos,"[38] conceived in a postchaise on 10 October 1774. Nowhere is the contrast between the "Lebensgefühl" of Goethe's *Sturm und Drang* and Classicism more evident than in these two poems; yet chronologically they are separated by just sixteen months. As a point of interest, "Der du von dem Himmel bist" was first published in 1780 under the title "Um Frieden" in a Christian magazine.[39] This points up nicely the prayerful character of these verses, which do indeed breathe a deep religious intensity with their cry for the peace of heaven in the human heart. The "Treiben," the "Schmerz und Lust" of which the speaker/singer is tired, refer generally to aspects of active living, which "Schwager Kronos" celebrates with zest and vitality: with Time as the postillion, the "Kraft-Genie" (as Goethe once termed himself) sets out on his up-and-downhill journey, that is life, to taste to the full all it has to offer; as in the end the path goes downhill and old age looms up in the distance, rather than allowing himself to be reduced to imbecility with its toothless gums and shaky bones, he urges Kronos to hurl him, to the sound of his horn and the roaring of his chariot, through the gates of Hell to a rousing Prince's welcome. For all their differences, these two poems belong together in that they render the two polar components of "wandering" in its broadest understanding: "Treiben," activity, on the one hand, "Ruhe," rest, on the other—breathing in and breathing out, the two mutually dependent motive forces of life.

While "Der du von dem Himmel bist" is a prayer for peace which the heart does not yet possess, "Über allen Gipfeln ist Ruh"— scribbled, on 6 September 1780, on a wall of a cottage situated quite literally "above all the hill-tops" surrounding the Kickelhahn near the town of Ilmenau—renders in uniquely Goethean simplicity and richness that rare moment of stillness of nature and the human soul which instills in the latter a sense of assured anticipation of ultimate peace. Many profound things have been written about the significance and beauty of these inimitable lines. Many settings have been produced, none capturing their spirit as sensitively and completely as Schubert's composition. It may be regrettable, on a personal level, that Goethe never heard it and that Schubert never received the appreciation he so richly deserved. Objectively, however, there is no cause for regret. Thanks to the elder poet's silence *vis-à-vis* the younger composer, the rift between the former's Classical and the latter's Romantic mind was not torn open and the musical genius informing Goethe's poetry could travel freely to inspire Schubert's song.

This, of course, lends substance to Hermann Abert's pronouncement that "without Goethe we would have no Schubert." However, since Schubert's Goethe-*Lieder* appear to afford us glimpses of a part of the poet's mind and soul which he, for his own reasons, strove to keep under lock and key, it seems only fair to add that without Schubert we would not have all of Goethe.

Notes

[1] This article was first published in *Carleton Germanic Papers*, Volume 22 (1994): 15–24.

[2] Hermann Abert, *Goethe und die Musik* (Stuttgart: Engelhorn, 1922), 67.

[3] Quoted from Joseph Müller-Blattau, *Goethe und die Meister der Musik* (Stuttgart: Klett, 1969), 63.

[4] See Abert, *Goethe und die Musik*, 49, 71–76; Müller-Blattau, *Goethe und die Meister*, 73.

[5] Samuel Fisch, *Goethe und die Musik* (Frauenfeld: Huber, 1949), 84.

[6] Willy Tappolet, *Begegnungen mit der Musik in Goethes Leben und Werk* (Bern: Benteli, 1975), 123.

[7] Abert, *Goethe und die Musik*, 76.

[8] Emil Staiger, "Goethe und Mozart," in Emil Staiger, *Musik und Dichtung* (Zürich/Freiburg i.Br.: Artemis, 1959), 441–60.

[9] Johann Wolfgang von Goethe, *Werke: Hamburger Ausgabe in 14 Bänden*, ed. Erich Trunz (Hamburg: Christian Wegner Verlag, 1949), Band 11, *Italienische Reise*, 437.

[10] Johann Peter Eckermann, *Gespräche mit Goethe in den letzten Jahren seines Lebens* (Wiesbaden: Insel, 1955), 626.

[11] Quoted from Fisch, *Goethe und die Musik*, 84.

[12] Alfred Einstein, quoted from Tappolet, *Begegnungen mit der Musik*, 122.

[13] Goethe, *Werke: HA, Band 12, Maximen und Reflexionen*, 487.

[14] Elizabeth M. Wilkinson and L.A. Willoughby, *Goethe: Poet and Thinker* (London: Arnold, 1962), 35.

[15] Dieter Arendt, "Der Mensch unterwegs. Wanderschaft und Reise in der Dichtung," *Zeitwende* 38 (1967), 688–98: 691.

[16] Goethe, *Werke: HA, Band 1*, 33–6.

[17] Erich Trunz, ed. in: Goethe, *Werke: HA, Band 1*, 33; Heinrich Henel, "Der Wanderer in der Not: Goethes 'Wanderers Sturmlied' und ‚Harzreise im Winter'," *Deutsche Vierteljahresschrift für Literatur und Geistesgeschichte*, 47 (1973), 69–94:69.

[18] Wilkinson and Willoughby, *Poet and Thinker*, 36.

[19] Goethe, *Werke: HA, Band 1*, 36–42.

[20] Goethe, *Werke: HA, Band 8*, 392.

[21] Goethe, *Faust I: HA Band 3*, 107, lines 3348–3349.

[22] Eusebius Mandyczewski, ed. *Schubert's Songs to Texts by Goethe* (New York: Dover Publications, 1979), 1.

[23] Mandyczewski, *Schubert's Songs*, 20, 24.

[24] Mandyczewski, *Schubert's Songs*, 29, 37.

[25] Mandyczewski, *Schubert's Songs*, 202, 205.

[26] Mandyczewski, *Schubert's Songs*, 59.

[27] Mandyczewski, *Schubert's Songs*, 26, 127, 132.

[28] Mandyczewski, *Schubert's Songs*, 83, 121, 129.

[29] Mandyczewski, *Schubert's Songs*, 124, 136.

[30] Mandyczewski, *Schubert's Songs*, 79

[31] Mandyczewski, *Schubert's Songs*, 75, 77 (1815); 138, 140 (1816); 225,233 (1826).

[32] Mandyczewski, *Schubert's Songs*, 183 (1821); 228 (1826).

[33] Mandyczewski, *Schubert's Songs*, 185, 231 (1826).

[34] Hannelore Schlaffer, *Wilhelm Meister: Das Ende der Kunst und die Wiederkehr des Mythos* (Stuttgart: Metzler, 1980), 40–51.

[35] Mandyczewski, *Schubert's Songs*, 52, 224.

[36] Wilkinson and Willoughby, *Poet and Thinker*, 36.

Goethe, *Werke: HA, Band 1*, 142.

[38] Goethe, *Werke: HA, Band 1*, 47–8.

[39] Trunz, ed., in Goethe, *Werke: HA, Band 1*, 533.

5
Полифункциональные лексемы как новое явление в грамматике русского языка

Ю.В.Рощина

1. Проблема грамматического описания лексем, которые в предложении могут быть актуализованы как различные части речи

В последние годы чрезвычайно возросла активность конструкций типа *бизнес-план, видео-салон, офис-менеджер, пиар-структуры, фитнес-клуб, рок-исполнитель, экспресс-опрос, шоу-премьера* и им подобные. Эти конструкции не остались незамеченными исследователями современного русского языка: они отмечались как случаи пополнения выделенного М.В.Пановым класса аналитических прилагательных.[1]

В лексикографии сочетания типа *бизнес-план* принято трактовать как сложные слова. Однако мы в данной работе исходим из того, что одна и та же языковая единица может быть описана по-разному на разных уровнях системы языка. Признавая теоретическую возможность рассмотрения соединений типа *бизнес-проект, аудио-коллекция, вип-места, интернет-олимпиада, шоу-таланты* и под. в качестве сложных слов на уровне лексикографии, а также морфемики и словообразования, мы, вслед за М.В.Пановым и многими другими исследователями, оставляем за собой право на уровне морфологии трактовать такие конструкции как словосочетания с первым компонентом—аналитическим определителем (в терминологии Панова—аналитом).

В то же время нельзя не отметить, что первые элементы упомянутых конструкций (*бизнес, видео, фитнес*...) и собственно аналитические прилагательные типа *беж* принципиально отличаются по характеру функционирования.

К аналитическим прилагательным относятся лексемы, выступающие в одной грамматической функции—морфологически неизменяемого определителя имени существительного (*брюки хаки, цвет индиго, полит-тусовка*).

Для лексем типа *бизнес, видео, медиа, офис, пиар, шоу* характерен более широкий круг синтаксических функций. Так, например, они активно функционируют в качестве существительных. Ср.: *ведение бизнеса через Интернет, классические медиа, увлекательное шоу, чёрный пиар*... Большинство из них зафиксировано словарями именно как существительные[2].

Все эти лексемы употребляются и в функции определителей имени существительного, и в таких случаях действительно могут быть рассмотрены как примеры аналитических прилагательных: *Бизнес-проект* Кремля (Версия, №22 16-22 июня, 2003); В этих тяжелых политических условиях коммунистам не осталось ничего иного, как уповать на свои *шоу-таланты* (МК, 04.05.02); *"Медиа-социум"*, владеющий лицензией на телечастоту (МК, 17.05.02); Пригласили бы *офис-леди* куда-нибудь... (Б.Акунин, Внеклассное чтение).

Таким образом, адъективная частеречная принадлежность первых элементов конструкций типа *бизнес-проект, интернет-олимпиада, вип-места* отнюдь не очевидна. Болееe того, возникает вопрос: не являются ли подобные конструкции словосочетаниями с первым компонентом—приложением, т.е. существительным? Чтобы ответить на этот вопрос, рассмотрим, как определяется приложение в русской грамматике.

Так, в «Кратком справочнике по современному русскому языку»[3] приложение определяется как «член предложения, который поясняет существительное и сам представлен существительным **в той же падежной форме**» (выделение наше—*Ю.Р.*). Ср. также в энциклопедии «Русский язык»: «Приложение согласуется с определяемым словом в падеже и числе: *телефон-автомат, телефона-автомата, телефоны-автоматы*»[4]. К исключениям отнесены следующие случаи:

а) географические названия (*на озере Байкал*);
б) если в качестве приложения выступает прозвище (*у Владимира Красное Солнышко*);
в) если приложением являются названия газет, учреждений, транспортных средств, литературных произведений и пр. (*из газеты «Московские новости», в издательстве «Русский язык», к пароходу «Федор Шаляпин»*).

В нашем случае (особенно это заметно на примере сочетаний типа *бизнес-план, вип-места*, в которых зависимый элемент потенциально может склоняться) согласования не происходит ни при каких условиях: *бизнес-плана, к бизнес-плану, о бизнес-плане, бизнес-планы…; вип-места, к вип-местам, о вип-местах…* Следовательно, подобные конструкции не могут рассматриваться как сочетания с первым компонентом — приложением.

В современном русском языке, по нашим данным, достаточно много подобных примеров. Все подобные лексемы объединяет то, что каждая из них представляет собой одну единицу грамматики и словаря, при этом в предложении они могут быть актуализованы как **р а з л и ч н ы е   ч а с т и   р е ч и**.

2. О понятии широкой (нестандартной) грамматической валентности

Для определения частеречного статуса таких полифункциональных слов мы предлагаем пользоваться понятием стандартной и **широкой (нестандартной)** грамматической валентности.

Лексема со стандартной грамматической валентностью обладает характерными для определенной части речи синтагматико-функциональными возможностями. Например, субстантивное слово *газета* требует согласованных форм слов-атрибутов и финитных глагольных форм (*свежая газета, газета выходит/вышла*), в предложении обычно является подлежащим или дополнением. Стандартная субстантивная грамматическая валентность этого слова предопределяет всё его функционирование в языке. У адъективного слова *великолепный* и адвербиального слова *экстремально* — иные особенности функционирования, связанные с тем, что каждое из них обладает стандартной для прилагательных и наречий грамматической валентностью (в указанном выше смысле).

Иначе ведут себя полифункциональные лексемы с широкой грамматической валентностью. Они формируют особый «надкатегориальный» (точнее, «надчастеречный») класс слов, при этом каждая из лексем данного класса реализуется как определенная часть речи *лишь в конкретном предложении*. Ср.: *онлайн* — 1) с у щ е с т в и т е л ь н о е: *расширять свое присутствие в о н л а й н е,* 2) п р и л а г а т е л ь н о е: *о н л а й н - издания, вопросы поступают в режиме о н л а й н,* 3) н а р е ч и е: *общаться о н л а й н;* также: *городское к а н т р и, музыка к а н т р и; политический э к с т р и м, э к с т р и м - с п о р т.*

Конкретную реализацию полифункциональной лексемы мы будем называть **морфологическим словом**[5]. Морфологические слова, представляющие полифункциональную лексему в предложении, распределены позиционно. Так, например, полифункциональная лексема *экстрим* может быть реализована двумя морфологическими словами: а) как субстантив (**Sub**) — *политический э к с т р и м,* б) как адъектив (**Adj**) — *э к с т р и м - спорт.*

Грамматическое значение конкретного морфологического слова определяется его позицией (окружением, контекстом). Позиционный подход к изучению грамматического значения слова представлен в работах М.В.Панова: «Слово, подчиняясь позициям и меняясь по их велению, может в одних случаях получать признаки одной части речи, а под влиянием другой позиции — признаки другой части речи»[6].

Явление полифункциональности — не новое в русской грамматике. Так, наряду со стандартными по признаку грамматического рода лексемами типа *учитель, учительница, Максим, Анна* в русском языке существует грамматический класс полифункциональных слов общего рода, реализующихся в разных контекстах то как существительные мужского рода (*староста сказал, наш Саша*), то как существительные женского рода (*староста сказала, наша Саша*)[7]. В сфере глагола выделяется грамматический класс полифункциональных двувидовых глаголов типа *женить, атаковать*, которые в разных контекстах реализуют свойства то совершенного, то несовершенного вида[8].

Подобные явления всегда трактовались как черты аналитизма в морфологическом строе русского языка[9]. Нетрудно заметить, что аналитическая тенденция реализуется в рассматриваемых случаях в рамках отдельной части речи—соответственно в рамках существительного (общий род) и глагола (двувидовые глаголы).

Очевидно, что появление нового грамматического класса полифункциональных слов, где нестандартная, широкая грамматическая валентность реализуется на уровне нескольких разных полнознаменательных частей речи (существительное ⇔прилагательное⇔наречие), является ярким проявлением аналитизма в морфологическом строе русского языка.

По происхождению полифункциональные лексемы—это, как правило, слова, заимствованные из языка с аналитическими, по преимуществу, средствами выражения грамматического значения. В первую очередь речь идет об английском. Заимствованные лексемы типа *шоу, бизнес, интернет, онлайн, пиар, рок, рэп* в родном для них языке могут функционировать как различные части речи без изменений формы слова (*to see a show; show business, show card, show house; to launch a business, to run a business; business class, business centre, business plan*). Их грамматическая функция в предложении определяется аналитически.

В процессе заимствования в язык попадает не какая-то определенная часть речи, а собственно слово, обозначающее какой-либо новый для русского языкового сознания предмет, понятие, явление. Причем очень часто заимствуется целое сочетание: *бизнес-класс, бизнесс-центр, бизнесс-план.* Ср. также: *rock music, rock festival—рок-музыка, рок-фестиваль; show business—шоу-бизнес, PR action—пиар-акция.* Поэтому в русском языке одновременно появляются имена существительные: *в мире бизнеса, прибыльный бизнес, интересное шоу, чёрный пиар* и аналитические прилагательные: *бизнес-центр, пиар-акция, шоу-бизнес.*

Важно отметить, что заимствуется не лексема как материальная, звуковая оболочка, и не лексема как единица словаря, а ее конкретные актуализации в предложении. Поэтому наряду с существительным *Интернет* в язык входят такие сочетания, как *интернет-услуги* [Internet service], *интернет-связь* [Internet connection], и далее по утвердившейся в языке модели 'аналитическое прилагательное + существительное' легко образуются многие подобные словосочетания: *интернет-публикации, интернет-программы, интернет-ресурсы, интернет-магазины*.

Как бы ни трактовались подобные конструкции, нельзя не отметить их очевидную идентичность английским сочетаниям с неморфологизованными определителями. Многочисленные примеры употребления нового класса полифункциональных лексем (в нашей картотеке содержится около 100 таких слов и более 2000 контекстов их употребления в функции приименного аналит-определителя, не считая их субстантивных и адвербиальных употреблений) являются ярким проявлением аналитизма в грамматической системе современного русского языка.

3. Характеристика полифункциональных лексем с точки зрения словообразовательной производности

Среди лексем с широкой грамматической валентностью можно выделить непроизводные и производные лексемы.

1) *Непроизводные на уровне синхронии лексемы представляют собой, как уже было отмечено выше, заимствования:* кантри, медиа, ретро, онлайн, шоу, бизнес, интернет, модерн, рок, фан, хит, *которые, встроившись в грамматическую систему русского языка, в некоторой степени сохранили свои сочетаемостные возможности, присущие им в языке-оригинале.*

Особо следует отметить заимствованные, т.е. непроизводные на уровне синхронии аббревиатуры типа *CD*, *DVD*, *PR* и *пиар*, *VIP* и *вип*, *SMS*. В русском языковом сознании такие аббревиатуры часто теряют связь с составляющими их производными словами. Об этом, в частности, свидетельствует тот факт, что далеко не все носители русского языка четко представляют, какие слова составляют аббревиатуры *DVD, PR, SMS*, но тем не менее знают значения этих слов. Еще одним подтверждением «непроизводности» таких слов в современном русском языке на уровне синхронии, является их написание строчными буквами: *дивиди, пиар, вип, эсэмэска*. Приведем примеры: Основным *пиар-достижением* партии власти стал торжественный проход демонстрацией по Красной площади (МК, 04.05.2002); Никакими <...> общественно-политическими *випами* публика не блистала (МК, 11.02.04).

2) *Производные* *полифункциональные лексемы представляют собой усеченные дериваты имен существительных и прилагательных, а также бывшие приставки и лексемы, извлеченные из состава сложных слов, которые обрели статус самостоятельной языковой единицы. Так, выделяется несколько подгрупп.*

а) Усеченные дериваты имен (*авто<автомобиль, автомобильный; авиа <авиация, авиационный; мини <минимальный*).

б) Лексемы, «извлеченные» из состава сложных слов (*аудио <аудиокассета, аудиокассетный; видео <видеокассета, видеокассетный*).

в) Приставки (интернациональные и русские), которые стали функционировать в русском языке как самостоятельные языковые единицы (*гипер, супер, ультра, экстра, сверх*).

г) Русские сокращения аббревиатурного типа (*ВИЧ, ТВ*).

В связи с вопросом о самостоятельности производных полифункциональных лексем типа *аудио, ультра* необходимо подчеркнуть отмеченные нами факты участившегося дефисного и раздельного написания в СМИ конструкций, для которых кодифицированным является слитное написание. Ср. примеры из современной публицистики: Меня обогнали *ультра-монархисты* (АиФ, 12.03.03); *Ультра-реальных* актеров я не признаю (Известия, 14.07.03); Придя в интернет-кафе, <...> старшеклассник полезет искать рефераты, писать письма друзьям, а не читать газету, пусть даже *супер-интересную* (Правда, 08.02.02); На каждом столбе по *мега звезде* (заголовок статьи, АиФ Суббота-воскресенье, 30.08.02); В водку были добавлены мед, молоко и другие *био-активные* элементы (КП, 17.04.03).

Отмечаются даже случаи употребления бывших приставок в постпозиции: В сети «Копейка» открылся супермаркет «*Копейка-*

супер» (АиФ Москва, 09.01.02), что также свидетельствует в пользу отдельности, словности употребляемых таким образом единиц.

4. Классификация лексем с расширенной грамматической валентностью *по типу полифункциональности*

Лексемы с расширенной грамматической валентностью различаются **по типу полифункциональности**. Проанализированный нами материал позволяет выделить следующие типы:

1) Лексемы, реализующие грамматические функции **двух частей речи** представлены различными возможностями функционирования:

а) В функции имени существительного и аналит-определителя выступает большинство полифункциональных слов (всего, по данным нашей картотеки, 64). Среди них отчетливо различаются:

— аналиты, неизменяемые (несклоняемые) в обеих функциях (*народное караоке, караоке-соревнование; выпустить свой CD, CD-пиратство*) (33 единицы) и

— слова, которые склоняются в субстантивном употреблении *бывшие фаны, российский VIPы*) и не изменяются в функции приименного определителя (*фан-движение, VIP-автомобиль*) (31 единица).

б) Встречаются и случаи употребления одной лексемы в функции аналит-определителя и наречия. Нами отмечены три такие единицы: *авиа* (*авиа-ЧП, отправить письмо — как? — авиа*); *био* (*центр Био Мир, био-активные элементы*); *сверх* (*сверх-Дарвин, сверх-элитный район*).

2) Лексемы, способные реализовывать грамматические функции **трех частей речи**: имени существительного, аналит-прилагательного и наречия. Таковыми являются, например: *онлайн* (*присутствие в онлайне, онлайн-технологии, работать онлайн*), *офлайн* (*жизнь в офлайне, офлайн-отделение, читать офлайн*); *ультра* (*индусские ультра, ультра-монархисты, ультра-реальный*).

К этому же типу относятся слова *гипер* (*признаки "гипера" —* имеется в виду компьютерный супергерой, *гипер-шанс, гипер-удобно*), *супер* (*первые "суперы" и "гиперы" —* имеются в виду супер-и гипермаркеты; *супер-внешность* и *фильм просто супер, супер-дешевый*), *мега* (*третья часть "Меги"* — *энциклопедии, мега звезда, мега-популярный; экстра* (*читать "Экстру"* — *газету, экстра-специалист, экстра-авангардный*). Однако следует учитывать, что, в отличие от *онлайн, офлайн* и *ультра*, лексические значения, которые выражают слова *гипер, супер, мега, экстра*, реализуя грамматические функции имени существительного, несколько отличаются от значений, реализованных в атрибутивном и адвербиальном употреблении, они конкретизируются, приобретая связи с определенным референтом. Например: *экстра* (существительное) — "газета", "соль" и др., *экстра* (аналит-определитель, наречие) — "высокая степень проявления признака". Всего в грамматических функциях трех частей речи употребляется семь из рассмотренных нами лексем.

Таким образом, полифункциональные лексемы могут принимать грамматические значения двух и трех частей речи. Самым распространенным является тип, в котором реализуются субстантивное и атрибутивное значения. Более половины таких слов являются полными аналитами (неизменяемыми в любой своей грамматической функции).

5. Виды семантических отношений между различными морфологическими словами в рамках одной лексемы

Конкретные морфологические слова, грамматически реализующие ту или иную полифункциональную лексему как существительное, прилагательное или наречие (*присутствие в онлайне* — **Sub**, *онлайн-технологии* — **Adj**, *работать онлайн* — **Adv**), связаны определенными отношениями семантической мотивации. Рассмотрим возможные виды таких отношений.

1) Семантические отношения в парах типа *бизнес — бизнес возможности* можно описать как отношения т р а н с п о з и ц и и (такие отношения, при которых морфологические слова обладают различными категориально-грамматическими значениями, сохраняя при этом одно лексическое значение[10]. Так, например, согласно пражской Русской грамматике[11] между личными, причастными и деепричастными формами глагола существуют особые отношения транспозиции: одна и та же лексема (одно лексическое слово) попадает то в собственно

глагольные позиции, то в неглагольные (соответственно адъективные и адвербиальные).

Подобные отношения мы наблюдаем и между морфологическими словами, составляющими полифункциональную лексему: в зависимости от позиции (субстантивной, адъективной или адвербиальной) будет реализовано соответствующее грамматическое значение определенной части речи. Ср.: *он был супером (Sub) — супер (Adj) агент — дела идут супер (Adv).*

Между различными морфологическими словами (субстантивными, адъективными и адвербиальными транспозиторами[12]) можно, как нам представляется, установить характер и направление мотивации.

Так, для большинства полифункциональных лексем, представленных в нашей картотеке, характерны такие отношения между морфологическими словами, в которых субстантив (Sub) воспринимается как мотивирующее (производящее) слово, а адъектив (Adj) как производное[13]. Ср.: *бизнес — бизнес-возможности, Интернет — интернет-олимпиада, сервис — сервис-менеджер, рэп — рэп-композиция.* Такие отношения можно представить следующим образом:

Sub → Adj

Все подобные примеры являют собой пример транспозиции, т.е. лексическое значение мотивированного слова (в данном случае адъектива) остается неизменным.

2) Вместе с тем в ряде случаев наблюдаются обратные отношения, когда адъектив воспринимается как мотивирующее слово, а субстантив как производное от него:

Adj → Sub

Ср.: *гос-ТВ — сдавать госы, спец-приз — местные спецы, евросувениры — курс евро.*

Заметим, что такое направление мотивации может быть отмечено только в связи с морфологическими словами производных полифункциональных лексем. При этом очевидна возможность двойной мотивации: конкретное морфологическое слово может также трактоваться как дериват соответствующего прилагательного или существительного, ср.: *государственный→гос-ТВ, госэкзамены →госы; специальный→спец-приз, специалист → местный спец; европейский → евро-сувениры, euro → евро* (денежная единица); *кибернетический—кибер-мир, cyber → кибер* (человекоподобный робот). Схематически этот вид семантических отношений можно представить так:

государственный   *госэкзамен*
↓   ↓
гос (**Adj**)   →   *гос* (**Sub**)

При участии иностранного корня отношения между лексемами очень похожи:

европейский   *euro*
↓   ↓
евро (**Adj**)   →   *евро* (**Sub**)

В подобных случаях субстантив по своему значению соответствует полному слову, от которого он произведен (усечением по аббревиатурному способу) и с которым связан отношениями эквивалентности (*гос = госэкзамен, спец = специалист*).[14] В случаях типа *евро* значение субстантива равно значению этого слова в том языке, из которого оно заимствовано (*евро = euro*).

В то же время субстантив может быть воспринят как производный от равного ему по форме адъектива *гос* (**Adj**) → *гос* (**Sub**); *евро* (**Adj**) → *евро* (**Sub**).

Описанные виды отношений (**Sub → Adj, Adj → Sub**) между морфологическими словами характерны для определенного типа полифункциональных лексем—таких, которые способны реализовывать грамматические функции двух частей речи: существительного и аналит-прилагательного.

3) Для полифункциональных лексем, реализующих грамматические функции аналит-прилагательного и наречия (*авиа-ЧП—отправить письмо авиа; Био Мир—био-*

активный), семантико-деривационные отношения между морфологическими словами будут представлены следующим образом:

Adj → Adv

Такой вид связи морфологических слов отмечен нами для производных полифункционалов (*авиа, био, сверх*). Здесь тоже вероятна двойная мотивация, которую схематически можно отобразить так:

биологический   *биологически*
↓   ↓
био (**Adj**)   →   *био* (**Adv**)

4) Особые отношения наблюдаются между морфологическими словами полифункциональных лексем, реализующих грамматические функции трех частей речи: существительного, прилагательного и наречия (*онлайн, ультра, супер*). Сравним, например, такие употребления единицы *супер*: *супер-предложения, супер-дешевый (супер-дешево), он был супером*. В подобных случаях субстантив воспринимается как мотивированный соответствующим аналит-прилагательным и наречием. Такие семантические отношения можно записать следующим образом:

(Adj → Adv) → Sub

При этом если отношения между аналит-прилагательным *супер* и наречием *супер* можно определить как транспозиционные (лексическое значение не меняется), то, как мы уже отмечали выше, субстантив, может обретать нетривиальную сему, новый элемент значения. Так, например, субстантив *супер* приобретает сему 'человек, существо', и даже имеет омонимы "супермаркет", "суперобложка": побывать в новом *супере*, словарь Мюллера в *супере* (ср. также указанные выше значения субстантивов *гипер, мега, экстра*).

В редких случаях транспозиционные отношения могут сохраняться между всеми тремя морфологическими словами.

Ср.: *онлайн-технологии* (**Adj**)→*работать онлайн* (**Adv**)→ *присутствие в онлайне* (**Sub**). Во всех своих грамматических реализациях полифункционал *онлайн* имеет одно и то же лексическое значение.

Интересно отметить, что многие полифункциональные лексемы, реализующие грамматические функции трех частей речи, по происхождению являются приставками (*гипер, супер, ультра, экстра*). При этом именно субстантивное употребление, как нам кажется, послужило основанием для языкового сознания воспринимать эти приставки как самостоятельные слова и в других функциях. Ср., например, следующие довольно распространенные субстантивные употребления приставок: Торговые центры, «*гиперы*» и «*суперы*» отличаются друг от друга дополнительным набором услуг (АиФ Москва, 21.02.01); Тем, кто обнаружил у себя все признаки классического «*гипера*», настоятельно советуем…(АиФ Москва, 05.06.02); Хотя это и не нравится *популярным ультра* (НГ, 10.06.02).

По аналогии восприятие таких приставок как самостоятельных единиц может распространяться, например, и на те приставки, которые не встречаются в субстантивном употреблении. Это, в первую очередь, относится к приставке *сверх*, которая также часто в газетах и журналах отделяется дефисом или пробелом. Приведем ряд примеров такого написания: Возможность застройки какого-нибудь *сверх-элитного* района в центре (Известия, 23.01.04); Он всего лишь жалкий филолог, тогда как нужно быть биологом, *сверх-Дарвиным* (НГ, 13.10.99); Ср. также: «…относитесь к словам (подчеркнуто нами—Ю.Р.) "*супер*", "*сверх*", "*эффективный*", "*чудодейственный*" чуточку скептически» (пример из романа О. Зайкиной "Житейские кружева"). Очевидно, что языковым сознанием такие приставки и части сложных слов воспринимаются как самостоятельные слова.

Итак, как показывают результаты исследования тенденций развития русского языка конца XX—начала XXI века, в современном русском языке есть основания выделять особый надчастеречный класс полифункциональных лексем, который возник как следствие развития тенденции к аналитизму в русской грамматике.

Полифункциональную лексему образуют морфологические слова, которые распределены позиционно. Если морфологическое слово в предложении является подлежащим, дополнением или именной частью составного сказуемого, имеет парадигматически или синтагматически выраженные признаки субстантива, то оно определяется как имя существительное (ср.: *шоу в онлайне, он был супером, индусские ультра*). В позиции при существительном та же материальная последовательность становится определителем, теряя при этом способность изменять свою форму, т.е. попадает в класс аналитических прилагательных (*онлайн-словари, супервнешность, ультра-спорт*). В позиции при прилагательном, наречии или глаголе та же единица выступает в адвербиальной функции, попадая таким образом в разряд наречий (*ультрареальный, супер-дешево, работать онлайн*).

Notes

[1] См., например: Голанова Е.И., О «мнимых сложных словах» (развитие класса аналитических прилагательных в современном русском языке) // *Лики языка. К 45-летию научной деятельности Е.А. Земской* (Москва, 1998); Земская Е.А., Активные процессы в русском языке последнего десятилетия XX века / http://www.gramota.ru/mag_author.html , 05.02.2001.

[2] См., например, словари: Захаренко Е.Н., Комарова Л.Н, Нечаева И.В. Новый словарь иностранных слов (Москва, 2003); Ефремова Т.Ф. Новый словарь русского языка: Толково-словообразовательный (Москва, 2000); Русский орфографический словарь Российской академии наук / Под ред. В.В.Лопатина (Электронная версия, «ГРАМОТА.РУ», 2001–2002); Толковый словарь русского языка конца XX века. Языковые изменения / Под ред. Г.Н.Скляревской (Санкт-Петербург, 1998).

[3] *Касаткин Л.Л., Клобуков Е.В., Лекант П.А.*, Краткий справочник по современному русскому языку (Москва, 1995).

[4] Русский язык. Энциклопедия / Под ред. Ю.Н.Караулова (Москва, 1997).

[5] О понятии морфологического слова как единицы грамматического описания полифункциональных лексем см.: Клобуков Е.В., Теоретические основы изучения морфологических категорий русского языка (морфологические категории в системе языка и в дискурсе) (Москва, 1995: 13).

⁶ Панов М.В., Позиционная морфология русского языка (Москва, 1999:123).

⁷ Зализняк А.А.,Русское именное словоизменение (Москва, 1967); Русская грамматика, Т.1. / Гл. ред. Н.Ю.Шведова (Москва, 1980).

⁸ Бондарко А.В., Буланин Л.Л., Русский глагол (Ленинград, 1967).

⁹ Русский язык и советское общество, Морфология и синтаксис современного русского литературного языка / Под ред. М.В.Панова (Москва, 1968); Русский язык конца XX столетия (1985–1995) / Под ред. Е.А.Земской (Москва, 1996: 326–343); Милославский И.Г., Морфологические категории современного русского языка (Москва, 1981); Камынина А.А., Современный русский язык: Морфология (Москва, 1999).

¹⁰ Современный русский язык / Под ред. В.А.Белошапковой (Москва, 1997: 362).

¹¹ Русская грамматика, Т.1. / Гл. ред. K. Horálek (Praha, 1979: §274).

¹² Термин транспозитор используется, например в [Русская грамматика 1979: 205–206].

¹³ Подчеркнем, что отношения мотивированности устанавливаются в данном случае между морфологическими словами: *бизнес* (Sub) и *бизнес* (Adj), представляющими определенную полифункциональную лексему. При этом сама полифункциональная лексема может быть как непроизводной (*бизнес, интернет, шоу*), так и производной (*супер, авиа, авто*).

¹⁴ Современный русский язык / Под ред. В.А.Белошапковой (Москва, 1997: 362).

6
A Culture of Suffering: Isaak Babel and
How It Was Done in Odessa

Regan Treewater

"He was no opponent of the Soviet system but he served his own talent rather than the authorities. Babel's real crime was his artistic independence" (Shentalinskii 2). Isaak Emmanuilovich Bobel was born on the 30th of June, 1894 (June 1st Old Style) within the oppressive, and ultimately inspirational, walls of Moldavanka, the Jewish quarter of Odessa, to Emmanuel and Feiga Bobel. The family would later change their surname from Bobel to Babel. The name Babel expresses more of an Ashkenazi derivation, and is perhaps an allusion to the Tower of Babel. Young Babel split his childhood between Odessa and the nearby suburb of Nikolaev, about 150 kilometres outside the city. In 1905, with the ratification of a constitutional monarchy as outlined in the October Manifesto, Nicholas II orchestrated vicious *pogroms*[1] throughout the southern regions of the empire. This included Nikolaev where Babel's family resided at the time. The family survived the violence by seeking refuge, hiding in the attic of Christian neighbours who denounced the hostility against Jews as unchristian. This time of his childhood would later inspire Babel's short story "V podvale" (In the Basement 1929)[2], which appeared in *Novyi mir* (New World) in October, 1931. Babel's grandfather was the only family casualty of the murderous campaign. The rest of the family was quite fortunate to escape the anti-Semitic terror unscathed. The death of his grandfather played a brief yet graphic role in "Istoriia moei golubiatni" (The Story of My Dovecote), which was published first in *Krasnaia gazeta* (Red Newspaper) in 1925.

Like Babel's elderly grandfather, hundreds of innocent people perished in the *pogroms*, their only crime, their Jewish heritage. But, when tensions had subsided, the Babel family relocated back to Odessa. Although the mass murders had ceased for the time being, anti-Semitic sentiment still persisted in the form of quotas and restrictions mandated upon Jews. Once the family had re-established themselves, this time in the city centre, attempts to enrol young Isaak in school were thwarted by limitations on the number of Jewish children allowed to matriculate. Thus, Isaak was schooled at home by private tutors. This ultimately proved highly beneficial for him, as he was able to complete the equivalent of two years of work in one. He received instruction in music and German as well as Talmudic studies. However it was his education in French language and literature that captured Babel's interests most and inspired his early efforts to write creatively. The first stories he ever put to paper were thus not written in his native Yiddish, or even Russian, but in French at the young age of only fifteen.

Babel's good friend Il'ia Ehrenhurg would one day write, "In the twenties there were many references in our papers to "scissors"; this did not mean the tailor's instruments but the growing discrepancy between the price of bread and the price of cotton fabrics for boots. It makes me think now of other kinds of "scissors": the discrepancy between life and the meaning of art; I spent the whole of my life with these "scissors". I often discussed with Babel. Passionate and in love with life, involved in it at every minute, he had been devoted to art from his childhood. It sometimes happened like this: a man has an important experience, he wants to relate it, it turns out he does it with talent, and a new writer is born" (70). Babel began to associate with his contemporaries and socialize in far more politically radical circles. He formed lasting friendships with such influential figures as Il'ia Ehrenburg (1891–1967), who would continue to follow and critique Babel's career throughout his life.[3] He also befriended literary critic and publisher Aleksandr Vronskii (1884–1937), a member of the *Proletkult*,[4] who would be killed in the Stalinist purges for his association to Trotsky. This would later bring Babel's own activities into question. However, his honest depictions of human existence with all its contortions and grotesque flaws earned him instant popularity among his peers and his readership

A Culture of Suffering   105

alike. Some of his works such as, "Moi listki" ("A Story" 1917),[5] were so graphic that officials deemed them pornographic, and in addition to censuring Babel, halted their publication. But with the upheaval of the October Revolution of 1917 these charges became of minor importance and went no further. "The first Jewish authors writing in Russia—Lev Lavanda, Grigori Bogrov and Osip Rabinovich—were, in essence, pleaders of their people's cause appealing to the Gentile world for understanding and compassion. None of these pioneers was remotely accepted in his time by the Russian public as an authentic Russian author" (Friedberg, "The Jewish Search in Russian Literature" 95). Babel however, remarkably found acceptance, and would go on to write more short stories, plays, and even film scripts.

The Russia in which Isaak Babel began his fledgling career was one of political turbulence and social instability. The proletariat was growing increasingly discontent with the gap between themselves and their bourgeois counterparts. In the midst of increasing polarity were the ghettoized Jews, isolated and oppressed, living under stifling administrative and social restrictions. For the inhabitants of Babel's native Moldavanka, life had never exhibited any stability. People simply lay in wait for the next onslaught of outlandish, and often inhumane anti-Jewish policies to be handed down by Russian officials. From the first *pogroms* sanctioned by the Tsar in the 1870s, to the eradication of an estimated 1.5 million Soviet Jews by the Nazi regime, campaigns of violence succeeded one after another (Israel x).

Most Russian Jews resided in the southwestern territories, as did Babel's family, in what is present-day Ukraine. The concentration of Russia's Jews in this specific region was the result of the partitioning of Poland between 1772 and 1795. The majority of Eastern Europe's Jews who had lived in contained self-governed communities within the Polish Kingdom now found themselves under the unforgiving and devoutly Orthodox rule of the Russian Empire. Although some territories were partitioned to the Austrian Empire, most of Poland's Jewry lived in the lands annexed to Russia. Communities of displaced Jews developed in the northeast of Ukraine as well as in Odessa along the Black Sea, outside of Yalta on the Crimea, and additionally in Bessarabia, now Moldova. The conglomeration of these areas came to be known as the Pale. In 1897 only a mere 4% of the population outside of the Pale had Jewish roots, while 14.5% of the population within the boundaries of the Pale, were Jewish (Schwarz, 11). With the emancipation of the serfs in 1861 and the Russian age of industrialization of the 1880s, even smaller, more isolated regions developed sustainable economies. According to Maurice Friedberg, during the Tsarist years following the abolition of serfdom, leading up to the official emancipation of Russian's Jewry by the government in March of 1917, in the months leading up to the Revolution, Russia's population of Jews was greater than anywhere else in the world (Friedberg, *How It Was Done in Odessa* 93). However, even as freed serfs spread throughout the country, Jews were still prohibited from residing in Moscow, or other major centers. "Throughout the history of the Jews under Tsarist rule, legislative and administrative restrictions slowed down or stopped completely the integration of Jewish masses in the economy. Scarcely any of the conditions of Jewish life even remotely approached normality" (Schwarz 9).

Like the majority of Russian Jews, Babel's mother tongue was Yiddish. In 1897 an astonishing 90% of Jews born in the Russian Empire were Yiddish speaking (Schwarz 13). To facilitate their education, regions with large Yiddish speaking communities provided schooling in Yiddish, although after the Ukrainian nationalist movement took hold of the country, and Ukrainian and Russian were both declared official languages, such schools were required to also teach either Ukrainian or Russian. In the early 1930s less emphasis was given to providing education to minority groups in their native language, and the Yiddish schools began to dwindle in number (Schulman 19). Additionally the number of Yiddish speakers declined significantly with the fall of imperialism. In 1926 only 70% of the Soviet population, 76% in Ukraine spoke Yiddish as their native language (Schwarz 17). Yiddish, a language that for all practical purposes is now considered dead, flourished during this time due to the closed Jewish communities. The ghetto walls proved strong. Not much was permitted entrance, and even less was permitted to exit. The poverty of the pre-revolutionary *shtetls* was described as follows. "The official who, in 1897, took part in the census, accustomed as they were since childhood to hearing about the tendency of Jews to exploit everyone, were literally shocked to see the conditions under which most of the Jews lived. Frightful overgrowing poverty, many beggars, and unemployment were the norm. In a cellar with little more than ten cubic meters of space, in one room where generally six to eight, and sometimes ten are crowded, two pieces of furniture, more or less resembling beds are to be found where a part of the family sleeps. The others sleep here and there on the floor. As for their food, a family of five members goes through entire days without eating more than two kilos of bread and a herring. All walk barefooted and are in rags. With hardly an exception the children are weak, pale, and carry within them the seeds of tuberculosis and other chronic illness" (Israel 71). Countless campaigns to coerce Jews to convert to Russian Orthodoxy were orchestrated by edicts of the Tsar. All attempts were minimally fruitful at best. Under Nicholas I (1825–1855) even sheep's blood on the door of every Jewish home would not have been enough to save all Jewish sons from mandatory conscription in the Russian Army. "Young Jewish boys were drafted into the military for terms of twenty-five years, sometimes undergoing pre induction military training for years that were added to their term of service. The aim was not so much to beef up what was already the largest standing army in the world, but to remove Jewish youngsters from their families and communities and thus to wean them away from their faith and people. It is estimated that 50,000 Jewish teenagers were drafted in this way, and that about half of them were lost to the Jewish people" (Gitelman 2). Legislation gradually tightened restrictions on matriculation of Jews in schools and universities. It was virtually impossible to attend Russian institutions of learning, as Babel himself would experience at all levels. Mounting aggressions by several gentile minority groups resulted in *pogroms* throughout the southern areas of the country in the latter half of the nineteenth century and the early twentieth century leading up to the Bolshevik Revolution.

In 1871, Odessa was the site of the first recorded *pogrom*. Raging anti-Semitism multiplied exponentially. Ten years later in 1881, during Russian Orthodox Easter and the Jewish high holiday of Passover (*Pesach*), an unprecedented 224 *pogroms* were inflicted upon Russia's Jews. The aggressors were locals, and Cossacks, as well as itinerant Greek merchants whose main competition for business were the Jews. The 1905 *pogroms* of Babel's childhood were even more violent and heartless than their predecessors. Over 690 independent *pogroms* intent on destroying Jewish lives took place during this single year (Israel 30). This rendered the *shtetls* uninhabitable, and utterly devastated. The laws prohibited Jews from leaving. After the bloodshed had subsided, these victims were forced to remain confined within the boundaries of their own agony. The result was the cultivation of a culture of suffering. Babel himself would capture in vivid and sometimes unbearably honest detail the essence of this tormented culture.

> She also said other things about our seed, but I no longer heard anything. I lay on the ground, the innards of the crushed bird trickling down the side of my face. They trickled, winding and dribbling, down my cheek, blinding me. The dove's tender entrails slithered over my forehead and I closed my uncaked eyes so that I would not see the world unravel before me. This world was small and ugly. A pebble lay in front of my eyes, a pebble dented like the face of an old woman with a large jaw. A piece of string lay near it and a clump of feathers, still breathing. My world was small and ugly. I closed my eyes so I wouldn't see it, and pressed myself against the earth that lay soothing and mute beneath me. This tamped earth did not resemble anything in our lives. Somewhere far away disaster rode across it on a large horse, but the sound of its hooves grew weaker, and vanished, and silence, the bitter silence that can descend on children in times of misfortune, dissolved the boundary between my body and the unmoving earth. The earth smelled of damp depths, of tombs, of flowers. I breathed in its scent and cried without the slightest fear" (Babel, "Istoriia moei golubiatni" 373).[6]

Despite Babel's adamant assertions that nothing of his own life ever made its way into his work, "Istoriia moei golubiatni" reflects the onset of the 1905 *pogrom*, which resulted in the murder of thousands of innocent Jews in Odessa. A decade later Babel defied legislative quotas and relocated to Petrograd despite thriving anti-Semitism and the dangers he would face. Whether in Odessa or Petrograd, Isaak Babel would never escape his own history, or the ingrained hatred of society.

On March 15th of 1917, Tsar Nicholas II abdicated his throne to his brother Grand Duke Mikhail. The collapse of the Romanoff dynasty was now not only imminent, but certain. All official policies that had held back Russia's Jews for centuries disappeared over night (Israel 114). But the immeasurable upheaval that would soon ensue made this a meagre victory. The Russian tradition of anti-Semitism was far too inherent in society to be defeated by the abolition of antiquated laws. "Nationalistic Jewish writers have repeatedly noted a certain anti-Semitic tradition in Russian literature from Pushkin to Chekhov. Some of them have been puzzled by the fact, as it seems to them, that Russian literature, so generally humanitarian in its aims and ideals has singled out only Jews for portrayal as either ludicrous or repulsive stereotypes" (Levin 13). In his foreword to his translation of Rogachevskii's *A History of Russian Jewish Literature*, Arthur Levin remarks on the long Russian tradition of the allegorical satire in literature of Jews. A prime example of such one-dimensional Jewish allegory can be found in Anton Chekhov's "Palata nomer 6" ("Ward Number 6," 1892). His character Moisek is a scavenger of trinkets, an entrepreneur even when institutionalized in an asylum. He guards his measly kopeks viciously. This is the image of Jews perpetuated through Russian literature.

In his 1926 publication, "Babel': Pechat' i revoliutsiia," Abram Lezhnev, an historical and literary critic, wrote regarding the legacy of Isaak Babel, "Babel' is the first Jew to enter Russian literature as a Russian writer, at least the first prose writer. Up until now we only had Jewish writers attached to Russian literature. Their work was interesting for the reader curious about the ethnographic details rather than the art. It is only in Babel''s hands that the life of the Jews of Odessa has acquired aesthetic value. The *Odesskie rasskazy* and "The Story of My Dovecote" prove that he is capable of transcending the limitations of anecdotal and ethnographic tendencies"[7] (Lezhnev 85).[8] Babel managed to capture the essence of the historical era of which he wrote. Lezhnev valued literary truth of form over psychological realism, which is perhaps why Babel appealed to him so strongly. He felt that a writer could easily become lost in the labyrinth of psychological character and neglect conflict, which he regarded as the key factor in narrative (Maguire 272). Babel's narrative style represented the antithesis of the much-celebrated poetic prose produced during the nineteenth century Russian Literary Golden Age. In essence, this directness of narration gave his work universality. Lezhnev once stated, "We need an art which will be able to reproduce life in its uninterrupted development, in its becoming, an art which in reality of today will be able to show the sprouts of what will be tomorrow, the kernels of what is to come, an art which will be capable of reproducing life in the constant renewing of its forms" (Maguire 279).

The *Proletkult* strove to reinvent the standards of Russian literature into a purely Soviet mould. Where once Aleksandr Sergeevich Pushkin had embodied the virtually unattainable ideals of prosaic and poetic perfection, modern thinkers like Lezhnev and Voronskii pushed for a literary rejection of the ornamental romanticism and supported the minimalist humanist realism of authors like Babel. Babel stated, "my reputation for literary 'independence' and as a 'fighter for quality' attracted those who were inclined towards formalism (Crowfoot 31).[9]

The 1920s in the Soviet Union proved a time of extremes, instability, and ultimately a futile struggle to establish some modicum of balance. "What did we talk about over a cup of tea? We told each other penitent tales about the old departed Russia in which, alongside the bad, there had been much that was good. Sentimentally we recalled the onion domes of the monasteries and the idyll of the small provincial towns. Even the Tsarist prisons were depicted in positive, sometimes moving terms, and the jailors and secret policemen of the day appeared in these stories to be slightly odd, not at all bad kinds of people. The Revolution was condemned for the mortal sin of under estimating so-called good men" (Crowfoot 32).[10]

The first decade of Soviet rule was perhaps the greatest era of universal change and transformation that Babel and his contemporaries would experience in their lifetimes. There was nothing gradual about this metamorphosis, and writers of this generation did not find a lack of subject matter of which to write. It was only that their creative voices would be quickly silenced.

A Culture of Suffering 111

With the death of Vladimir Lenin[11] in 1924 the USSR was seized in a battle over who would succeed the father of Socialism. The main contenders were Lev Trotsky[12] (1879–1940) and Joseph Stalin (1878–1953)[13] who advocated two very different practices of Socialism. Stalin assumed control of the Central Committee in 1922 when Lenin's health declined. Trotsky and Stalin clashed on their fundamental philosophies, and despite Stalin's position as the head of government, Trotsky and his brand of Communism boasted much support. Stalin regarded both Trotsky and his followers as a threat to the consolidation of his power. At Stalin's behest, his top officials stripped Trotsky of his citizenship. He was exiled and settled in Mexico. Ultimately, a Soviet agent loyal to Stalin assassinated him.

On December 1st 1934, a man named Leonid Nikolaev shot Sergei Mironovich Kirov (1886-1934) in Leningrad. Kirov was a popular cabinet minister with a vision of a more moderate government, gaining him support early on in his career. A monumental search for the culprits behind the assassination ensued. Stalin believed it to be an act by extremist Trotsky sympathizers. The NKVD scoured the nation in pursuit of Trotskyites who Stalin believed threatened Communism. This hunt escalated to what is now known as the Great Stalinist Purges. Those targeted included any persons known to have had ties to Trotsky, or those who spoke out against Stalin.

Modern scholars debate the sincerity of Stalin's attempts to capture and bring to justice the killer of Sergei Kirov. As one looks back at the destruction of Stalin's Great Terror and the estimated thirty million lives that were lost, it becomes clear that Kirov's death was used as a convenient excuse for Stalin to rid himself of those he considered a threat. It has even been suggested, rather convincingly, that it was in fact Stalin himself who arranged the murder.

Isaak Babel became of particular interest to the NKVD because of his friendship with Aleksandr Vronskii, who was a known Trotskyite. He was a prominent writer, and in Stalinist Russia, writers were the most potentially damaging to the regime. Even firm supporters of Communism, and the Soviet state were brought under close scrutiny. In essence, no one was safe. "I believe that in every human being in whom there beats a Soviet heart, an honest and incorruptible Soviet heart, every man who passionately, intently and purely without vanity or pretence, tries to master the summits of the arts and the sciences, every student of our workers' colleges, every member of the Young Communist League, every college student and Red Army man who approaches art and learning with the same self discipline and passion as did Furmanov—that these are the ones who are pursuing this cause directly" (Babel, *Isaac Babel The Lonely Years* 402).[14] In spite of his public and ardent support of the Soviet vision Babel was still labelled a traitor and Trotskyite. These allegations were strengthened in the eyes of the NKVD by Babel's ties to the west. Trips to see his daughter Nathalie in Paris, and his mother and sister in Brussels were seen as excuses venturing abroad and spreading elicit materials and information. The majority of the Soviet Union's creative community of this time, found an untimely end in the Lubianka and Butyrka prisons in Moscow. Others would be deported to the farthest regions of Siberia, leaving their loved ones in constant wonder of their fate. The West would know of this for decades as the information smuggled out of the USSR was scant (Souvarine 413, 1929). The NKVD would arrest suspects under the cover of night, many of whom would never be heard from again. "The arrested man was left no opportunity to take his own life. The procedure had been minutely thought out and planned. By stripping the individual of each last item that still linked him to everyday life and his family they rendered him insignificant and helpless. What was an unshaven and unwashed man, in ill fitting lace-less shoes and falling trousers, against the might of the all-powerful state" (Shentalinskii 23)

The height of the Stalinist Terror was in 1937 and 1938. By the time Babel was arrested in May of 1939, the mass sweeps of arrests had begun to subside. Nevertheless the stern finger of accusation had been pointed at Babel. Abruptly roused from sleep, he and his wife were taken forcibly by the NKVD to Moscow. Despite the dire straights of his situation Babel's dark humour stayed with him through the bitterest of times. It is reported that along the midnight drive to Moscow, Babel joked with his captors musing, "You don't get much sleep do you?" (Crowfoot 23).

Nine boxes full of manuscripts, folders of letters, and even unfinished sketches, essentially everything he had written was confiscated. These documents would be reviewed for any hint of incriminating evidence. Isaak Babel's innocence or guilt was an inconsequential matter as far as the NKVD was concerned. He was now seen as an enemy of the Soviet Union, and evidence against him would be obtained at any cost. Interrogation methods were so heinous that in the end authorities could get a man to confess to absolutely anything. Vsevolod Meyerhold (1874–1940)[15] details these techniques vividly in a letter written from inside the Lubianka prison to Viacheslav Molotov (1890–1986).[16] "The investigators began to use force on me, a sick, 65-year-old man. I was made to lie face down and then beaten on the soles of my feet and my spine with a rubber strap. They sat me on a chair and beat me on my feet from above with considerable force. For the next days when those parts of my legs were covered with extensive internal haemorrhaging they again beat the red, blue, and yellow bruises with the strap, and the pain was so intense that it felt as though boiling hot water was being poured on these sensitive areas. I howled and wept from pain. They beat my back with the same rubber strap and punched my face, swinging their fists from a great height. When they added the "psychological attack" as it's called, the physical and mental pain aroused such an appalling terror in me that I was left quite naked and defenceless. My nerve endings, it turned out, were very close to the surface of my body and the skin proved as sensitive and soft as a child's. The intolerable physical and emotional pain caused my eyes to weep unending streams of tears. Lying face down on the floor I discovered that I could wriggle, and twist and squeal like a dog when its master whips it. One time my body was shaking so uncontrollably that the guard escorting me back from such an interrogation asked me "have you got malaria?" When I lay down on the cot and fell asleep, after 18 hours of interrogation in order to go back in one hour's time for more, I was woken up by my own groaning and because I was jerking around like a patient in the last stages of typhoid fever. Fright arouses terror, and terror forces us to find some means of self-defence. "Death, oh most certainly death is easier than this," the interrogated person says to himself. I began to incriminate myself in the hope that this, at least, would lead quickly to the scaffold" (Meyerhold, qtd. Crowfoot 25, 26).[17]

The interrogators, who questioned Vsevolod Meyerhold, were the same NKVD officers who interviewed Isaak Babel. No doubt similar methods were carried out on him, although this is simply conjecture as such details were not recorded in Babel's interrogation files. Just as Meyerhold indicated in his account, Babel too began to confess to crimes he did not commit, simply to rid himself of the immediate and unrelenting pain being subjected upon his person.

Although Babel would confess his guilt in an act of desperation, implicating members of his social circle, he would later rescind these statements and write several letters on behalf of those he accused. He pleaded for leniency on their behalf; knowing full well what fate would await them within the walls of the Lubianka.

After his arrest and subsequent execution, Babel's works would no longer be published in the Soviet Union. Only after Stalin's death in 1953, and Khrushchev's renouncing of Stalinism, would Babel's words be seen, and even then exclusively in censored forms. Any person who exercised the slightest iota of creativity or personal conviction was treading on thin ice during this time. It is evident that the environment in which Babel wrote was not one of freedom, all the more dangerous for him to practice his innovative and unconventional style. This style, although seemingly simplistic, is deceptively complex. According to Andruszko, Babel's narrative gift lay in minimalism, and minimalism continues to be the most difficult of the literary forms for an author to maintain with any consistency (Andruszko 71). It is this literary minimalism in depicting a culture of suffering which has ensured that the few but poignant words that Babel left behind still survive.

Notes

[1] "The Russian word meaning 'pillage' but in this case it describes a mob action either conducted by the Tsarist authorities or with their tacit consent, calculated to ruin or exterminate the Jews." (Israel, ix)

[2] "In the Basement" was published originally in the book *Story of My Dovecote* which consisted of four short stories detailing the experiences of a young narrator during the *pogroms* of the early century.

[3] In 1954 Ehrenburg published his most influential novel *The Thaw*, which told the stories of three average Soviet citizens from astoundingly different perspectives. This novel coined the name for Khrushchev's era of de-Stalinization, now referred to as the Thaw.

[4] The term *Proletkult* is a compound Russian term Proletarskaia kul'tura (пролетарская культура) meaning proletariat culture. This movement existed predominantly in the early years of the Soviet Union and aimed to

define a Socialist culture that rejected the decadence of Imperialism and the perceived frivolity of the bourgeois.

⁵ A later version of this same story would be published in a truncated form under the title "V shchelochku" ("The Bathroom Window" 1923).

⁶ Она еще сказала о нашем семени, но я ничего не слышал больше. Я лежал на земле, и внутренности раздавленной птицы стекали с моего виска. Они текли вдоль щек, извиваясь, брызгая и ослепляя меня. Голубиная нежная кишка ползла по моему лбу, и я закрывал последний незалепленный глаз, чтобы не видеть мира, расстилавшегося передо мной. Мир этот был мал и ужасен. Камешек лежал перед глазами, камешек, выщербленный, как лицо старухи с большой челюстью, обрывок бечевки валялся неподелеку и пучок перьев, еще дышавших. Мир мой был мал и ужасен. Я закрыл глаза чтобы не видеть его, и прижался к земле, лежавшей подо мной в успокоительной немноте. Утоптанная эта земля ни в чем не была похожа на нашу жизнь и на ожидание экзаменов в нашей жизни. Где-то далеко по ней ездила беда на большой лошади, но шум копыт слабел, пропадал, и тишина, горькая тишина, поражающая иногда детей в несчастье, истребила вдруг границу между моим телом и никуда не двигавшейся землей. Земля пахла сырыми недрами, могилой, цветами. Я услышал ее запах и заплакал без всякого страха.

⁷ Translated from the Russian by Gregory Freidin.

⁸ Бабель — первый еврей вошедний в русскую литературу как русский писатель. До тех пор имелись лишь еврейские писатели при русской литературе. Одним из них являлся Юшкевич. Несмотря на весь свой талант он представлял для читателя больше интерес этногафически-бытовой, чем художественный. Только в руках Бабеля одесский быт приобретает художественную ценность. Как это ни странно покажется на первый взгляд, но именно Бабель, несмотря на то что формально все его Одесские рассказы представляют свобой хорошо рассказанные анекдоты, быть может, единственный из изобразителей еврейского быта вышел за пределы анекдота. (Lezhnev 85)

⁹ This is an excerpt taken from an interrogation conducted in the Lubianka during the summer of 1939. In the entirety of the statement Babel is making, he is clearly acquiescing to the authorities.

¹⁰ О чем говорилось за стаканом чаю? Перепевались покаянные рассказы о старой ушедшей России, в которой наряду с плохим было так много прекрасного; с умилением вспоминали монастырские луковки, идиллию уездных городов; царская тюрьма — и та изображалась в легких, иногда трогательных тонах, а тюрмщики

и жандармы выглядели по этим рассказам чуть вывихнутыми неплохими людьми. Недооценка так называемых хороших людей (Babel', qtd. Shentalinskii 37).

[11] Vladimir Il'ich Ulianov, (Владимир Ильич Ульянов), (1870–1924) would later change his surname and use the *nom de guerre* Lenin (Ленин).

[12] Lev Davidovich Trotskii (Троцкий) was born Lev Davidovich Bronstein (Лев Давидович Бронштейн), but changed his name in order to sever any associations the surname might have with Judaism.

[13] The Georgian born dictator chose the *nom de guerre* Stalin (Сталин) as a reference to steel.

[14] This is an excerpt from a speech given by Babel at a 1936 writer's conference in Moscow. He is speaking in regard to a 1934 Soviet film, *Chapaev*, based on the novel by Dmitry Furmanov. The film chronicles the life of a famous Red Army commander Vassilii Ivanovich Chapaev (1887–1919). It celebrates the endurance of the Soviet vision and spirit.

[15] Meyerhold was a director who was celebrated for the experimental nature of his work. He was an original member of the Moscow Art Theatre, and performed in their debut production, Anton Chekhov's *Chaika (The Seagull)*.

[16] Viacheslav Molotov was the Chairman of the Counsel of the People's Commissar under Stalin.

[17] Когда следователи в отношении меня, подследственного, пустили в ход физические методы... меня здесь били, больного 65-летного старика, клали на пол лицом вниз, резиновым жгутом били по пяткам и по спине. Когда сидел на стуле той же резиной били по ногам сверху с большой силой. В следующие дни, когда эти места ног были залиты обильным внутренним кровоизлиянием, то по этим красно-сине-желтым кровоподтекам снова били этим жгутом и боль была такая, что, казалось, на больные чувствительные места ног лили кругом кипяток, и я кричал и плакал от боли. Меня били по спине этой резиной, руками меня били по лицу размахами с высоты, и к нам присоединили еще и так называемую психическую атаку, и то и другое вызвало во мне такой чудовищный страх, что натура моя обнажилась до самых корней своих, нервные ткани мои оказались расположенными совсем близко к телесному покрову, а кожа оказалась нежной и чувствительной, как у ребенка; глаза оказались способными (при нестерпимой для меня боли физической и боли моральной) лить слезы потоками. Лежа на полу лицом вниз я обнаруживал способность извиваться и корчиться и визжать как собака, которую плетью бьет ее хозяин. Конвоир, который вел меня однажды с такого допроса, спросил меня "У тебя малярия?" — такую тело мое обнаружило способность к нервной дрожи. Когда я лег на

койку и заснул с тем чтобы через час опять идти на допрос, который длился перед этим восемнадцать часов, я проснулся разбуженный своим стоном и тем, что меня подбрасывало на койке так, как это бывает с больными, погибающими от горячки. Испуг вызывает страх, а страх вынуждает к самозащите. "Смерть (о, конечно!), смерть легче этого!" — говорит себе подследственный. Сказал себе это и я. И я пустил в ход самооговоры в надежде, что они-то и приведут меня и на эшафот. (Meyerhold, qtd. Shentalinskii 30, 31).

Bibliography

Andruszko, Czesław. *Zhizneopisanie Babelia Isaaka Emmanuilovicha*. Poznań: Uniwersytet im Adama Mickiewicza w Poznaniu, 1993.
Babel', Isaak. *Odesskie rasskazy*. Moscow: EKSMO, 2006.
_____. *Antologiia satiry i iumora Rossii XX veka*. Moscow: EKSMO, 2005.
_____. *The Collected Short Stories*. trans. Constantine, Peter. Ed. Natalie Babel. New York: W.W. Norton and Company, 2002.
Borenstein, Eliot. *Men Without Women; Masculinity and Revolution in Russian Fiction 1917–1929*. Durham: Duke University Press, 2000.
Ehrenburg, Ilya. "The Wise Rabbi (Memoirs)" *Modern Critical Views: Isaac Babel*. ed. Harold Bloom, New York: Chelsea House Publishers, 1987, 67–77.
Freidin, Gregory. "Justifying the Revolutions as an Aesthetic Phenomenon" *Nietzsche and Soviet Culture: Ally and Adversary*. Rosenthal, Bernice. Oxford: Oxford University Press, 2004.
_____. "Between the Stalin Revolution and the West: Isaac Babel's Career in the 1920s and Early 1930s" *Standford Slavic Studies* 4–2 1991.
Friedberg, Maurice. *How Things Were Done in Odessa: Culture and Intellectual Pursuits in a Soviet City*. San Francisco: Westview Press, 1991.
_____. "The Jewish Search in Russian Literature" *Proqftexts*, 4, i (1984): 93–105.
Gitelman, Zvi. "Soviet Jewry Before the Holocaust" *Bitter Legacy: Confronting the Holocaust in the USSR*. Bloomington: Indiana University Press, 1977.
Israel, Gérard. *The Jews in Russia*. Trans. Chernoff, Sanford L. New York: Saint Martin's Press, 1975.
Kravets, A. S. *Kto takoi Misha Iaponchik*. Moscow: Vneshsigma, 1994.
Levin, F. *I. Babel'*. Moscow: Khudozhestvia literatura, 1972.
Lezhnev, A. *Literatura revoliutsionnogo desiatiletiia 1917–1927*. Moscow: Proletarii, 1929.
_____."Babel'", *Pechat' i revoliutsiia* 6 (1926): 119–128.
Paustovsky, Konstantin. "I Promise You Maupassant" *Modern Critical*

Views: Isaac Babel. Ed. Harold Bloom, New York: Chelsea House Publishers, 1987, 113–123.

Pirozhkova, Antonia. *Sobranie sochinenii v chetyrekh tomakh*. Moscow: Vremia, 2006.

Poggioli, Renato. "Isaak Babel in Retrospect" *Modern Critical Views: Isaac Babel*. ed. Harold Bloom, New York: Chelsea House Publishers, 1987, 47–57.

Rogachevsky, V. Lvov, *Russko-evreiskaia literatura*. Tel Aviv: Antiquarian Booksellers, 1972.

Rosenthal, Raymond. "The Fate of Isaak Babel: A Child of the Russian Emancipation" *Modern Critical Views: Isaac Babel*. ed. Harold Bloom, New York: Chelsea House Publishers, 1987, 15–21.

Schulman, Elias. *The History of Jewish Education in the Soviet Union*. New York: Ktav Publishing House Inc. 1971.

Schwarz, Solomon M. *The Jews in the Soviet Union*. Syracuse: Syracuse University Press, 1951.

Shentalinsky, Vitaly. *Arrested Voices: Resurrecting the Disappeared Writers of the Soviet Regime*. Trans. Crowfoot, John. New York: Martin Kessler Books, 1993.

Shklovskii, Viktor, "Isaac Babel: A Critical Romance" *Modern Critical Views: Isaac Babel*. ed. Harold Bloom, New York: Chelsea House Publishers, 1987, 9–14.

Shrayer, Maxim D. *Anthology of Jewish Russian Literature*, Armonk: M.E. Sharpe, 2007.

Sicher, Efraim. *Jews in Russian Literature After the October Revolution*. Cambridge: Cambridge University Press, 1995.

_____. "Midrash and History: A Key to the Babelesque Imagination" *Modern Critical Views: Isaac Babel*. ed. Harold Bloom, New York: Chelsea House Publishers, 1987, 215–230.

Simmons, Ernest J. Ed. *Through the Glass of Soviet Literature*. New York: Columbia University Press, 1954.

Sinyavsky, Andrey. "Isaac Babel" *Modern Critical Views: Isaac Babel*. Ed. Harold Bloom, New York: Chelsea House Publishers, 1987, 87–95.

Slomin, Marc. *Soviet Russian Literature; Writers and Problems*, New York: Oxford University Press, 1964.

Souvarine, Boris. *The Two Russian Revolutions*. Amsterdam: Dekker and Nordemann, 1980.

_____. *Stalin; A Critical Survey of Bolshevism*. New York: Longmans, Green and Company, 1939.

Struve, Gleb. *Russian Literature Under Lenin and Stalin 1917–1953*. Oklahoma: University of Oklahoma Press, 1971.

Trilling, Lionel. *Beyond Culture*. New York: Viking Press, 1955.

Vronskii, Aleksandr. "Isaac Babel", *Twentieth-Century Russian Literary Criticism*. Ed. Erlich, Victor, New Haven: Yale University Press, 1975.

Zavalishin, Vyacheslav. *Early Soviet Writers*. New York: Frederick A. Praeger Publications, 1958.

Zholkovsky, Alexander. "How a Russian Maupassant Was Made in Odessa and Yasnaya Polyana: Isaak Babel' and the Tolstoy Legacy" *Slavic Review* 53.3 (1994): 671–693.

7
Intertextualität und Vampirismus bei Patrick Süskind und Adolf Muschg

Peter Gölz

Intertextualität ist eines jener Reizworte, die im Zuge strukturalistischer und post- strukturalistischer Theorien in den letzten Jahrzehnten populär wurden. Der Begriff selbst lässt sich auf Julia Kristeva zurückführen, die auf Bakhtin aufbauend beschrieb, wie sich diese Theorie von auf den ersten Blick verwandt scheinenden Einflußstudien oder Stoff- und Motivgeschichten unterscheidet.[1] Im Sinne des unter anderem von Roland Barthes weiterentwickelten Textbegriffs handelt es sich bei der Intertextualität um ein Phänomen, das Ausdruck der allgegenwärtigen und unendlichen Texte ist[2] und sich nicht nur auf literarische Kunstprodukte beschränkt. Laut Barthes sind ‚Texte' in diesem Sinne denn schlechterdings alles, was uns umgibt, von Proust zur Tagezeitung und zum Fernsehen.[3] Alle werden ‚gelesen' und verkörpern das unausweichliche kulturelle Gesetz der Intertextualität.[4]

Um die Beziehungen, die zwischen dermaßen weitgefassten Texten bestehen, darzustellen, haben verschiedene Theoretiker versucht, durch Neologismen und Abstrakta ihre Auffassung von der Intertextualität auf einen Punkt zu bringen: so etwa als „Palimpsest" (Genette), „Echokammer" (Barthes), „Dialogizität" (Bachtin/Lachmann), „Hypogramm" (Riffaterre),[5] oder als Para-, Meta, Archi-, Hyper- und Hypotextualität.[6] Gemein ist diesen Begriffen, dass sie das dialogische Verhältnis von Texten verdeutlichen sollen. Ohne jedoch hier näher auf die Unterschiede eingehen zu wollen, soll hier gezeigt werden, wie Mythen bildhaft das beschreiben, was die Intertextualität auszeichnet.

Solche mythologische Beschreibungen werden gewählt, um dem jeweiligen theoretischen Ansatz eine historische Dimension zu verleihen, die der eigenen Position größeres Gewicht verleiht und sie gleichzeitig verallgemeinert. Dies geschieht oft durch antithetische Formulierungen. Semantische Inversionen sind aber nicht nur für mythologische Beschreibungen typisch, sondern sind ein Merkmal verschiedener Theoretiker, die sich auf solche Weise distanzieren, man denke an Barthes' für die Intertextualität zentrale Unterscheidung von Werk und Text,[7] an Derridas Spielbegriff,[8] oder an Richard Rortys Begriffspaar ‚metaphysisch' und ‚ironisch', das er benutzte, um festgefahrene Verständnismuster des ‚final vocabulary' in Frage zu stellen.[9]

Gemein ist ihnen allen, dass sie auf ‚Altem' aufbauend ihr ‚Neues' schaffen. Bezüglich der Mythen heißt das, dass man einen klassichen Mythos unter einem neuen Gesichtspunkt liest, der der jeweiligen Zeit und Methode angepasst wird. Dies soll zuerst am Mythos des Orpheus veranschaulicht werden, da diese Darstellung des Künstlers in den letzten Jahrzehnten beispielhaft neu interpretiert wurde.

Bei Ovid, dessen *Metamorphosen* meist als Grundlage gewählt werden,[10] begab sich der Sänger in die Unterwelt, nachdem er Eurydike durch den Biss einer Schlange verloren hatte. Dort schlug er mit seinem Gesang nicht nur die Götter in seinen Bann, sondern ließ auch die Qualen der dort leidenden Helden kurzzeitig verstummen. Als die Mänaden (auf Geheiß des Dionysos) ihn später mit Speeren und Steinen töten wollten, bestätigte er seine Kunst nochmals, indem selbst ihre Waffen ihm nichts anhaben konnten, denn er sang steinerweichend schön. Wer oder was ihm lauschte war von seiner göttlichen Kunst betört. Die Kunst zeigte sich von ihrer besten Seite und es bedurfte (scheinbar) keiner Interpretation, um den Sinn dieses ‚unsterblichen Werkes' zu verstehen.

Diese gängige ‚offensichtliche' Lesart wurde von Klaus Theweleit[11] und in der Folge von Volker Elis Pilgrim[12] umgekehrt, und Orpheus erschien plötzlich in einem ganz anderen Licht. Theweleit sieht die Bedingung der Kunst des Orpheus darin, dass er Eurydike bei ihrer gemeinsamen Rückkehr aus dem Totenreich nicht verlor, sondern dass er sie seiner Kunst opferte: nach ihrem Verlust begann seine Sangeskunst erst wirklich, das liest man auch bei Ovid. Diese

Idee weitete Theweleit in seinem *Buch der Könige* dahingehend aus, dass er sie verallgemeinerte und das Frauenopfer geradezu zu einer Voraussetzung ‚männlicher' Kunst wurde, dargestellt an Benn, Kafka, Brecht, Hamsun und anderen.

Eine entsprechende Neuinterpretation findet man auch bei Ihab Hassan,[13] der sich jedoch auf einen ganz anderen Aspekt des Mythos konzentrierte. Für ihn dient Orpheus als Personifizierung der Postmoderne. Eurydike gänzlich ausklammernd inkorporiert Hassan Orpheus in seine Theoreme indem er beschreibt, wie er quasi post-mortem, nachdem er von den Mänaden zerrissen worden war, im Hebros schwamm. Kopf und Leier tönten weiter, schöner als zuvor. Für Hassan ist dies der mythologische Ausdruck der postmodernen Grenzüberschreitungen und Samples, deren endgültige Bedeutung nicht festzumachen ist, und denen es (mythologisch gesprochen) an einem auffindbaren ‚Grund' fehlt.

Doch sind es bei weitem nicht nur klassische Mythen, die Theoretiker für ihre bildhaften Darstellungen heranziehen. Anstatt ein kanonisiertes Mythenverständnis umzukehren oder sich auf einen anderen Punkt der Geschichte zu konzentrieren, findet man immer öfter bislang negativ konnotierte Bilder, die die Intertextualität beschreiben sollen.

Der Vampir ist eine Figur, die, mythologisch gesprochen, Orpheus geradezu ablöst. Er unterscheidet sich zwar von klassischen Mythen durch sein kurzes Leben, erst im 18. Jahrhundert wurde er literarisiert, doch war man von seiner realen Existenz überzeugt, so wie nach Nietzsche jeder ehrliche Athener sicher war, dass ihm eines Tages Athene auf dem Markt begegnen könne.[14] Und bezüglich der ihm zugeschriebenen übermenschlichen Eigenschaften handelt es sich beim Vampir allemal um eine Götter- oder Heldenfigur.

Vergleicht man ihn mit Orpheus, so finden sich mehrere inhaltliche Übereinstimmungen bzw. Entsprechungen, wie der Unterweltsbesuch, die Frauenopfer, die Macht über Tiere und Natur, als auch die Auflösung strikter Grenzen und ihr Schwebezustand. Der Vampir wird nicht nur von vielen Theoretikern als Paradigma herangezogen, sondern ist auch die Figur, die als Verbildlichung aller Aspekte der Intertextualität benutzt werden kann.

Für Tzvetan Todorov und Linda Hutcheon ist es naheliegend, den Vampir als Metapher für die Literatur zu verstehen, da er als

Fantasiefigur oder Mythos durch seine betonte Fiktionalität immer ein Zeichen für die Sprache ist, die ihn beschreibt:

> Das Übernatürliche entspringt aus der Sprache, es ist zugleich ihre Folge und beweist sich an ihr: nicht nur, dass Teufel und Vampire ausschließlich in den Wörtern existieren, allein die Sprache ermöglicht auch zu begreifen, was stets abwesend ist: das Übernatürliche.[15]

Doch nicht nur als Beschreibung der Metafiktion bietet sich der Vampir an. Das dialogische Verhältnis von Texten aller Art ist eine der Grundbestimmungen der Intertextualität. ‚Vampirisch' verhalten sie sich zueinander, da sie andere zum Überleben benötigen, so wie der Vampir das Blut seiner Opfer braucht. Bereits Northrop Frye bezeichnete dies so: „Poetry can only be made out of other poems; novels out of other novels."[16]

Intertextuell sind sie aber auch deshalb, weil Autoren selbst Leser sind, die mit ihrem Textvorrat an die Arbeit gehen, so wie Leser an ihre. Dadurch stehen Texte nicht nur in einem Verhältnis zu vorangegangen ‚Werken' (im Sinne von Einflussstudien), sondern werden durch den von Lesern an sie angelegten Apparat bei der produktiven Lektüre erweitert, was die Chronologie des Einflusses aufhebt und immer neue Lesarten ermöglicht und fordert.[17] Damit stellt sich die Frage nach der Trennung von Primär- und Sekundärtexten.

Abrams bezeichnete literaturwissenschaftliche Kritik als parasitär, da sie sich von einem Originaltext nährt.[18] In J. Hillis Millers Replik auf Abrams' „The Deconstructive Angel", die er bezeichnenderweise „The Critic as Host" nannte,[19] erklärt Miller diese Notwendigkeit zur Möglichkeit, indem er die von der kritischen Auseinandersetzung ausgelösten Diskussionen als neue oder weitere Originale versteht, die den Text erweitern. Auf diese Weise ist der Kritiker kein passiver Rezipient (Parasit) mehr, der den ‚offensichtlichen' Sinn eines Textes aufzufinden sucht, sondern wird zum Wirt, der durch die produktive Rezeption den Primärtext ins Leben ruft, und mit ihm einen Dialog führt, der nie abzuschließen ist.[20] Ein solcher Dialog, schreibt Miller, bezieht sich aber nicht nur auf Text und Kritik, sondern auch auf das Verhältnis kritischer Theorien zueinander:

On the one hand, the ‚obvious or univocal reading' always contains the ‚deconstructive reading' as a parasite encrypted within itself, as part of itself, and, on the other hand, the ‚deconstructive' reading can by no means free itself from the metaphysical, logocentric reading which it means to contest. The poem in itself, then, is neither the host nor the parasite but the food they both need.[21]

An diesem vermeintlichen Parasiten liegt es, aus der Literatur etwas zu machen, denn wie sonst kann sie ihre Zeit überdauern? Vampirisch den Text benutzend, erhalten einige Texte das Geschenk, das der Vampir seinen Opfern macht: die Unsterblichkeit.

Ein weiterer Aspekt solch vampirischer Kritik findet man bei Gilbert und Gubar,[22] die einen anderen Teil des Vampirmythos betonen: nicht dessen Essenzentzug, sondern das Erotische, das Vampirgeschichten auszeichnet. Dies verbinden sie mit Barthes' „Lust am Text" und beschreiben mit diesen Kategorien französische Theoretikerinnnen wie Kristeva, Cixous und Irigaray als „vamp school", deren post-strukturalistisches Textverständnis sich in ihren Schriften äußert, die Kategorien von Primär- und Sekundärliteratur ‚lustvoll' überschreiten. Sie beschreiben diese Vamps folgendermaßen: "Recovering the 'Undead' repressed pre-Oedipal female self that, they claim, has been staked and beheaded throughout history, they suck the blood of male theory, thieving a language they wish to destroy."[23]

Doch nicht nur in theoretischen Schriften greift der Vampir um sich. Als populärer, wie Frost behauptet, sogar als populärster Mythos des 20. Jahrhunderts,[24] findet man ihn (oder sie) in einer Übermenge von Filmen und Fernsehserien als auch kommerziellen Produkten. Und in der Literatur zeigt er sich von seiner besten Seite als wahres Paradebeispiel der Intertextualität, schon allein deswegen, weil Vampirismus als Energietransfer Teil des kreativen Prozesses ist.[25]

Im deutschen Sprachraum erschienen in den 80er Jahren zwei Romane, die dies veranschaulichen: Adolf Muschgs *Das Licht und der Schlüssel*[26] und Patrick Süskinds *Das Parfum*.[27] Der Protagonist in Muschgs Roman ist der Vampir Constantin Samstag, von Beruf Therapeut und Autor. Er beschreibt sich folgendermaßen:

Ich bin kein Mensch; der Sage nach bin ich eine menschliche Fledermaus mit blutigen Reißzähnen...Ich bin weder tot noch lebendig, wenn ich schreibe; das Schreiben ist eine eigene Verfassung, ein dritter Zustand, eine Reduktion auf leeres Papier, die gespannte Erwartung auf nichts als Zeichen, die sich statt meiner rühren.[28]

Das Ziel dieses Vampir-Autors ist es—wie bei Süskinds Grenouille—ein Kunstwerk zu schaffen, das alle anderen daneben verstummen läßt. Dem absoluten Parfum, das Grenouille schaffen will, entspricht bei Muschg die Suche nach der absoluten Kunst in Form eines Stilllebens, und vielleicht auch in Form dieses Romans. Dabei gehen beide vorbildlich intertextuell vor.

Samstag soll im Auftrag eines im Hintergrund bleibenden Magnaten das absolute Stillleben auffinden und es beschreiben, denn der blinde Auftraggeber sucht das vollkommene Bild, das ihm seine Sehkraft zurückgibt, „das die Mauer sinken läßt, an der es hängt; die Mauer, die den tiefsten Einblick trennt von der vollkommenen Blindheit."[29] Obwohl der Vampir als Einäugiger für diesen Aufgabe nicht gerade prädestiniert ist, gelingt es ihm doch, in gewisser Weise seinen Auftrag zu erfüllen.

Auf den ersten Blick sind beide Vampire Genies, die durch ihre Kunst das Unvorstellbare (eigentlich: das Nur-Denkbare) leisten. Sie können das, weil sie anderen etwas entziehen. Grenouille muss lernen, wie man einen Duft einfängt und haltbar macht, bevor er daran gehen kann, ihn seinen Opfern zu rauben. Samstag nimmt von seinen Patientinnen deren Blut und deren Geschichten, was beiden das Überleben ermöglicht. Zuerst sind sie aber hilflose Geschöpfe, Säuglinge, die Ziehmütter brauchen. Sie müssen erst lernen, wie ‚richtige' Vampire, auch wieder etwas zurückzugeben, und nicht nur zu kannibalisieren. Im Gegensatz zum klassischen Vampir, der seinen Opfern ein ewiges Leben ermöglicht, gibt der literarische seinen ‚Opfern' ein Geschenk und macht die ‚unsterbliche' Kunst zum Thema.

An intertextuellen Zitaten ohne Anführungszeichen fehlt es beiden nicht. Einer der vielen Unterschiede ist jedoch, dass sich Muschg mehr auf die Parodie verschiedener Genres konzentriert, Süskind jedoch, wie es Judith Ryan darstellte, mit der einen Hand schreibt und mit der anderen eine Lyrik-Anthologie hält, aus der er Versatzstücke in seinen Roman einbaut.[30] Die Bewusstmachung des solchermaßen parodierten Schöpfungsprozesses ist bei beiden ein Hauptanliegen.

In Muschgs Roman, mit dem Untertitel *Erziehungsroman eines Vampirs*, finden sich Anleihen beim Kriminal-, Horror- und Bildungsroman, Märchen und Mythen, als auch bei der Freudschen Psychoanalyse, feministischen Theorien und der Feuilleton-Kritik. Weniger versteckt als bei Süskind übernimmt Muschg oft direkt Personen aus seinen Vorlagen, so zum Beispiel von Bram Stoker's *Dracula*, indem er, wie ehemals Murnau in seinem Film *Nosferatu*, nur die Namen der Hauptpersonen ändert: bei Muschg wird aus Mina eine Mona (die auch mal Lisa heißt), die drei Bräute des Vampirs sind nun seine drei Patientinnen, und van Helsing heißt weiterhin van Helsing, mit leicht verändertem Berufsbild: nicht mehr Vampirjäger, sondern nun auch Kunstpolizist.

Muschgs Intertexte stammen jedoch nicht nur von anderen Autoren. Er verweist ausführlich auf sich selbst, genauer gesagt auf zwei andere Romane. Am Ende von *Das Licht und der Schlüssel* erfährt man, dass der Vampir eine Figur ist, die Muschg schon sehr lange mit sich herumträgt. Er tauchte bereits zweimal auf, in seinem ersten Roman *Im Sommer des Hasen*[31] als der Werbefachmann Bischof, und ein weiteres Mal in *Albissers Grund*[32] als der Graphologe und Therapeut Constantin Zerutt, der das Auge verlor, das dem Vampir Constantin Samstag immer noch fehlt. Eine wirklich wichtige Figur, so Muschg, läßt einen eben nicht los, sie besucht einen immer wieder und ist Teil des einen Textes, an dem man sein ganzes Leben schreibt.[33]

Solche Textlichkeit wird in Süskinds Roman zum Programm. Obwohl er offensichtlich von einem Geruchskünstler handelt, liest man immerzu, dass das Hauptproblem dieser Figur nicht die Zusammenstellung von verschiedenen Geruchskombinationen ist, sondern die sprachliche Vermittlung.[34]

> All diese grotesken Mißverhältnisse zwischen dem Reichtum der geruchlich wahrgenommenen Welt und der Armut der Sprache, ließen den Knaben Grenouille am Sinn der Sprache überhaupt zweifeln; und er bequemte sich zu ihrem Gebrauch nur, wenn es der Umgang mit anderen Menschen unbedingt erforderlich machte.[35]

Er lernt ein „Vokabular von Gerüchen, das ihn befähigte, eine schier beliebig große Menge neuer Geruchssätze zu bilden."[36] Diese verwertet er, indem er „alles, alles fraß... [und] in sich hinein (saugte)."[37] Dies ist genau das, was der Text mit seinen ungenannten Zitaten macht und erzählt daher ‚eigentlich' die Geschichte seiner Entstehung, als „ironische Allegorie", wie Ryan es nannte.[38]

Doch nicht nur der intertextuelle Sampler wird vorgestellt, auch die Leser solcher Literatur werden gleich mit-beschrieben. Der ‚Leser' ist in diesem Sinne innerhalb des Romans der Vater von Grenouilles letztem Opfer, der langsam aber sicher das Prinzip erkennt, nachdem Grenouille und Süskind arbeiten:

> Wenn man sich nämlich—so dachte Richis—all die Opfer nicht mehr als Individuen, sondern als Teile eines höheren Prinzips vorstellte und sich in idealistischer Weise ihre jeweiligen Eigenschaften als zu einem einheitlichen Ganzen verschmolzen dächte, dann müßte das aus solchen Mosaiksteinen zusammengesetzte Bild das Bild der Schönheit schlechthin sein.[39]

Wie manche Kritiker, die nach den Einflüssen, Stoffen und Motiven suchten, sich über ihre Funde freuten, so freut sich Richis über seine Erkenntnisse. Die Hochachtung vor dem Plünderer toter Häute und toter Dichter[40]—dem ‚Vampir' anderer Texte—ist gleichzeitig Bestätigung des eigenen kritischen Talents, Grenouille/Süskind auf die Schliche gekommen zu sein, durch den eigenen „feinen analytischen Verstand"[41] das „Destillat"[42] erkannt zu haben. Denn im Gegensatz zu der Kritik der ersten Stunde, die von den ungeahnten Fähigkeiten dieses neuen Autors schwärmte und die von ihm parodierten und zitierten Texte nicht als solche erkannte, sondern sie für das Werk des ‚Großen Süskind' hielt, zeigt sich bei der Beschreibung des genialen Duftkünstlers, dass er ohne seine anderen Texte nicht existieren kann. „Die Großen Erzählungen," betonen auch Kissler und Leimbach, „lassen sich nicht mehr glaubwürdig darstellen."[43] „Perfekt verpackt", wie es im *Parfum* heißt,[44] entpuppt sich die jeweilige Genialität als Spiel mit Versatzstücken, und Grenouille und Süskind zeichnen sich beide durch ihre ‚guten Riecher' aus.

Intertextuell zeigt sich sowohl in Muschgs als auch in Süskinds Roman der Versuch, strikte Genres und Konventionen aufzuheben, genauso wie die genannten theoretischen Texte fiktive Elemente inkorporieren. Der populäre Vampir verwässert jedoch nicht solch strikte Grenzziehungen, sondern stellt dar, wie durch neue Kombinationen und unter Heranziehungen vielleicht auf den ersten Blick etwas ungewöhnlich scheinender Bilder Beschreibungen der Intertextualität gesucht werden, die weniger trocken Sinnzusammenhänge darzustellen vermögen. Postmodern ist hierbei die Verbindung von populären Elementen, die auf diese Art einem breiteren Publikum die auf die Intertextualität bezogenen Konzepte vorstellen.

Der Vampir ist daher eigentlich der krasse Gegensatz zum göttlichen Sänger im Streit zwischen Apollo und Dionysos. Ihm machen die Götter keine Leier zum Geschenk und er muss sich nicht vor deren Rache fürchten. Sein Haupt wird nicht an Land gespült, um in einem Tempel ausgestellt zu werden. Er nimmt, was er braucht, und er spielt dafür einen Riff der gesampelten Musik, während seine furchterregende Fratze sich über die Grenzen lustig macht, die wir immer noch ziehen.

Notes

[1] Julia Kristeva, "Word, Dialogue, Novel," in Toril Moi, Hrsg., *The Kristeva Reader* (New York: Columbia University Press, 1986) 34–61.

[2] Roland Barthes, *The Pleasure of the Text*, Richard Miller, Übers. (New York: Hill and Wang, 1975) 36.

[3] Barthes, *Pleasure of the Text*, 36.

[4] Joann Blais, "The Ashes of Intertextuality", *Comparative Literature in Canada: Interaction in Progress* (Fall 1992) 35.

[5] Ingeborg Hoesterey, *Verschlungene Textzeichen: Intertextualität von Literatur und Kunst in der Moderne/Postmoderne* (Frankfurt/M.: Athenäum, 1988) 13.

[6] Michael Worton und Judith Still, Hrsg., *Intertextuality: Theories and Practices* (Manchester & New York: Manchester University Press, 1990) 22.

[7] Roland Barthes, "From Work to Text," in Stephen Heath, Trans., *Image—Music—Text* (London: Fontana, 1977) 155–64.

[8] Jacques Derrida, "Structure, Sign, and Play in the Discourse of the Human Sciences," in R. Macksey und E. Donato, Hrsg., *The Structuralist*

Controversy: The Languages of Criticism and the Sciences of Man (Baltimore: Johns Hopkins, 1972) 247–65.

⁹ Richard Rorty, *Contingency, Irony, and Solidarity* (Cambridge: Cambridge University Press, 1989) 75.

¹⁰ Ovid, *Metmorphosen*, Michael von Albrecht, Hrsg. und Übers. (München: Goldmann, 1989).

¹¹ Klaus Theweleit, *Buch der Könige. Band 1. Orpheus und Eurydike* (Basel, Frankfurt/M.: Stroemfeld/Roter Stern, 1988).

¹² Volker Elis Pilgrim, *Der Vampirmann: Über Schlaf, Depression und die Weiblichkeit: Eine Forschungsnovelle* (Düsseldorf: Claasen, 1989).

¹³ Ihab Hassan, *The Dismemberment of Orpheus: Toward a Postmodern Literature* (New York: Oxford University Press, 1971).

¹⁴ Friedrich Nietzsche, „Über Wahrheit und Lüge im aussermoralischen Sinn," in Giorgio Colli und Mazzino Montinari, Hrsg., *Sämtliche Werke 3,2* (Berlin: de Gruyter, 1967–77) 381.

¹⁵ Tzvetan Todorov, *Einführung in die fantastische Literatur*, Karin Kersten, Senta Metz und Caroline Neubaur, Übers. (München: Hanser, 1972) 75. Siehe auch: Linda Hutcheon, "Metafictional Implications for Novelistic Reference," in Anna Whiteside und Michael Issacharoff, Hrsg., *On Referring in Literature* (Bloomington and Indianapolis: Indiana University Press, 1987) 9.

¹⁶ Northrop Frye, *Anatomy of Criticism*, 1957 (Princeton: Princeton University Press, 1990) 97.

¹⁷ Owen Miller, "Intertextual Identiy," in Mario J. Valdés und Owen Miller, Hrsg., *Identity of the Literary Text* (Toronto: University of Toronto Press, 1985) 30.

¹⁸ M.H. Abrams, "The Deconstructive Angel," *Critical Inquiry* 3 (1977) 425–38.

¹⁹ J. Hillis Miller, "The Critic as Host," *Critical Inquiry* (Spring 1977) 439–47.

²⁰ Robert Con Davis, Hrsg., *Contemporary Literary Criticism: Modernism Through Poststructuralism* (New York, London: Longman, 1986) 6.

²¹ Miller, "Critic as Host," 444–45.

²² Sandra M. Gilbert und Susan Gubar, "The Mirror and the Vamp: Reflections on Feminist Criticism," in Ralph Cohen, Hrsg., *Future Literary Theory* (New York: Routledge, 1989).

²³ Gilbert und Gubar, "The Mirror and the Vamp," 152.

²⁴ Brian J. Frost, *The Monster With a Thousand Faces: Guises of the Vampire Myth in Literature* (Bowling Green: Bowling Green State University Popular Press, 1989) 112.

²⁵ James B. Twitchell, *The Living Dead: A Study of the Vampire in Romantic Literature* (Durham, N.C.: Duke UP, 1981) 143.

[26] Adolf Muschg, *Das Licht und der Schlüssel—Erziehungsroman eines Vampirs* (Frankfurt/M.: Suhrkamp, 1984).

[27] Patrick Süskind, *Das Parfum: Geschichte eines Mörders* (Zürich: Diogenes, 1985).

[28] Muschg, *Das Licht und der Schlüssel*, 50–51.

[29] Muschg, *Das Licht und der Schlüssel*, 463.

[30] Judith Ryan, „The Problem of Pastiche: Patrick Süskind's *Das Parfum*," *German Quarterly* 63 (Fall 1991) 396.

[31] Adolf Muschg, *Im Sommer des Hasen*, 1965 (Frankfurt/M.: Suhrkamp, 1975).

[32] Adolf Muschg, *Albissers Grund* (Frankfurt/M.: Suhrkamp, 1976).

[33] Adolf Muschg, „Die Oberfläche als Ort der Kunst: Aus einem Gespräch mit Adolf Muschg über Schreiben und *Das Licht und der Schlüssel*," in Manfred Dierks, Hrsg., *Adolf Muschg* (Frankfurt/M.: Suhrkamp, 1989) 335: „Oft werde ich mit einer Figur nicht fertig—etwa mit Zerrutt (in *Albissers Grund*) dann kommt sie eben wieder, ohne dass ich gleich merke, mit wem ich es zu tun habe. Sie hat sich ja auch verändert, in diesem Fall: zum Vampir; die Identitäten der Figuren wechseln, aber das Geschäft, das ich mit ihnen habe, scheint im Grunde immer dasselbe."

[34] Hutcheon, "Metafictional Implications," 52.

[35] Süskind, *Parfum*, 34.

[36] Süskind, *Parfum*, 35.

[37] Süskind, *Parfum*, 48.

[38] Ryan, "The Problem of Pastiche," 396.

[39] Süskind, *Parfum*, 259.

[40] Gerhard Stadelmauer, „Lebens-Riechlauf eines Duftmörders," *Die Zeit* (22. März 1985).

[41] Süskind, *Parfum*, 260.

[42] Süskind, *Parfum*, 127.

[43] Alexander Kissler und Carsten S. Leimbach, *Alles über Patrick Süskinds Das Parfum* (München: Heyne, 2006) 210.

[44] Süskind, *Parfum*, 276.

8
Vancouver Island Croatians in the Coal Strike of 1912–1914, and the Internment Operations of 1914–1918 in Canada

Želimir B. Juričić

According to the 1912 Canadian Collieries (Dunsmuir) Limited *Record Book*, there were over fifty Croatian miners living in Ladysmith. Most were young, married men, in their thirties, with some half-dozen men as old as fifty and fifty-five-years of age.[1] Almost all were employed by the Dunsmuir's Wellington-Extension Collieries' mines in Extension, eleven-miles north of the city. The membership in the St. Nicholas Lodge for that year stood at seventeen members. They were: Janko Kuljaj, Ilija Kuljaj, Mile Kuljaj, Josip Sebelja, Grga Berdik, Alojz Jurkas, Janko Dragelj, John Zbayovsky, Ilija Badovinac, Jure Popovic, Daniel Radakovic, Marko Popovic, Janko Brdar, Janko Grubacevic, Janko Popovic, Marko Grubacevic, and Andrija Putica.[2] Joseph (Joe) Berdick, also known as Grga Berdik, a Croatian miner from Zagreb,[3] a long-standing member of the Lodge, become naturalized in 1911, and had permanently settled in Ladysmith. In subsequent months, his two friends, Mark (Marko) Radatovich and John Michek (Micik)[4] also took out Canadian citizenship, and thus, under the Canadian Immigration Act, acquired the status of 'natural-born British subjects.'[5] It is not known how many more Croatians in Ladysmith were naturalized.

The following three years, 1912–1915, were crucial in the development of the small but socially and culturally burgeoning Croatian community in Ladysmith. Two events had affected it profoundly. During the strike of 1912–1914, the longest labour dispute in Vancouver Island history, it had been radically reduced in size, and, during the war years, 1914–1918, it had been further weakened when, under the cloud of suspicion and mistrust by the Canadian government, many of its members, both naturalized and non-naturalized, either left the Island and Canada for the United States, returned to the 'old country,' or spent a number of years behind the wire fences of internment camps in Nanaimo and the mainland. Between 1912 and 1914, Ladysmith found itself in the middle of one of the bitterest, and at times the most violent, strikes in the history of Canada. The strike, which was called by the United Mine Workers of America, U.M.W.A., against the Dunsmuir Collieries, was permeated with violence and bitterness unparalleled in the city's history. The strike pitted the international union against the coal companies, the companies against the workers, strikers against the strikebreakers, the militia against rioters, neighbours against neighbours. When in 1913 the mines temporarily opened, and some of the men returned to work, the houses belonging to working miners were burned and looted. The militia was brought in to keep order. The strike touched the lives of everyone in the city, including the members of the Croatian community.

Staunch unionists, the Croatian miners resented with increasing anger the scabbing that went on while they struggled to live on meager strike pay. The strike relief was hardly sufficient for adequate support, particularly for miners with families. George Badovinick (Badovinac) recalled years later:

> My father never worked for three years. There was four of us, and it took three years before he got another job, before they opened up more places, see. How did we live during that time? Well I don't know, it was a struggle. But he never went to work anyway. He stuck it out with the rest. Yes. They were getting a little bit of relief. From the miners around Montana, because they were collectin', see. They sent millions of dollars up here, you know. But, the whole Island was on strike—Nanaimo and Cumberland, see? There wasn't many Croatians in Nanaimo, about four, I guess. But in Ladysmith there were about 50 or 60. All from the same locality in Croatia. They were all pretty near friends,

like...you know. Like during the strike of 1912, there was a lot of single men, see. And they stayed there for about a year, a year and a half—and then no sign, they took off to the States. Some went to Idaho, some went to Montana, and Colorado. They were all single men. But the married men, well, they couldn't go. They had their families in Ladysmith, like my father, and these others, so they stuck it out, see. No Croatians went to work during the strike. No Croatians. I know that for sure. Croatians were no scabs.[6]

Writing in the newspaper *Zajednicar* [*Fraternalist*], the voice of the 24,500 strong National Croatian Society, Janko Grubacevic, the Secretary-Treasurer of St. Nicholas Lodge, describes hardships other Croatian miners experienced during the strike:

It's been over a year-and-a half now, since 3, 500 miners in Ladysmith went on strike. Despite this long and ugly strike, we stand firm and united, and will remain so until a just agreement is signed between the mining companies and our union, the United Mine Workers of America. As for our lodge, we have as many members now as we had before the strike. There are not very many of us, but we are united and trust each other. I believe that as soon as this strike is over, our lodge will prosper as never before. Most of our members in Ladysmith are *Zumbercani*, from the Zumberak area in Croatia. Of all of us who went on strike, not one went back to work—no one went 'skebati' [scabbing], and no one will until the strike is finished and we get what we wanted. However, several months ago, four Croatian men, ...originally from Lika, were brought in as 'scabs,' and there might have been others whose names I do not know. These people never worked here before. It appeared that some soulless agent brought them here under false pretenses, as strikebreakers. These men are not members of our organization, for if they were, they would surely have been instructed about the true situation here and that it was a shame to fight against their own brothers. I will report again when I have more encouraging news.[7]

The strike had a devastating impact on the activities of Ladysmith's various social and cultural organizations. The St. Nicholas Lodge was no exception. By the end of 1912, as a result of their meager strike pay, many a member could ill afford to keep up his membership in the Lodge, which soon found itself in a dire financial situation.[8] 'As long as we're on strike' [dokle budemo na strajku],[9] wrote Janko Kuljaj, the president of the Lodge, to the CSU's headquarters in Pittsburgh, 'we wish to be excluded from all the activities of the National Union, because we are in great poverty [jerbosmo u velikoj biedi].'[10] 'We're not accepting any new applications for membership,' he continued, ' and are even forced to expel some members for their strikebreaking activities. We will not tolerate scabs in our midst... the names of all known Slavic strikebreakers [slavenskih strajkolomaca] in Ladysmith, should be published in *Zajednicar*, the society's newspaper, to let our brothers and sisters in Canada and the United States know who these turncoats are,' concluded Kuljaj.[11]

With few exceptions, all throughout the strike the discipline, morale and camaraderie of the striking Croatian miners remained at a very high level. Union business and one's personal affairs, were the two subjects never to be discussed with anyone, anywhere, save with their compatriots and in trusted circles. This was a lesson learned by a Pinkerton agent, hired by mining interests to find out how the miners felt about their labour organization and their own lives in light of the prolonged work stoppage. The agent came up empty when trying to extract information from a Croatian miner named Nanick (Nanic), on a Ladysmith street:

> The Ladysmith men are a distinctly lower order of people and display the traits employed by the ignorant and savage. Foreigners seem to predominate. By foreigners, ...means Italians or Slavonian or the like. ...On September 14, 1913, Sunday, in the morning near the Post Office, we wanted to find about how the strikers feel about their union and how business was progressing by interviewing one Slavonian striker named Nanick(sic), but could not find anything from him.The miners are being coached to maintain absolute silence regarding their affairs and thus dwarf efforts to gain their secrets.[12]

The strike, which finally ended in August 1914, transformed the once prosperous town of Ladysmith into a deserted, derelict community. Many businesses closed, and many a miner left town never to return. Without question, the protracted labor dispute had broken the spirit of optimism that had permeated the city before 1912.[13]

The strike also left a deep scar on the Ladysmith's small Croatian community. Its already thin ranks were further depleted by a number of men, predominantly those young and single, who left the city in search of work elsewhere. Married Croatian men with large families, relying as always on their backyard gardens and resourceful methods of food provision, stayed if they were able to find work. Some, like Janko Brdar, never did learn the outcome of the long, bitter labour dispute; he died several months before the strike ended.[14] With the old, long-standing members leaving the organization, either through retirement or death, and the potential new members who were counted upon to replenish its ranks having left town for work elsewhere, the growth of the NCS in Ladysmith stagnated, even shrank. By August 1914, the St. Nicholas Lodge had fewer members than in 1912. They were: Janko Kuljaj, Ilija Kuljaj, Josip Sebelja, Grga Berdik, Janko Dragelj, Alojz Jurkas, John Zbayovsky, Ilija Badovinac, Jure Popovic, Marko Popovic, Daniel Rajakovic, Janko Grubacevic, Mile Kuljaj, Janko Popovic, Marko Grubacevic, and Nikola Popovic.[15]

The largest and one of the most bitterly contested strikes of British Columbia's history, pales in comparison with what confronted the Vancouver Island Croatians in subsequent years. The senseless killing of the Austrian Archduke at Sarajevo, near their own homeland of Croatia, precipitated a chain of diplomatic maneuvers that ultimately led to war. Canada's entry into World War I had dramatic consequences, not only for the hundreds of thousands who were mobilized, but also for the entire civilian population. In British Columbia, where anti-alien feeling was even stronger than elsewhere in Canada, the future of Canadian Croatians became complicated and obscured. Along with other non-ethnic Austrians and Germans from the Austro-Hungarian territories, such as the Bohemians, Ukrainians, Hungarians, Poles, Slovenes, Czechs, Slovaks, and others, Canada's fledgling Croatian communities were suddenly caught on the wrong side, and over the next six years various repressive measures would be directed against them. These would be swift and harsh, resulting in large numbers of Croatians being put behind Canadian barbed wire in internment camps, receiving stations, detention centers, provincial jails, and scores of military lock-ups established throughout the country, from Halifax to Nanaimo. It is estimated that at the end of 1914, only a few months into the war, 'some 3,400 aliens had been interned, nearly all as a result of being destitute or not reporting to the local authorities, the latter brought on by the well-grounded fear of being discovered as unemployed and subsequently interned.'[16] And during the course of the war, 8,579 men of enemy-alien origin were interned in Canadian prison camps. Eventually a total of 81 women and 156 children were to share imprisonment, although quarters were available for them only at the camps at Vernon and Spirit Lake, in British Columbia.[17] The Vancouver Island Croatians were among the first to be taken from their homes and deprived of their property under no other process of law than regulations drawn under the War Measures Act.

On 28 June 1914, a warm, sunny day greeted Countess Sophie Chotek and her husband, the Archduke Francis Ferdinand, heir to the thrones of Austria-Hungary, on their ceremonial visit to Sarajevo. The Bosnian capital was in a festive mood. Municipal officials in the Town Hall, where a reception was being held for the distinguished visitors, and the crowds outside, cheered as the royal couple made ready for a short ride to the nearby military base at Ilidze. In honour of the distinguished visitors, elaborate military maneuvers were to be conducted by the seventy-thousand-strong Austrian garrison stationed there. The motorcade slowly wove its way through the narrow, crowded, city streets. As it halted momentarily on the embankment near a bridge spanning the river Miljacka, a young man leapt out of the crowd, drew his revolver, and shot the Archduke in the heart. With the second bullet he killed the Countess, also. The young assassin was apprehended as he tried to empty his revolver into the third official in the royal limousine. 'It all happened so quickly,' remarked an eyewitness. [But] 'The Archduke had no chance. There were seven men in the street to shoot him if Gavrilo Princip, the nineteen-year-old-pro-Serbian-student-assassin, failed.'[18]

Surely the most lurid prophets of doom in their wildest fantasies could not have foretold that a sordid political killing in a remote Balkan town, orchestrated by a handful of young, obscure revolutionaries, was to unleash upon the world such bloody wars and revolutions as it had never known before. In just over a month following the assassination, more than a dozen countries were making plans for war. On July 28, 1914, Austria-Hungary declared war on Serbia. Within a week, Germany declared war on Russia and France and invaded Belgium. On August 4, Great Britain declared war on Austria-Hungary and Germany. Canada soon followed suit. By the thousands young Canadian men and women flooded enlistment centres across Canada, eager to sign up.[19] Many went directly to England, to enlist. By late fall, war hysteria had spread over four continents engulfing their populations.

While the war raged in Europe, taking an unprecedented toll in human lives and rapidly transforming the map of that continent, Canadian authorities, fearing a major internal threat to its security, became increasingly concerned about the activities of the many thousands of people living in Canada whose birth and background lay outside the boundaries of the British Empire. According to the Canadian Census of 1911, of the total Canadian population of 7,206,643, well over ten per cent were known to be 'foreign born.' Included in this category were over half a million 'enemy aliens', people born in countries at war with Canada: 393,320 were of German origin, 129,103 were from the Austro-Hungarian Empire, 3,880 came from the Turkish Empire, and several thousands came from Bulgaria.[20]

Although the vast majority of these people had long been established in Canada, and had become naturalized, at the opening of the war there were some 80,000 non-naturalized enemy aliens living in the Dominion, of whom approximately 60,000 were males of military age—twenty-one years old or over—who had undergone military service, and were liable to be called to the colours.[21] Upon the completion of their military training, soldiers' instructions specially provided that in the eventuality of their respective countries becoming engaged in war they would be required to serve the Fatherland, no matter where they might be. For example, the Austro-Hungarian ambassador in the United States, Konstantin Dumba, instructed all of his consular staff in that country to remind Austro-Hungarian citizens of their obligation to report to their country's consulates within twenty-four hours and to be ready to join the Austro-Hungarian army.[22] In Chicago, Hugo Silvestri, the Austro-Hungarian consul, on instructions from his government, published a *Proclamation* in all immigrant newspapers in that city, demanding that "all persons younger than 37 years of age ...should report to the Consulate and be ready to leave for Austria-Hungary."[23] Those not complying with the order were threatened with the confiscation of property and the persecution of family back home. The call to serve extended also to the citizens of Germany and Austria-Hungary residing in Canada. Since neither the German nor the Hapsburg government recognized Canadian naturalization, even those who had taken out citizenship papers in Canada were not exempt from such a call. The consular staff of enemy governments in Canada worked feverishly to expedite the flow of their reservists from Canada back through the neutral United States to Europe.[24]

To counteract this threat, Canadian authorities instituted a series of measures for dealing with the enemy-alien residents of the country whose loyalty was suddenly being questioned. The result was that thousands of Canadian immigrants of enemy-alien origin were interned and spent the war in Canadian prison camps scattered throughout the country. Besides the Germans and Austrians, also included here were the members of the various minority ethnic groups whose roots lay somewhere within the boundaries of the vast Austro-Hungarian Empire, such as the Bohemians, Ruthenians, Hungarians, Slovaks, Dalmatians, Slovenians, Croatians, and others.

The news of the war in Europe reached Vancouver Island mining communities by surprise. As one miner remembers:

> My family used to camp at Departure Bay in a tent each summer and Dad worked at Brechin mine. The summer of 1914 there was a party on the Loudon property at Wellington and a group of us walked up from Departure Bay. They had chairs and tables set up on this huge lawn around their huge gray house. All of a sudden someone came running out of the house and he said: We're at war! We're at war with Germany. It was August 4, 1914.[25]

Within a week of the declaration of war, and throughout the month of August, a series of proclamations and Orders-in-Council directed at immigrants from enemy countries were introduced by the Canadian government. The proclamation of 15 August 1914, stated that former subjects of enemy states were liable to arrest and detention by the Militia if they attempted to leave Canada. The aim of the proclamation was to block the flow of immigrants, especially the German and Austrian officers or reservists, across a long, virtually unpatrolled border with the neutral United States. Assurances were given to those immigrants of German and Austro-Hungarian background who quietly pursued their usual avocations that they would not be detained or interfered with, although they too might be apprehended and detained if there were reasonable grounds to believe that they were engaged in or suspected of participating in any acts of a hostile nature—espionage, transmitting or attempting to give information to the enemy regarding war preparation or troop movements, sabotage, subversion, or even helping others to escape—or were found to be contravening any Canadian law, Order-in-Council or proclamation.[26] Shortly afterwards, the power already vested in the Militia to make arrests and detentions was extended to the Dominion Police and the Royal North-West Mounted Police. Provision was made for the release of any enemy-alien who signed an *Undertaking* to report at regular intervals, to observe the law and strict neutrality, and to refrain from acts of hostility towards the Government of Canada. A person issued an *Undertaking* was requested to report monthly, until the termination of the war, at designated centers and, later, to local police stations. On the back of the *Undertaking* it was stated that its bearer was not subject to interference as long as he complied with its provisions, though refusal was made punishable by internment under the Militia of Canada. Alien reservists and anyone else whose departure might be helpful to the enemy might be locked up; only those who were considered of no value to the enemy were to be allowed exit passes.[27] Alien immigrant workers and visitors were forced to curtail any plans they had for traveling in Canada, to the United States, or returning to their native homeland in Europe.

Also in August 1914, the Provincial Government of British Columbia formed the Department of Alien Reservists—the only one of its kind in Canada—, which was to observe and report upon the aliens in the Province and coordinate the activities of the various policing forces. Lt. Col. W. Ridgway Wilson was appointed to head the newly created Department, and the facilities were provided by the provincial government at Nanaimo and Vernon for the detention of enemy aliens found to be in breach of stated regulations. For those who could read between the lines, the intent of the War Measures Act, which gave the government sweeping powers to override the rights of individuals, various Orders-in-Council, and the creation of the Department of Alien Reservists in British Columbia, was clear. No one was free from arbitrary arrest and possible imprisonment for even the slightest noncompliance with these laws and regulations.

As the early patriotic euphoria about the war became supplanted by fear and uncertainty, no doubt due to the early setbacks of French and British forces in the trenches in Europe, the public opinion towards enemy aliens on Vancouver Island quickly hardened. 'Fellow countrymen,' warned the *Times Colonist* in its August issue, 'the enemy is among us, thousands of them right here amongst you. In Canada today there are at least 30,000 of our foes. No fools, mind you, but soldiers born and trained, many of them highly educated officers, who know the science of warfare to a degree, and make use of every piece of information. Trumpet's call is music to their souls, and the military band thrills every fiber of their bodies.'[28] Another Island newspaper was not entirely free of suspicion of the new immigrants, either. In an article entitled *We do not want them*, the *Ladysmith Chronicle* offered its readers the following solution on what to do with all those Austrians, Ruthenians, Poles, Bulgarians, Croatians, and other foreigners in their midst: 'They should be deported wholesale and replaced with new settlers coming into the area who are very superior, being almost entirely British and American settlers, men with money and willing to work the land.'[29] In a later issue, the same paper showed downright contempt for its alien immigrant population, which, at the time, constituted the backbone of the city labour force: 'The time has come when subjects of the powers with which we are at war, should without exception be gathered into concentration camps, and be kept there under the strictest guard, until the war is over. There is a further consideration that if matters continue as at present, something worse may happen.'[30]

A series of measures taken by the Dominion government concerning the movement and behavior of enemy aliens, and the public suspicion of them, at times bordering on the hysterical, indicated to immigrants of enemy nationalities that although Canada might be remote from the actual fighting, hostility did not necessarily diminish with distance. Fearing their nationality could be a source of difficulty and contempt in troubled times and places, and because Canadians with limited knowledge of European history or geography tended to brand any central or eastern European as an enemy alien, various measures were taken by the aliens of enemy nationality to cushion the government and public wrath which had suddenly descended upon them. There was an unprecedented number of applications for citizenship before the courts. The members of immigrant communities in the province readily swore allegiance to His Majesty without hesitation, stating that this was their adopted home and they would willingly serve in defense against anyone.[31] On 9 September 1914, in only one day, nearly five hundred applications for naturalization were made in the naturalization court in Vancouver.[32] However, judges in British Columbia tended to decide against enemy-alien applications. G.H. Thompson, a county judge in the Kootenay district held in one case that 'No enemy alien has a right to apply to the civil courts during war. His civil rights are suspended.'[33] Generally, enemy aliens applying for citizenship failed to receive their papers. As a means of expressing his loyalty or of protecting his private interests, naturalization of the enemy aliens was not a viable option in maintaining his status in a society at war.

There was also a noticeable increase in the flow of migrant labourers—by both legal and illegal means—across a virtually unpatrolled border with the United States. Many of those on the move were unemployed and impoverished enemy alien workers, having been dismissed from their jobs in Canada for 'patriotic reasons.'[34] The Secretary of State, Bryan, assured them of fair treatment in his country, which was observing strict neutrality. He ruled,

> 'The United States is not a party to any treaties, under which persons of foreign origin residing in this country may be compelled to return to their country of origin for military

service, nor is there any way in which persons may be forced into foreign armies against their will as long as they remain in the United States.'[35]

Early in September, the British Columbia police dragnet produced the first casualties of the very stringent government regulations imposed on enemy aliens in the province. Headed by a man named Orlich, probably a Croat, a group of workers, possibly from Ladysmith, were apprehended in Sidney, B.C., while attempting to escape via the sea route to the neutral United States:

> About 9 am on Tuesday 15 September 1914, an Austrian Mike Orlich, by name came up to me on the streets of Sidney [B.C.] an asked me if I knew where he could hire a boat. He seemed excited at the time and was a foreigner. I guessed that he wanted to get out of the country, so I told him that I had a boat myself and would hire to him, and I asked him where he wanted to go. He said he wanted to go a long way, and asked where my boat was and how big it was. I took him down to the breakwater and showed him a large boat moored there and said it was mine. He asked me when I could go, and I said right away and again asked him where he wanted to go, and he said "to the other side" [presumably the United States]. He said there was 18 of them altogether wanted to go; I told him I would take them across for twenty dollars. He agreed to the price and offered me 5 dollars extra but I said 20 was enough. He said I was to be ready to start at 6 pm. as the men were in Victoria and were coming out on the train due Sidney at 6 o'clock. I told him that 9 of them ought to come out on the B.C.E.R [British Columbia Electric Railway] and nine on the V and S [Victoria and Sidney] Railway. As soon as he left me I told Prov. Const. Macdonald, and came into Victoria on the noon train. Orlich was on the same train, but did not see me. When I got to Victoria, I pointed Orlich out to Const. Owens.[36]

Soon afterward, another Croatian, Mike Ivitch, was apprehended in Cloverdale, and a group of Austrians including one Pete

Durrowvich (sic.), probably a Croat, were arrested in White Rock, for intending to illegally cross the border.[38] Another escape-route used by the alien nationals to reach the United States was through Osoyoos, in the Okanagan. This route was popular on account of the customhouse in Osoyoos being isolated, and short-staffed; only one customs officer worked the crossing. There was a long stretch of open country, roads and trails where, according to a police report, 'it was not difficult to pass over at almost any point, especially at night.'[39] In late August 1914, Chief Constable John Simpson instructed H.J. McDougal, the Provincial Constable in Fairview, B.C., to keep a close eye on any foreigner that may be passing between Canada and the U.S., especially Austrians and Germans. "If any of these nationalities try to make their way to their native countries, detain them...."[40]

In September and October, a number of Croatians were arrested in Victoria; among them were Sam Andjelich (a native of Dalmatia), John Uzelac, S. Babich (a native of Kropa, Bosnia), Ivan Corak (who had seven dollars, two pocket books and a container of shaving cream on his person when apprehended), Joseph Corak (apprehended with a knife and two notebooks), Karl Kasovich (apprehended with a watch, chain, notebook and some papers), Mike Mataja (apprehended with a notebook and some money), M. Perich (a native of Mostar), George Kolak (apprehended with $248.60 in cash), George Vicich (a native of Crikvenica), Joe Uremovich (apprehended with a gold ring, pin, gold watch, tobacco, knife, and $7.40 in cash) and Joseph Hecimovic. The last two were confined by the Militia Department first at the Saanich prison farm on Wilkinson Road, and then in the internment camp in Nanaimo, and the rest were required to sign an *Undertaking*, to take an oath of allegiance to Great Britain and Canada, and to report monthly to the provincial police in Victoria.[41] Despite the tightening of measures at various border-crossings, and some success experienced by the police in this operation, a number of Croatians negotiated the border—allegedly at $25.00 a head on small launches to Anacortes or via small sea planes—and entered the United States undetected.[42]

Struggling to keep in step with Canadian public opinion, which whetted a public appetite for vengeance, a drive to identify all enemy aliens intensified in the fall of 1914. Colin S. Campbell,

Superintendent, Provincial Police, Victoria, instructed all police chiefs in the province to have the following *Notice* prominently displayed at all police stations, post offices, and places where immigrant workers were likely to conglomerate—hotels, saloons, boarding houses, train stations and the like, and other points throughout their jurisdiction which were not included in any municipality.[43] C.G. Allen, the Chief of Police of the City of Ladysmith, had the *Notice* conspicuously displayed not only at his police station but, in order to ensure it had reached as wide an audience as possible, had a copy placed in *The Ladysmith Chronicle*. The *Notice* read:

> *Notice to all Subjects of Germany and Austria-Hungary.*
> Notice is hereby given that all persons who are subjects of Germany and Austria-Hungary, who reside or enter the city of Ladysmith, are required forthwith to present themselves to the Chief of Police of the City of Ladysmith, B.C., there leave their names and addresses and descriptions and make such report and give such other information and follow such directions as shall be required or directed by the Chief of Police. All keepers of boarding houses in the city of Ladysmith are also required to submit the names of all persons of German or Austro-Hungarian nationality domicile on the premises to the Chief of Police of the city of Ladysmith, B.C. And further take notice that any such persons who are subjects of the countries aforesaid who do not comply with the above requirements forthwith, will be proceeded against. Signed C.G. Allen, Chief of Police of the City of Ladysmith, B.C.[44]

For the remainder of 1914, and indeed for the rest of the war, the Croatians of British Columbia were required to report their movements, occupations and addresses to the authorities. By late October, the system of registration and internment had been established which was to last throughout the war. Hundreds of male Croats, many of whom had been resident in British Columbia for years as fishermen and miners, were required to report their whereabouts each month. The police records reveal, for example, that there were many miners in the Nanaimo, Ladysmith, and Wellington areas on

Vancouver Island, that some of these who had been in the country for several years and were naturalized citizens were required to report along with those single men who had recently left their Austrian regiments and were still considered reservists by Austrian and Canadian authorities.[45] The real intent of the *Notice* was unmistakably clear—non-compliance with its provision was punishable by imprisonment. And it did not take long for the authorities to produce results of its new regulations.

By February 1915, there had been 35,620 citizens of enemy countries registered in Canada—Austro-Hungarians 27,840, Germans 7,410 and Turks 370. The total of male prisoners actually interned numbered some 8,579. They included 5,954 Austro-Hungarians (Ruthenians, Slovaks, Czechs, and Croats), 99 Bulgarians, 2,009 Germans, 205 Turks, and 312 of various other nationalities. They were arrested generally throughout the Dominion, many at the border leaving or coming into the country, while 817 were received from the British Islands of Jamaica, Barbados, Bermuda, St. Lucia, and British Guiana.[46] They were interned in a number of detention camps: Halifax 156, Kingston, 196, Petawawa, 564, Spirit Lake, Quebec 362, Kapuskasing, Ontario, 400, Lethbridge, 35, Brandon, 220, Vernon, 63, and Nanaimo, 123 internees.[47] By June 1915, all enemy aliens in Canada had been registered and then either interned, paroled, or given permission for temporary absence.

By an Order-in-Council (No.301) of 6 November1914, issued under the authority of the War Measures Act, Major-General Sir William Dillon Otter, K.C.B., C.V.O., was called out of retirement and appointed as Director Commanding of all Canadian Internment Operations. His headquarters were in Ottawa, where the Director reported to the Minister of Justice. The duties of Otter's office, as prescribed by the Order-in-Council, included the obtaining of provisions as were necessary for the maintenance of aliens of enemy nationality interned as prisoners of war, requiring such prisoners to do and perform such work as was prescribed, and the quartering and rationing of the troops employed.[48] The three branches of police, the Department of Militia, the Royal North-West Mounted Police and the Dominion Police and the secret service, were placed at his disposal. In order to meet these financial requirements, the issue of credits out of the war appropriation fund was authorized.

Also in November, Lieutanant-Colonel W. Ridgway-Wilson, who had been appointed by the Province of British Columbia to observe and report upon the aliens in the province, and whose headquarters were at Work Point Barracks, Esquimalt, B. C.,[49] was co-opted to Major-General Otter's staff. Although the overall control of the internment camps had been entrusted to Otter, his responsibility was that of taking 'care only'[50] of enemy aliens, not in matters relating to their original arrest. Registration of enemy aliens and their arrests rested with the regional Registrars of enemy aliens, the police units, and in some cases, with other specially appointed persons. In British Columbia, the Registrar of enemy aliens was located in Victoria. Thus, by early November 1914, a new, standardized, nation-wide military organization was finally created for properly and uniformly administering all internment operations in the country.[51]

Within a matter of days of the Order-in-Council, a receiving station opened in the Immigration Building in Montreal, Quebec, and the first prisoners were handed over to the internment authorities there. The second internment camp to be opened was in Fort Henry, in Kingston, Ontario. Other camps were soon set up in Petawawa, Toronto, and Kapuskasing, Ontario, and in Montreal and Spirit Lake, Quebec. Other smaller camps were soon in operation in Brandon, Manitoba, Halifax, Nova Scotia, Lethbridge, Alberta, and Vernon and Nanaimo, British Columbia. Eventually, twenty-four camps and stations were established throughout the Dominion. Each camp was managed by a Commandant, who was aided by an adjutant, a Supply Officer, a Medical Officer, and a number of subordinate staff, such as a Sergeant Major, a Supply Sergeant, an Orderly Room Sergeant, an Interpreter (civilian), and a Matron (in camps where women and children were interned). In smaller stations and camps, there were not as many appointments. Through all the operation Otter and his staff had to be mindful of the international regulations of the Hague Convention and to keep in touch with the Bureau of Information of England.[52]

The first internment camps to be established in the Province of British Columbia were in Vernon (opened 18 September 1914– closed 20 February 1920), where a commodious provincial government building with ten surrounding acres was pressed into military service, and, on Vancouver Island, in Nanaimo (20 September

1914–17 September 1915), which also operated out of a provincial government building. Other camps were soon located in Revelstoke-Field, Fernie-Morrissey, Edgewood, and Monashee-Mara Lake. A number of camps in British Columbia were in operation for a short time only, as an effort was made to reduce Internment expenditures through amalgamations and readjustments as soon as the relief of initial pressures made this possible. During this process of readjustment, the Fernie camp was moved to Morrissey, the Monashee camp to Mara Lake, and the Revelstoke camp to Field. It was in the detention facility in Nanaimo, which was in operation for less than a year, and which met the needs of most of Vancouver Island, that many a Croatian miner was interned in the early years of the war. When in the Fall of 1915, Vernon became the central, permanent camp for the Province, the Nanaimo camp closed and the remaining prisoners were transferred to that and other camps in the interior of the Province.

The internment camp at Nanaimo officially opened on 20 September 1914. It was situated in the Provincial Government Building on Steward Avenue near the intersection with Townsite Road. The site overlooked Newcastle Island Channel, and was enclosed by strong wire fencing.[53] Under the regulations instituted by Major-General Otter, in all camps sentries were to guard the enclosures and buildings, to escort work parties, and to supervise prisoners' quarters.[54] In Nanaimo, a system of guards and sentries was in operation at all times; their boxes formed the final outposts of the establishment. The guards were billeted in the old Agricultural Hall on Machleary Street, about a mile south-west of the internment camp.

The Commandant of the Nanaimo facility was Major A. Rowan, 6th Regiment (Duke of Connaught's Own Rifles), a Vancouver B.C. Militia unit. He worked in close cooperation with the numerous provincial and municipal law-enforcement agents on the Island, including W.J. Bowser, Attorney-General of B.C., Major W. Ridgeway-Wilson, B.C.'s own internment officer, Colin S. Campbell, Superintendent, B. C. Provincial Police, Constables McDonald (Sidney), Stephenson (Nanaimo), Neen (Nanaimo City Police), Mills (Cumberland), Kemp (Ladysmith), Frier (Ganges), Kier (Duncan), and others in charge of smaller Island communities.[55]

Several days prior to the Nanaimo camp receiving its first prisoners, Superintendent Campbell sent out instructions to all chiefs of Police in the Province regarding the costs of transporting the prisoners to the camps and how the Province planned to utilize its two main internment centres. The instructions read in part:

> ...the military authorities will assume the cost of transportation and necessary escort for all prisoners of war from the various gaols and lock-ups [in the Province] to the internment camps at Nanaimo and Vernon; those from Vancouver, New Westminster, and the island going to Nanaimo, and all those from the upper country to Vernon.[56]

On 22 September 1914, only days after it was officially opened, the Nanaimo camp received its first prisoners. They were 14 Austrian and Croatian nationals who had been taken in charge by the police and military authorities in Victoria and escorted under guard to the newly opened detention facility in the mid-Island city.[57]

They were soon joined by an unspecified number of enemy alien men apprehended and detained by the police in various locations on the Island, although they had registered their names in accordance with the recent federal and provincial regulations.[58] By November, according to one press source, 'a considerable number of aliens, are now being confined in that city.'[59] By April 1915, the prisoner population in the Nanaimo camp stood at about 90 men.[60] In the following month, that number had sharply increased, forcing the camp commandant Rowan to close the camp due to overcrowding, and to redistribute the overflow of Island prisoners to the jails and lock-ups in Victoria, and to the internment camp in Vernon. The worsening situation at the war front, and the new, tougher policies towards enemy aliens in the Province had a direct impact on this, sudden, dramatic increase in the enemy alien internee population on Vancouver Island.

The European campaign of 1915 raised the Central Powers to the zenith of their military fortunes. The Russian armies were in retreat, Poland went the way of Belgium, Serbia was subdued, and Italy's offensive against Austria produced insignificant results. French, British and Canadian offensives in the West were everywhere repulsed. Casualties were heavy on both sides. Headlining the valiant and heroic efforts of the Canadians in the Battle of Ypres, the Vancouver Island press regularly carried long lists of casualties suffered by Canadians in that bloody offensive. Such headlines as 'More wounded come from here,' 'The list of officers killed in Battle North of Ypres,' 'Casualty roll still growing,' 'Another long list of casualties,' which listed Vancouver Island men who had fallen in the field of Battle,[61] deeply moved and awed readers. Knowledge of the events on the war front was heightened through personal letters received from men in the trenches or in prisoner-of-war camps in Germany. In a letter to his brother Joe, Jack Lapsansky, a son of a large Croatian-Canadian mining family from Ladysmith, wrote about the horrors of war and the loss of his pals in the trenches in Europe:[62]

> I performed a delicate mission last night so I wrote a letter to Mrs. Parks informing her of her son Henry's death, the poor woman must be terribly heartbroken, for I know how I feel myself. Poor Henry worked with me in Courtenay for a couple of years and then came down to Vancouver and enlisted with me, and we have soldiered together ever since. I know one thing, brother, the next time we get into close quarters with these cowardly devils, woe betide them. I only pray to God that he shall spare me until I have the pleasure of bayoneting about six of them. Yes Joe, it is a pleasure to finish them off, for they are the worst enemy we ever had. I say, Joe, it was pretty hard to come back here and find a lot of my pals have gone, but war is war and they couldn't have died a better death. Your affectionate brother, Jack.[63]

Such letters exposed many people to the horrors of the conflict their loved ones experienced half a world away, in Europe. The suffering imposed by the loss of relatives in the trenches precipitated an emotional distress among British Columbians that tended to find its outlet in retribution on enemy aliens who were close at hand.

Another event which brought the patience of British Columbians to the breaking point, and even made them resort to direct action against the Austro-German nationals both in Victoria and other parts of the Province, was the sinking of the Cunard liner *Lusitania*, on 7 May 1915. Torpedoed by a German submarine in St. George's Channel, off the southern coast of Ireland, as she was heading for Liverpool, the luxury liner sank in just eighteen minutes. Of her 1,959 passengers and crew, three-fifths perished in the disaster. More than a dozen Victorians went down with the ship, among them Lt. James Dunsmuir (son of the Hon. James Dunsmuir, a former Lieutenant Governor), who was on his way to the front with the Canadian Mounted Rifles, a regiment which trained in Victoria.[64] The anger and shock created by this act of war swept around the world. British Columbians, too, reacted with ire and disbelief to this supreme outrage. 'It never entered the mind of men, outside of Germany, that anyone could have been found willing to perpetrate so dreadful a crime,' wrote the *Colonist*.[65] The news of the German action on the high seas broke the patience and ignited the feelings of some Victorians, who took immediate action to redress their personal grievances against the Germans and other enemy aliens in the city. On Saturday, 8 May 1915, a mob of nearly 300 anti-German demonstrators stormed the Blanshard Hotel, demanding that the bartender produce a Union Jack. The hotel, located on the southwest corner of Blanshard and Johnson Streets, was previously called the *Kaiserhof*, a name which was still used by the members of the city's German club who frequented the hotel and often used it for meetings and special occasions. In the ensuing melee, the unruly crowd smashed one of the bar's plate glass windows, and, fueled by the beverages of the bar, proceeded to demolish the premises. Nearly 500 rioters took the hotel apart, while a crowd estimated at between 2,000 and 3,000 watched and orally supported the destruction, singing 'Rule Britannia' and other patriotic songs. The disturbance, henceforth referred to as the 'Lusitania riot,' subsided only when the military and the civil authorities were brought in.[66] The Blanshard Hotel losses were estimated at between ten and fifteen thousand dollars.

There were demonstrations in other parts of the city as well and businesses known to have been owned by Germans suffered considerable damages: Simon Leiser claimed to be out thirty thousand dollars, Moses Lenz's losses stood at between ten and fifteen thousand, and such other smaller establishments as The Phoenix Brewing Company, the German Club premises, Pither and Leiser, Popham Brothers, E.F. Geiger, and Max Kilburger, also sustained substantial damages.[67] In order to calm the situation in the city, which appeared to have gotten out of hand despite increased security, Victoria Mayor Alex Stewart imposed the Riot Act on 10 May, requesting 'all residents of Victoria to remain in their homes or places of business...until popular excitement has abated.'[68]

The sinking of the *Lusitania*, however, had other repercussions on the enemy aliens on Vancouver Island. Although the rowdy anti-German audiences were removed from Victoria's streets, no doubt due to Mayor Stewart's warning that rioters would be persecuted, the attitudes of citizens and communities in the Province towards enemy alien took a turn for the worse—they hardened. Demands were placed on both the provincial and federal governments to take action in the matter of interning enemy aliens or, in some cases, of expelling them from the country altogether.

In the days following the *Lusitania* riot, in an effort to prove their loyalty and protect their businesses, business after business in Victoria and the Island, advertised that they did not employ any enemy alien labor—in some cases they dismissed them if they had— and that they were operated entirely by Canadians or British.[69] The citizens of Oak Bay, after a lengthy meeting in that Victoria municipality, forwarded to the Dominion government in Ottawa several resolutions calling for the expulsion of all enemy aliens from Canada or their internment for the duration of the war, and that all certificates of naturalization hitherto issued to them be revoked.[70] The City Council in North Vancouver also called for the internment of all enemy aliens until the end of the war, as well as for immediate confiscation and sale of their properties.[71] The English-speaking miners of Coal Creek and Fernie, B.C., working for the giant Crow's Nest Coal Company, threatened strike action unless all enemy alien miners were dismissed. The miners' resolution, which was forwarded to both the provincial and federal governments, read in part: 'We, as Britishers and other than aliens, are willing and will work, but not under present conditions, that is to say, with alien enemies.'[72] Bowing to the demands of his Anglo-Canadian constituents to do something concrete about the enemy alien problem in the Province, Hon. W. J. Bowser, Attorney General of B.C., traveled to Ottawa and succeeded in persuading the Dominion Government to consent to the internment of enemy aliens employed in the coal mines in the Province of British Columbia. 'Affected by that order,' wrote the *Colonist*, 'will be considerable number of Germans and Austro-Hungarian men, for there are a number of them employed in the coal mines on Vancouver Island.'[73] Within hours of the government's new policy, a large group of miners of enemy nationality, both single and married, were removed from the coal pits in the Bevan, Cumberland, Extension, Ladysmith, South Wellington, Union Bay and Nanaimo areas, and locked up.[74] According to the list of enemy aliens working in Vancouver Island mines at the time, and of those receiving relief in Ladysmith and Extension,

> there were 17 alien enemies on the relief list at Ladysmith and Extension, 12 were single men, and 1, a married man, who was naturalized in 1907. There were 23 enemy alien miners working in the mines at Ladysmith and Extension, of these 12 were single men, two of whom are naturalized, and 8 of the married men were naturalized. At South Wellington there were 27 men of enemy nationality working there, 13 of these were single men. Among these there was but one German and he was naturalized.[75]

Among the more than 60 men taken prisoner in May 1915, police round-up of enemy alien miners from the Island coal pits were a number of Croatian miners including Vukosic, the Pavic brothers, Sverko, Nordolski, Trinka and others. Some were married with children.[76] The two long-standing members of the St. Nicholas' lodge in Ladysmith, Janko Dragelj and Josip Sebelja, were also 'uzeti u prisoner' (taken prisoner) at this time.[77]

Among the reasons given for the internment of these men was the creation of working vacancies 'for bona fide British subjects who have their families and homes in the district.'[78] By mid-September, 1915, due to the overcrowding at the Nanaimo camp, the camp commandant Rowan was forced to redistribute the owerflow of Island prisoners—some 115 alien miners—to the jails and lock-ups in Victoria, and to the internment camps in Vernon, Revelstoke-

Field, Fernie-Morrisey, Edgewood, and Monashee-Mara Lake.[79] In the fall of 1915, Vernon became the central, permanent camp for the province, the unsuitable and overcrowded Nanaimo camp closed for good (17 September), and some 120 remaining prisoners were either transferred to that and other camps in the interior of the province or, save those considered most dangerous, released by the authorities on parole to work for private companies.[80] At the request of Attorney General Bowser, the coal and railway companies agreed to rehire some unemployed miners. Bowser was anxious to get these men, particularly heads of families, off the relief roles.[81] Some 30 people, including Croatians Smiljanic, Marich, Lukanich, Borovich, and others found work in Canadian Collieries in Extension, while others moved to Field and Winnipeg, to work for the Canadian Pacific Railway.

And there were some who, rather than face an uncertain future in Canada, decided to 'pack it up' and return to the 'old country.' In October, 50 to 60 miners from Ladysmith and Cumberland joined a group of more than 200 people in Vancouver for the trip to Europe.

> Asked why, one Croatian returnee replied: Why am I leaving?
> Well, what is there for me to do here? Look, I came to this country to escape economic and political exploitation at home. I came here to work for a better life, and to help build this country. Instead, almost overnight, and of no fault of my own, I became despised, suspect, discriminated against, and, worst of all, without a trial or anything, interned in prison and treated like a criminal. What did I do to deserve this? And now, we're the first to be fired, and last to be hired. I'm leaving, come what may.[82]

Notes

[1] *Canadian Collieries (Dunsmuir) Limited Record Book* (Ladysmith, Ted Knight Collection).

[2] *Glavna knjiga i imenik Odsjeka broj 268, H.B.Z., u Ladysmithu* (Nanaimo, Archives of the Croatian Fraternal Union St. Nicholas Lodge No. 268), 281.

[3] 'Oath of Residence and Oath of Allegiance of Joseph Berdick, and Notice of Intention of Joseph Berdick to apply for Naturalization' (Ladysmith, 13 June 1911), in possession of the author.

[4] 'Oath of Residence and Oath of Allegiance of Mark Radatovich and Notice of Intention of Mark Radatovich to apply for Naturalization' (Ladysmith, 21 February 1911), in possession of the author. Also 'Oath of Residence and Oath of Allegiance of John Michek and Notice of Intention of John Michek to apply for Naturalization' (Ladysmith, 11April 1913), in possession of the author.

[5] *Annual Report of the Department of the Interior for the fiscal year ending March 31, 1915* (Ottawa: King's printer, 1915), 202.

[6] Interview Myrtel Burgen with George Badovinick. (Victoria, 9 Februay 1979), Coal Tyee History Project, B.C.P.A., transcript 4051,14.

[7] 'Hrvati na strajku u Kanadi', *Zajednicar* (Pittsburgh, 1 April 1914), 1.

[8] 'Hrvati na strajku u Kanadi', 138.

[9] 'Hrvati na strajku u Kanadi', 149.

[10] 'Hrvati na strajku u Kanadi', 146.

[11] 'Hrvati na strajku u Kanadi', 156, 157.

[12] Pinkerton reports re strike at Nanaimo, Cumberland, Extension, Ladysmith South and elsewhere, B.C.Provincial Archives, GR 429, Box 19.

[13] Richard Goodacre, *Dunsmuir's dream, Ladysmith, the first forty years* (Victoria: Porcepic books, 1991), 60.

[14] Richard Goodacre, 143.

[15] Richard Goodacre, 278.

[16] Bohdan S. Kordan and Peter Melnycky, eds., *In the shadow of the Rockies* (Edmonton: Canadian Institute of Ukrainian Studies Press, 1991), 15–16.

[17] William Otter, *Internment Operations, 1914-1920* (Ottawa: King's Printer, 1921), 6.

[18] Rebecca West, *Black Lamb and Grey Falcon* (New York: The Viking Press, 1958), 375.

[19] 'Canada to call army division', *The Daily Colonist* (Victoria, 6 August 1914), No. 203, 1.

[20] *Canada in the Great World War* (Toronto: United Publishers of Canada), II, 145.

[21] Colin Campbell, 'Canadian Internment Camps Of World War One', *The Canadian Philatelist*, II, 120.

[22] Josip Cizmic, *History of the Croatian Fraternal Union of America* (Zagreb: Golden Marketing, 1994), 144.

[23] *Ibid.*, 145.

[24] 'Austrians in Canada Liable to Call Home', *Times-Colonist* (Victoria, 4 August 1914).

[25] Lynne Bowen, *Boss Whistle* (Lantzville: Oolichan Books, 1982), 199.

[26] *Report of the Secretary of State of Canada for the year ending March 31, 1915* (Ottawa: King's printer, 1915), 224.

[27] B.C.Provincial Archives, B.C. Police, Alien Enemies Correspondence and Reports (1914–1918), GR 57, vol. 20, ff.20.

[28] 'The enemy among us', *Times-Colonist* (Victoria, 14 August 1914).

[29] 'Wholesale Deportation Are Contemplated', *Ladysmith Chronicle* (Ladysmith, 11 July 1914), 69.

[30] 'Strangers within our gates', *Ladysmith Chronicle,* VII, No. 30 (Ladysmith, 14 November 1914), 1.

[31] 'Become Citizens', *Times-Colonist* (Victoria, 13 August 1914), 6.

[32] *Times Colonist* (Victoria, 9 September 1914), 2.

[33] Tracy Raynolds, *A case study in attitudes towards enemy aliens in British Columbia 1914–1918* (M.A Thesis, University of British Columbia, April, 1973), 47.

[34] Donald Avery, *Dangerous Foreigners* (Toronto, McClelland and Stewart, 1988), 67.

[35] 'Foreigners in States', *Times-Colonist* (Victoria, 14 August 1914).

[36] B.C.Provincial Archives, B.C. Police, Alien Enemies Correspondence and Reports (1914–1918), GR 57, vol. 8, ff.1-22. H.A.E.Teats' statement to the Superintended of Provincial Police re: arrest of Austrian reservists at Sidney, 15 September 1914.

[37] B.C.Provincial Archives, B.C. Police, Alien Enemies Correspondence and Reports (1914–1918), GR 57, vol. 07, ff.1264-A to 1264-D. Correspondence from Chief Constable John Simpson to Colin S. Campbell, Superintendent, Provincial Police, Victoria, B.C., dated Greenwood, British Columbia, 27 August 1914.

[38] B.C. Provincial Archives, B.C. Police, Alien Enemies Correspondence and Reports (1914–1918), GR 57, vol. 07, ff.1264-A to 1264-D. Correspondence from Warden Turnbull Warden, Provincil Goal, New Westminster, B.C., to Colin S. Campbell, Superintendent, Provincial Police, Victoria, B.C., dated 26 August 1914, at New Westminster, B.C.

[39] B.C. Provincial Archives, B.C. Police, Alien Enemies Correspondence and Reports (1914–1918), GR 57, vol. 07, ff.1264-A to 1264-D. Correspondence from A.T. Turnbull, Warden, Provincil Goal, New Westminster, B.C., to Colin C. Campbell, Superintendent, Provincial Police, Victoria, B.C., dated 27August 1914, at New Westminster, B.C.,

[40] B.C. Provincial Archives, B.C. Police, Alien Enemies Correspondence and Reports (1914–1918), GR 57, vol. 07, ff.1264-A to 1264-D. Correspondence from Chief Constable John Simpson to H.J McDougal, Provincial Constable, Fairview, B.C., dated 27 August 1914.

[41] Prisoners' Effects Book, Saanich Prison Farm, Victoria, B.C., B.C.P.A., GR 306, vol.7.

[42] Anthony Rasporich, *For a Better Life. A History of Croatians in Canada* (Toronto: McClelland and Stewart, 1982), 77.

[43] B.C.P.A., B.C. Police, Alien Enemies Correspondence and Reports (1914–1918), GR 57, vol. 07, ff.1264-A to 1264-D. Correspondence from Colin S. Campbell, Superintendent, Provincial Police, Victoria, B.C., to Chief Constables and to Constables McDonald in Sidney, Fryer in Ganges, and Krier, at Duncan, dated 15 September 1914, at Victoria.

[44] 'Notice to all subject of Germany and Austria-Hungary', *Ladysmith Chronicle,* VII, No. 11(Ladysmith: 12 September 1914), 1.

[45] Rasporich, 76

[46] Otter, *Internment Operations,* 6.

[47] Donald M. Santor, *Canadian Scrapbook. Canadians at war 1914–1918* (Scarborough: Prentice-Hall, 1978).

[48] Otter, *Internment Operations,* 3.

[49] Internment Camp Appointment of 'Visitor', District Orders, 28 April 1916, Sheet 4 (Victoria, 5th (BC) Regiment, R.C.A. Museum and Archives).

[50] Otter, 4.

[51] Otter, 3.

[52] Otter, 4.

[53] Otter, 5.

[54] Otter, 6.

[55] B.C. P. A., B.C. Police, Alien Enemies Correspondence and Reports (1914–1918), GR 57, vol. 07.

[56] B.C. P.A., B.C. Police, Alien Enemies Correspondence and Reports (1914–1918), GR 57, vol. 07, ff.1264-A to 1264-D. Correspondence from Colin S. Campbell, Superintendent, Provincial Police, Victoria, B.C., to T. Smith, Chief Constable, Vancouver, B.C., dated 19 September, 1914.

[57] 'Aliens taken to Nanaimo', *Colonist* (Victoria, 22 September 1914).

[58] *The Nanaimo Free Press* (Nanaimo, 18 September 1914), 4.

[59] *Colonist* (Victoria,15 November 1914) 6.

[60] *Colonist* (Victoria, 17April 1915), 4.

[61] *Colonist* (Victoria, from 1 May, 1915–7 May, 1915).

[62] Viola Cull, *Chronicle of Ladysmith and District* (Ladysmith: New Horizons Historical Society, 1980), 184.

[63] 'Latter from J. Lapsansky', *The Ladysmith Chronicle,* VII, 87 (Ladysmith, 1 June 1915), 1.

[64] 'Submarine gets over 1,400 victims', *Colonist* (Victoria, 8 May 1915), 1.

[65] 'Murder Most Foul', *Colonist* (Victoria, 8 May 1915), 4.

[66] For details see Charles Humphries, 'War and patriotism, the Lusitania riots', *British Columbia Historical News,* V,1 (November, 1971), 15-23.

[67] 'Reads riot act to quell distrurbances', *Colonist* (Victoria, 11 May 1915), 5.

[68] 'Notice from the Mayor', *Colonist* (12 May 1915), 1.
[69] See *Colonist* (Victoria, 11 May 1915, pp. 2, 3, 4, 5, 6, 7; 12 May 1915, pp. 2, 4.
[70] 'Suggest internment of alien enemies', *Colonist* (Victoria, 21 May 1915), 10.
[71] *Colonist* (26 May 1915), 5.
[72] 'Opposed to working with 'Alien Enemies'', *Fernie Free Press* (Fernie, 18 June 1915),
[73] 'Takes enemy aliens from Island mines', *Colonist* (26 May1915), 10
[74] J.Colin Campbell, 'WWI Internment at Nanaimo, and a Scarce Censor Mark', *Postal History Society of Canada Journal* (Toronto, June, 1989), 28–29.
[75] Letter to Hon. W.J. Bowser, Attorney General, Victoria, B.C., from Colin S. Campbell, Superintendent, Provincial Police, Victoria, B.C., dated 25 May 1915. I wish to thank Mr. Colin Campbell for giving me a copy of this document.
[76] List of Alien Enemies, Superintendent Provincial Police, Victoria, B.C., 18 May 1915. Correspondence from Colin S. Campbell, Superintendent, Provincial Police, Victoria, B.C., to Chief Constables and to Constables McDonald in Sidney, Fryer in Ganges, and Krier, at Duncan, dated Victoria, 15 September 1914. I wish to thank Mr. Colin Campbell for giving me a copy of this document.
[77] *Glavna Knjiga i Imenik Odsjeka 268 u Ladysmithu, B.C.* (Ladysmith, 21 October, 1903).
[78] 'Takes enemy aliens from Island mines,' *Colonist* (Victoria, 26 May 1915), 10.
[79] 'Alien miners are to be replaced', *Ladysmith Chronicle* (Ladysmith, 26 May 1915), VII, No.85, 1.
[80] Avery, *Dangerous foreigners*, 68.
[81] Lynnne Bowen, *Boss Whistle* (Lantzville: Oolichan books, 1982), 199.
[82] Interview, Zelimir B. Juricic with Tom Kulaj (Nanaimo, 18 August, 1991). Kulaj heard this quote from a friend.

9
Evtushenko and the Legacy of "Babii Iar"

Amy Safarik

In 1961 Evgenii Aleksandrovich Evtushenko (born E. A. Gangnus, 1932–) dared to speak out on the controversial issues of Soviet anti-Semitism and the accountability of Communist Party members for their involvement in past and present injustices in his best-known literary work, "Babii Iar." The poem is named for a ravine located in Kyiv, Ukraine (between the districts of Lukyanovka, Kurenyovka, and Syrets) where thousands of primarily Jewish Soviet citizens were brutally massacred by Nazi forces and local collaborators during World War II.[1] Despite the poem's prevalence in historical, socio-political and literary studies, the artistic aesthetics and formal elements of the work largely remain free of any detailed investigation. The aim of the present paper is to provide a comprehensive analysis of the artistry behind the political phenomenon that Evtushenko's "Babii Iar" created. I approach the subject using a methodology of close examination, a formal and structural analysis of the poem that incorporates the influence of Maiakovskii and Ozerov on Evtushenko's work, against a backdrop of relevant social, political, and historical conditions.

The human butchery at Babi Yar occurred over two days in the fall of 1941. On 28 September 1941, Nazis distributed two thousand posters in Kyiv calling for all Jews to gather near the Russian and Jewish cemeteries on the morning of 29 September 1941 with their documents, money, valuables, and warm clothing. The order stated that any Jews who disobeyed would be shot, and any citizen who attempted to enter the emptied apartments and steal property or hide

Jews would be shot. Most Jews in Kyiv were unaware of Hitler's anti-Jewish policies, the treatment of Jews in Germany, or of the large Jewish communities in Bialystok and Lviv that had already been exterminated. Soviet officials deliberately suppressed this information after the German-Soviet Non-Aggression Pact was established in August 1939. As a result, many Jews believed the Nazi propaganda that they would be resettled and obeyed the order. On 29 September 1941 Nazis and local collaborators herded the massive crowd that had gathered towards the ravine, stripped the Jews of their belongings and clothing, and systematically drove them out in groups to the edge of the ravine. There the Jews were gunned down in front of their fellow sufferers. The wounded victims and lifeless bodies fell into the pit below; children were thrown into the ravine alive. The next group was then forced to the edge or made to lie over the layers of bodies and shot.[2] The account of Einsatzgruppe C,[3] dated 2 October 1941 and entitled "Operational Situation Report USSR No. 101," documents the massacre: "Sonderkommando 4a in collaboration with Einsatzgruppe HQ and two Kommandos of police regiment South, executed 33,771 Jews in Kiev on September 29 and 30, 1941."[4] Among the tens of thousands of Jews executed in the mass murder were some Ukrainians, Russians, Poles, and Roma. The extent of the brutality of the massacre becomes apparent when considered in a broader historical context: Stephen Berk stated in his 28 November 2006 lecture, "Death in the Ukraine," that throughout the Holocaust, the Nazis claimed the most deaths in the shortest period of time at Babi Yar.[5]

The killings continued into the first week of October 1941, and the Nazis continued to use Babi Yar as an execution site for the duration of their occupation of Kyiv, ending in 1943. By the time the Nazis had arrived in Ukraine, nearly all able-bodied Jewish men had been conscripted into the Red Army or evacuated to work at factories, and the most vulnerable and innocent members of society remained in their communities where they would perish at the hands of the Nazis. Wendy Lower writes that "[in] Zhytomyr the Germans and their local collaborators killed as many as 180,000 Jews between the summer of 1941 and the autumn of 1943—most of the women, children, elderly, and infirm died in August and September 1941."[6] When the Red Army approached Kyiv to retake the city in 1943, the Nazis began what Anatolii Vasil'evich Kuznetsov (1929–1979) describes in *Babii Iar: roman-dokument* [Babi Yar: A Document in the Form of a Novel] as "the final phase of Babi Yar" and "the first attempt to erase it from the pages of history."[7] The Nazis forced Soviet prisoners of war to exhume the corpses, burn them, and pulverize the bones to eradicate the evidence of their heinous crime, but there were too many bodies for the prisoners to destroy.[8] Thick gray human ashes with bits of bones covered the land,[9] clearly marking the location of a mass grave.

Evtushenko's poem has been influential in drawing international attention to the massacre at Babi Yar; however, there are many mass graves that have been identified in Ukraine that still do not have any commemorative markers and countless others that have yet to be uncovered. Father Patrick Desbois, President of Yahad-In Unum, and his team have located more than 600 mass graves out of an estimated 2,500 in Ukraine through interviews conducted with hundreds of living witnesses and by working closely with the United States Holocaust Memorial Museum.[10] Joshua Rubenstein stated in his 26 October 2007 lecture, "The Holocaust in German-Occupied Soviet Territories and the Response by Soviet Jewish Intellectuals," that in addition to Babi Yar, the most widely known killing sites located in the former Soviet Union include Ninth Fort in Kaunas, Ponary near Vilnius, Rumbula Forest near Riga, Maly Trostenets in Minsk, Drobitsky Yar in Kharkiv, and Bogdanovka in Odessa.[11] Thus, practically any occupied township in Lithuania, Latvia, Belarus, Ukraine, and Poland has such a tragic place. In *Holocaust in the Ukraine*, Boris Zabarko cites the number of Jews killed during the Nazi occupation of Ukraine at approximately 1.5 million,[12] and Babi Yar has become a powerful symbol of the Holocaust in all of Ukraine.

Soviet officials blatantly refused to acknowledge that of those killed at Babi Yar—Jews, Russians, Ukrainians, Poles, and Roma—the vast majority were Jews, specifically targeted because of their Jewish heritage in the Nazi attempt to eradicate the Jewish population.[13] After World War II, the Soviet government targeted Jews in their anti-Western campaign of cosmopolitanism, as well as for bourgeois nationalism during the period of *Zhdanovism*, 1946–1953. Soviet authorities, for example, became suspicious of the Jewish Antifascist Committee, which worked with Jewish groups abroad to publicize the Soviet war, because of its ties to the West and forced its closing in 1948.[14] Actor Shloyme Mikhailovich Mikhoels (1890–1948), the head of the committee, was executed the same year, and other leading members, including David Bergelson, Itsik Fefer, Perets Markish, and Leib Kvitko, were arrested and executed four years later on 12–13 August 1952, now known as *Noch' kaznennykh poetov* [Night of the Murdered Poets].[15] The Doctors' Plot of 13 January 1953 further illustrates Stalin's continuous ploy of using anti-Semitism as a political weapon, since eleven of the thirteen doctors who were alleged to have poisoned Party officials were Jews. In *Censorship in Soviet Literature, 1917–1991*, Herman Ermolaev notes that in the 1955 reprint of Vladimir Dal's 1880–1882 edition of *Explanatory Dictionary of the Living Great Russian Language*, the entry for "yid" in both neutral and negative connotations was eliminated, for which he attributes to "no more than a part of the smoke screen concealing the anti-Jewish sentiment smoldering in the upper echelon of the ruling Party."[16] Although monuments were erected at some sites of Nazi crimes in the Soviet Union following the war, Babi Yar was purposefully neglected, and all attempts to have a memorial built were overruled. On 10 October 1959, Viktor Platonovich Nekrasov (1911–1987), a writer and journalist who was raised in Kyiv, published an impassioned plea in *Literaturnaia gazeta* to have monuments placed at locations of mass graves and protested against building a stadium at Babi Yar. Richard Sheldon notes that although Nekrasov attempted to keep his arguments neutral by deliberately not referring to Babi Yar as a Jewish tragedy, little was done to honour the victims.[17]

Several authors began to commemorate the massacre in their writings, creating a canon of works on Babi Yar. Ol'ga Nikolaevna (Shteinberg) Anstei (1912-1985), a witness of the atrocity, wrote the poem "Kirillovskie Iary" [Kirillov's Ravines] in 1941; Ukrainian author Savva Evseevich Golovanivskii (1910-19??) composed the poem, "Abraham" in 1943; Itsik Kipnis (1867-1974) addressed Babi Yar in a 1944 article and 1947 story written in Yiddish; Perets Davidovich Markish (1895-1952) included the massacre in his epic poem "Milkhome" [War, 1941-1948]. Lev Adol'fovich Ozerov (1914-1996) wrote his poem "Babii Iar" in 1944-1945, and his essay "Kiev,

Babi Yar" was included in Erenburg and Grossman's *Black Book*. Erenburg also wrote a poem, "Babii Iar," in 1945 and describes "Hannah and her granddaughter being sent to their deaths at Babi Yar" in his 1947 novel, *Buria* [The Storm].[18] When heavy rains on 13 March 1961 caused the dam built at one end of Babi Yar to collapse, killing approximately 145 people, Evtushenko and fellow writer Kuznetsov immediately traveled to Kyiv to view the site following the disaster.[19] Shortly afterwards Evtushenko composed his famous poem "Babii Iar." Kuznetsov's *Babi Yar*, a documentation of the author's experiences as a child growing up in German-occupied Kyiv, contained previously unknown information about the city during the time of upheaval and includes the testimony of Dina Mironavna Pronicheva, one of the few survivors of the Babi Yar massacre. Kuznetsov's *Babi Yar* first appeared in *Iunost'* in 1966, but was heavily censored. Once Kuznetsov defected to England in 1969, his original manuscript was published in Germany a year later under the name of A. Anatoli. By identifying the previously banned text in a bold typeface, Kuznetsov sheds light on such issues as the Party's attempt to minimize Soviet anti-Semitism. In an analysis of the censored material, Ermolaev states that "the official policy interdicted singling out the Jews among the victims of the Babii Yar executions," "played down the hostility shown against Jews by Soviet citizens," and "[concealed] the fact that a part of the local population applauded the mass murder of the Jews and some helped the Germans carry it out."[20] In addition to Evtushenko and Kuznetsov, Iosef Brodskii is among authors who wrote on Babi Yar in the post-Stalin period.[21]

Prior to the publication of Evtushenko's "Babii Iar," literary works focused solely on the tragedy of the Babi Yar massacre. Evtushenko's poem uniquely confronts the presence of anti-Semitism in the Soviet Union and immediately received international attention, as the subject of anti-Semitism resounded with individuals around the world. Rather than reflecting on the social situation subtly or as an underlying current in his poem as he did in some of his earlier civic works, Evtushenko deals with the controversial issue in an overt manner. The poem opens: "Над Бабьим Яром памятников нет. / Крутой обрыв, как грубое надгробье."[22] [No monument stands at Babi Yar. A steep drop as a crude gravestone.] Evtushenko directly addresses the absence of a monument at Babi Yar and attributes this to the anti-Semitism of Soviet officials. The only thing to mark the presence of the grave is the steep drop of the ravine itself. This strong and direct opening targets the officials in power and their decision not to acknowledge this horrendous crime. The poem's haunting tone and ghostly atmosphere reflect the site of Babi Yar, where "[все] молча здесь кричит"[23] [everything here screams silently]. Although Evtushenko is not Jewish himself, he feels for those who died and is unable to comprehend the injustices committed by the Soviet government.

The poem is structured on a series of parallels, as Evtushenko (the speaker) imagines himself as various Jews persecuted for their Jewish heritage. Because the poem is based on a highly personal experience of the author and is narrated in the first person, the narrator can be identified as a persona of Evtushenko. He relates to the victims, as though he, too, has experienced their pain. "Babii Iar" follows the poetic embodiment of Evtushenko throughout the history of the Jewish nation, beginning as a Jewish man in ancient Egypt; to Dreyfus (a French artillery officer who was imprisoned at Devil's Island in 1894 for his Jewish decent under the guise of betraying military secrets); then moves to a young Jewish boy suffering in Bialystok; and to Anne Frank hiding from approaching enemies. Using the poetic device of anaphora, Evtushenko writes: "Мне кажется сейчас—я иудей." "Мне кажется, что Дрейфус— это я." "Мне кажется—я мальчик в Белостоке." "Мне кажется— я—это Анна Франк."[24] [Now I seem to be a Jew. I seem to be Dreyfus. I seem to be a child in Bialystok. I seem to be Anne Frank.] In "The Transformations of Babi Yar," Sheldon comments on the success of Evtushenko's passage on Anne Frank, but he criticizes the "quick successions" (the series of parallels) as the following: "[…] this extravagant, presumptuous list of parallels imparts to the poem a bombastic, egocentric quality that does not accord well with the subject matter."[25] Conversely, Evtushenko's extensive use of first-person narration serves to counteract the depersonalization of mass murder and strengthens the personification in the poem. By drawing on specific figures, Evtushenko individualizes those who were killed to heighten the emotional reaction of his audience (or reader). Furthermore, through the repetition of the phrase, "мне кажется," Evtushenko clearly draws a parallel from one figure to the next. He identifies Jews in various countries—Egypt, France, Poland, Russia, Germany, Ukraine, and others—and throughout history to connect their sufferings together as one, the most significant aspect of his poem. In lines 73–81, Evtushenko ends his poetic embodiment with all those who perished at Babi Yar:

> И сам я,
> как сплошной беззвучный крик,
> над тысячами тысяч погребенных.
> Я—
> каждый здесь расстрелянный старик.
> Я—
> каждый здесь расстрелянный ребенок.[26]

> And I myself
> am one massive, soundless scream
> above the thousands and thousands buried here.
> I am
> each old man here shot dead.
> I am
> every child here shot dead.

He feels the pain of every innocent life destroyed by the inhumane acts of violence. The shift from the impersonal or passive structure "мне кажется" [it seems to me] to the personal construction "Я" [I] symbolizes the speaker's empowerment to fight against anti-Semitism in the culmination of his outrage.

Evtushenko rejects the notion, which was then widely accepted in the Soviet Union, that Soviet Jews had no connection to Jews elsewhere in the world. Moreover, he rejects the view that Babi Yar was an isolated tragedy. In his epic poem, Evtushenko links the massacre at Babi Yar to other acts of persecution against the Jews, insisting and proving that the Jews are united as one culture or people. Furthermore, Evtushenko brings forth the issue of accountability in relation to the shameful period of pogroms in Imperial Russia and the anti-cosmopolitan campaign in the Soviet Union. In lines 28-30, the pogrom bullies who beat the young Jewish boy shout:

"Бей жидов, / спасай Россию!" [Beat the Kikes, Save Russia!] This issue of xenophobia sounds hauntingly familiar in contemporary Russia, where Russian nationalists, skinheads, and fascists are taking Slavophil notions to the extreme to purify Russia of Jews and people from the Caucasus. Evtushenko writes against anti-Semitic sentiments in both the past and present in Russia and other countries in one clear outrage. The poem closes with Evtushenko's passionate declaration:

> Еврейской крови нет в крови моей.
> Но ненавистен злобой заскорузлой
> я всем антисемитам, как еврей,
> и потому —
> я настоящий русский![27]

> In my blood there is no Jewish blood.
> In their callous rage, all anti-Semites
> must hate me now as a Jew.
> For that reason
> I am a true Russian!

Evtushenko does not hesitate to attack Soviet anti-Semitism, knowing that he will be hated by anti-Semites as if he was a Jew. The poem's final lines emphasize Evtushenko's message that anti-Semitism is not a national characteristic of Russia.

Evtushenko draws on both Erenburg and Ozerov's poems on the Babi Yar massacre to strengthen his own poem. Erenburg's "Babii Iar" (1944–1945) contains sentiments of sorrow as the author grieves over the lives mercilessly taken by the Nazis. His occasional use of first person narration heightens the personalization of the poem, which ends with an ominous message that together with the deceased:

> Мы понатужимся и встанем,
> Костями застучим — туда,
> Где дышат хлебом и духами
> Еще живые города.
> Задуйте свет. Спустите флаги.
> Мы к вам пришли. Не мы — овраги.[28]

> We'll gather all our strength and rise,
> Our bones will clatter as we wend—
> We'll haunt the towns still left alive,
> Where bread and perfumes waft their scent.
> Your candles sputter. Flags rip out their seams.
> We've come to you. Not we—but the ravines.[29]

Erenburg likens the heavy burden of the loss and memories of his friends to "каторжник ядро" [a convict hauling cannon].[30] The phrase "когда я был с живыми" [when I still lived among the living][31] implies that he feels as though he has been killed by the devastation and despite not knowing the victims, he has the sense that he is connected to them all.

Ozerov's poem, also written in 1944-1945 and entitled "Babii Iar," is narrated solely in the first person and opens with the speaker standing at the site of Babi Yar, as does Evtushenko's poem. Evtushenko draws on Ozerov's lines 2–4: "Если возраст у горя есть, / Значит, я немыслимо стар. / На столетья считать—не счесть."[32] [If age was grief, Then I would be inconceivably old. To measure by centuries—too many to count.] and echoes: "Мне сегодня столько лет, / как самому еврейскому народу."[33] [Today I am as old in years, as all the Jewish people]. Evtushenko slightly revises Ozerov's metaphor and equates the indescribable feeling of grief to the lengthy history and ancient tribal origins of the Jewish people. A prominent feature of Ozerov's poem is his delicate and tender images of nature. His speaker seeks an explanation for the devastation at Babi Yar and asks the land to break the silence. He then pleads to the maple trees: "[…] ответьте. / Вы свидетели—поделитесь."[34] [reply. You are witnesses—share.] Similarily Evtushenko writes, "Деревья смотрят грозно, / по-судейски"[35] [The trees look ominous, like judges], emphasizing that few survived at the ravine, and the only remaining life is found in nature. The haunting environment at Babi Yar transports Ozerov's speaker to those two horrific days in 1941, and in the second section of the poem, he describes the scene as if he had witnessed the massacre firsthand. Evtushenko's speaker, however, does not take the distanced stance of a bystander, but identifies with the victims as though he himself had been one. This perspective intensifies the emotional reaction of the reader. Through Ozerov's beautiful, yet haunting images of nature, his use of light to symbolize life and darkness to represent death, and his quiet lyricism, the reader is drawn into a personal and inner meditation. In contrast, Evtushenko responds to Babi Yar in a clear outrage, and his poem demands to be shared and read aloud.

Evtushenko draws on Maiakovskii's works to create the highly oratory qualities of his poem, "Babii Iar." Most obvious is Evtushenko's use of the stepped line known as *lesenka* or *lestnitsa*, first developed by Belyi and used extensively by Maiakovskii to reflect the natural pauses in speech. His poem is structured on quatrains written in iambic pentameter that are fragmented and dispersed with the use of *lesenka*. Lines are split into "steps" and staggered on the page. Because Evtushenko does not add any spaces at the end of his original quatrains, the poem contains no visual divisions or recognizable stanzas. He makes no regular use of rhyme, and any patterns in the original stanzas are lost in the stepped lines. These "steps" can be interpreted as a visual signal to the reader indicating a pause longer than that of an internal caesura, but less than a regular line break. The placement of the lines creates additional emphasis and may possibly reflect how Evtushenko intended his poem to be read aloud. Evtushenko most often follows Maiakovskii's later use of the stepped line, placing each "step" below and to the left of the end of the final word in the line above, rather than at the beginning of that word. For example, Evtushenko positions lines 3–4 as the following:

   Мне страшно.
                     Мне сегодня столько лет,
rather than:

   Мне страшно.
      Мне сегодня столько лет,

The result of this placement is that the eye travels smoothly through the reading, traveling down the page, rather than darting back and forth. Evtushenko punctuates his poem like a prose work, capitalizing the beginning of new sentences, rather than the beginning of each line. Typical of Evtushenko's works is the use of alliteration and unusual rhyming, tender and powerful language, as well as the repetition of phrases and sounds. In the tradition of Maiakovskii, Evtushenko and the young poets resurrected the poetry recitation during the Thaw period, 1953–1963. Soviet youth were especially drawn to their poetry, and enormous crowds filled halls, schools, city squares, and stadiums to hear the recitations. These uninhibited displays of emotion helped to foster the reawakening of a Soviet national conscience that had been trained to be silent under Stalin. The tradition of *Den' poezii* [Poetry Day] was born in September 1955, when the young poets gathered at Maiakovskii's statue in Moscow to recite their poems. A formal and structural analysis of Evtushenko's "Babii Iar" emphasizes the poet's deliberate and successful attempt at creating a highly oratorical poem that could be shared and circulated among the masses.

Evtushenko first recited "Babii Iar" at the Moscow Polytechnical Museum in September 1961. The poem circulated in *samizdat* and was published in *Literaturnaia gazeta* on 19 September 1961, the twentieth anniversary of the massacre.[36] Evtushenko was harshly criticized. Aleksei Markov refuted Evtushenko's poem with his own, "Moi otvet" [My Reply], which appeared in the newspaper *Literatura i zhizn'* on 24 September 1961. Although Markov did not mention Evtushenko, the opening lines of "Moi otvet" are an obvious reference to "Babii Iar." He challenges Evtushenko's claim of being a "настоящий русский," declaring: "Какой ты настоящий русский, / Когда забыл про свой народ."[37] [What kind of true Russian are you, When you have forgotten your own people]. He also criticizes Evtushenko for having forgotten the "свастикою ржавой" [rusty swastika] and the suffering the fascists inflicted upon the Russian nation during World War II.[38] Furthermore, Markov accuses Evtushenko of dishonouring the young Russian soldiers who were killed in World War II. In the final lines of his poem, Markov writes: "Пока топать погосты будет / Хотя б один космополит, — / Я говорю: я русский, люди!"[39] [As long as graves will be trampled on by even a single cosmopolitan, —I say: I am Russian, people!]. Three days later, on 27 September 1961, *Literatura i zhizn'* published Dmitri Starikov's denunciation of "Babii Iar" in his article, "Ob odnom stikhotvorenii" [On One Poem]. Starikov finds similar faults in Evtushenko's poem as Markov, though he makes no attempt whatsoever to conceal the target of his attack in his article.[40]

The editors of *Literaturnaia gazeta* supported Evtushenko and did not run an apology for the publication of "Babii Iar"; however, Valerii Kosolapov, the editor who was responsible for publishing Evtushenko's poem, was fired as expected.

The controversy surrounding Evtushenko's poem continued upon Dmitrii Dmitrievich Shostakovich's (1906–1975) composition of his famous, *Symphony No. 13, Op. 113* subtitled "Babii Iar" for bass soloist, chorus, and orchestra. The opening movement is set to the text of Evtushenko's "Babii Iar" followed by four additional poems of his: "Iumor" [Humor, 1960], "V magazine" [At the Store, 1956], "Strakhi" [Fears, first published in 1966], and "Kar'era" [A Career, 1957]. Official controversy over "Babii Iar" affected the symphony before it even premiered: both the original conductor, Evgenii Aleksandrovich Mravinskii (1909-1988), and bass soloist, Boris Romanovich Gmyria (1903–1969), withdrew from the project, leaving Kirill Petrovich Kondrashin (1914–1981) to conduct and understudy Vitalii Aleksandrovich Gromadskii (1928–) to perform. Furthermore, when the symphony premiered in Moscow on 18 December 1962, the customary text was banned from the programs. After the performance, the Soviet government threatened to ban the symphony, because Evtushenko did not specifically refer to the non-Jewish citizens who were murdered at Babi Yar. Twenty years after the tragedy, Soviet officials continued to inaccurately portray the massacre as a crime against Soviet citizens, and not the deliberate slaughter of the Jewish community. Evtushenko modified his poem in a version that never appeared in print, afterwards stating he did so upon Shostakovich's request—not the insistence of officials. He replaced lines 5–8 with the following:

> I stand here, as if by a well,
> That gives me faith in our brother.
> Here Russians lie and Ukrainians;
> They lie with Jews in the same earth.[41]

Thus, he retracts the focus on the Jews. He also referred to the Nazis by substituting lines 43–46 with:

> I think of Russia's exploit
> when it barred the way to
> Fascism with its own body;
> To the tiniest drop
> Russia is dear to me in its whole substance and fate.[42]

Despite these changes, the third performance was delayed until 10 February 1963 and the fourth was not until 20 November 1965; however, the symphony was met with outstanding success. *Symphony No. 13* had a deep cleansing effect on Soviet society, breaking the taboo of discussing issues of anti-Semitism, and became a kind of memorial itself to those who perished at Babi Yar. In one of Evtushenko's most recent publications dedicated to the sixty-fifth anniversary of the Babi Yar tragedy, *I Came to You, Babi Yar...*, Evtushenko writes:

> After WWII, the theme of Babi Yar completely disappeared from the pages of the Soviet Press. Cold War, Iron Curtain, mutual mistrust created [a] poisoned climate for epidemic, anti-Semitism. When I saw, in 1961, that the burial place of tens of thousands of innocent victims had become a dump, I wrote a poem that broke the conspiracy of silence. Shostakovich's *Thirteenth Symphony*, based upon my words, due to such mighty music, became the first sound monument over Babi Yar.[43]

Evtushenko's poem was published shortly before the Twenty-Second Party Congress and the introduction of Khrushchev's de-Stalinization campaign, which marked the beginning of the third period of liberalization during the Thaw period, 1953–1963. Because of this brief interval of creative relaxation, as well as Evtushenko's international fame, Evtushenko was not severely reprimanded for "Babii Iar," as he most certainly would have been in the past. However, once the Thaw ended in 1963, "Babii Iar" was not republished in the Soviet Union until 1989. On 8 March 1963, Khrushchev gave a speech to Party officials and leading cultural figures in the USSR on Soviet literature and art, during which he spoke about Evtushenko's "Babii Iar":

174   Amy Safarik

> What was the poem being criticised for? It was criticised because the author was unable truthfully to show and condemn the fascist, particularly the fascist criminals who were responsible for the mass slaughter at Babi Iar. The poem represents things as if only Jews were the victims of the fascist atrocities, whereas, of course, many Russians, Ukrainians, and Soviet people of other nationalities were murdered by the Hitlerite butchers. The poem reveals that its author did not show political maturity and was ignorant of historical facts.[44]

Khrushchev fails to mention anti-Semitism, instead stating:

> Since the October Revolution Jews have enjoyed equal rights with the other peoples of the Soviet Union in all respects. There is no Jewish question in our country, and those who invent it are slavishly repeating what other people say.[45]

The cited criticism not only reflects both the official and dominant political attitude toward Jews, but also indicates Evtushenko's courage to publish "Babii Iar." In 1976 an official monument of people entwined was erected to commemorate the Soviet citizens who died at Babi Yar. The plaque states in Russian, Ukrainian, and Hebrew: "Here in 1941–43 German Fascist invaders shot over 100,000 citizens of Kyiv and prisoners of war"; there is no specific mention of the mainly Jewish citizens who were slaughtered. A memorial of a large menorah for the Jewish victims was finally added in 1991, but it was the Jewish community, not the Soviet government, who was responsible for its construction. Finally, on the sixtieth anniversary of the Babi Yar massacre a commemorative stone was laid at the site. Evtushenko's poem is now displayed at the United States Holocaust Memorial Museum in Washington, DC as part of the exhibit on Babi Yar.

The devastation of the Babi Yar massacre resounds today. On 5 June 2007 *BBC News* reported that several thousand Holocaust victims were found in a mass grave in the village of Gvozdavka-1 in Ukraine.[46] As recent as 27 October 2007, *BBC News* reported that Ukrainian authorities gave proper burials to approximately two thousand victims of Soviet terror who were found at the site of Bukovnia near Kyiv.[47] In Evtushenko's essay, "Kamni—v Bulgakova" (Stones at Bulgakov), the poet describes how in 1991 he was astonished to see revolting graffiti aimed at Jews in the center of Kyiv in a cruel act of anti-Semitism.[48] An article in *International Herald Tribune*, published on 4 February 2008, states that swastikas and other offence signs were painted on Jewish graves in Southern Hungary, demonstrating the continued presence of anti-Semitism.[49] A recent three-day conference entitled *In the Shadow of Babi Yar: Holocaust Commemoration in Soviet and Post-Soviet Ukraine* was held at the University of Maryland and dedicated to the legacy of Babi Yar. Scholars Wendy M. Lower, Joshua Rubenstein, Zvi Gitelman, Larissa Dedova, film director Sergey Bukovsky, and Evtushenko participated in the conference. Evtushenko's work was not only prominently featured at the event, but was the central point of the gatherings. In addition to his presentation, "The Making of Babi Yar," Evtushenko gave a poetry reading, his film *Pokhorony Stalina* [Stalin's Funeral] was screened, and the University of Maryland Symphony Orchestra and the Men of University of Maryland Choirs performed Shostakovich's *Symphony No. 13*, during which Evtushenko recited the opening reading of "Babii Iar." As a civic poet, Evtushenko has been instrumental in breaking the decades of silence that resulted from Stalin's oppressive leadership. Evtushenko's greatest literary achievement, "Babii Iar," is a poem that impacted the Russian nation's approach to the issues of collaboration, complicity, accountability, and indifference to Nazi genocide and continues to draw international attention to the Holocaust in Ukraine and anti-Semitism.

Notes

[1] The standard Western spelling of the ravine, Babi Yar, is retained, except in quotations.

[2] For survivor and witness testimonies on the Babi Yar massacre, see Boris Zabarko ed., *Holocaust in the Ukraine*, translated by Marina Guba (London: Vallentine Mitchell, 2005); Ilya Ehrenburg and Vasily Grossman, *The Complete Black Book of Russian Jewry*, translated and edited by David Patterson (New Brunswick, New Jersey: Transaction, 2002); A. Anatoli [Kuznetsov], *Babi Yar: A Document in the Form of a Novel*, translated by David Floyd (London: Jonathon Cape, 1970).

[3] Einsatzgruppen, or "task forces," were Nazi mobile killing units composed of police and security services forces initially formed to arrest and murder active and potential political opponents and to annihilate Jews. Their primary function eventually became the mass murder of Jews.

[4] Yitzhak Arad, Shmuel Krakowski, and Shmuel Spector, eds., *The Einsatzgruppen Reports: Selections from the Dispatches of the Nazi Death Squads' Campaign against the Jews, July 1941–January 1943*, translated by Stella Schossberger (New York: Holocaust Library, 1989) 168.

[5] Stephen Berk, "Death in the Ukraine," *University of Waterloo Jewish Studies Program's Better Communities Foundation Annual Lecture*, St. Jerome's Siegfried Hall, Waterloo, Ontario, 28 Nov. 2006.

[6] Wendy Lower, *Nazi Empire-Building and the Holocaust in Ukraine* (Chapel Hill: University of North Carolina Press, 2005) 70.

[7] A. Anatoli [Kuznetsov], *Babi Yar: A Document in the Form of a Novel*, translated by David Floyd (London: Jonathon Cape, 1970) 373.

[8] Kuznetsov, *Babi Yar* 370-398.

[9] Kuznetsov, *Babi Yar* 16-17.

[10] Patrick Desbois, interview, "Voices on Antisemitism: A Podcast Series," *United States Holocaust Memorial Museum* 8 Nov. 2007, transcript 24 Feb. 2008 <http://www.ushmm.org/museum/exhibit/focus/antisemitism/voices/transcript/index.php?content=20071108>; Elaine Sciolino, "The Saturday Profile: A Priest Methodically Reveals Ukrainian Jews' Fate," *New York Times* 6 Oct. 2007, 24 Feb. 2008 <http://www.nytimes.com/2007/10/06/world/Europe/06priest.html?scp=2&sq=october+6+2007&st=nyt>.

[11] Joshua Rubenstein, "The Holocaust in German-Occupied Soviet Territories and the Response by Soviet Jewish Intellectuals," *In the Shadow of Babi Yar: Holocaust Commemoration in Soviet and Post-Soviet Ukraine*, University of Maryland, College Park, MD, 26 Oct. 2007.

[12] Zabarko, *Holocaust in the Ukraine* xiii.

[13] Anti-Semitism has existed in Russia and Ukraine for centuries. Prior to the first partition of the Polish-Lithuanian Commonwealth in 1772, Jews were banned from entering the Russian Empire, and afterwards they were legally authorized to reside in the Pale of Settlement until the restrictions were lifted in 1917. Following the assassination of Tsar Aleksandr II in 1881, anti-Jewish pogroms were prevalent in major cities and reoccurred in 1903, in 1905–1906, in 1918–1919 after the October Revolution, and throughout the civil war that followed. Lower explains that during Simon Petliura's fight for Ukrainian independence in 1918–1919, thousands of Jews were killed with the worst pogroms occurring in Zhytomyr, Vinnytsia, and Berdychiv [*Nazi Empire-Building* 14].

[14] John D. Klier, "Outline of Jewish-Russian History, Part 1: 1772–1953," *An Anthology of Jewish-Russian Literature: Two Centuries of Dual Identity*

in Prose and Poetry, Volume 1: 1801–1953, edited by Maxim D. Shrayer (Armonk: M.E. Sharpe, 2007) 629–630.

[15] Klier, "Outline of Jewish-Russian History" 630.

[16] Herman Ermolaev, *Censorship in Soviet Literature, 1917–1991* (London: Rowman and Littlefield, 1997) 169.

[17] Richard Sheldon, "The Transformations of Babi Yar," *Soviet Society and Culture: Essays in Honor of Vera S. Dunham*, edited by Terry L. Thompson and Richard Sheldon (Boulder: Westview, 1988) 133–134.

[18] Sheldon, "The Transformations of Babi Yar" 128.

[19] Sheldon, "The Transformations of Babi Yar" 135.

[20] Ermolaev, *Censorship in Soviet Literature* 208–209.

[21] For additional poems on Babi Yar by Russian, Ukrainian and Jewish writers, see: *Bol': poeticheskii sbornik*, compiled by I. A. Zaslavskii (Kyiv: MIP "Oberig", 1991).

[22] Evgenii Evtushenko, "Babii Iar," *Literaturnaia gazeta*, Moscow, 19 Sept. 1961, lines 1–2. All citations of poems refer to line numbers.

[23] Evtushenko, "Babii Iar" 69.

[24] Evtushenko, "Babii Iar" 6–7, 11–12, 22–23, 43–44.

[25] Sheldon, "The Transformations of Babi Yar" 138.

[26] Evtushenko, "Babii Iar" 73–81.

[27] Evtushenko, "Babii Iar" 88–92.

[28] Il'ia Erenburg, "Babii Iar," *Strofy veka: antologiia russkoi poezii*, compiled by E. Evtushenko (Moscow: Polifakt, 1995), *Stikhiia: luchshaia poeziia*, 3 Nov. 2007 <http://www.litera.ru/stixiya/authors/erenburg/k-chemu-slova.html> 19–24.

[29] Alyssa Dinega Gillespie, trans., "Babi Yar," by Ilya Ehrenburg, *An Anthology of Jewish-Russian Literature: Two Centuries of Dual Identity in Prose and Poetry, Volume 1: 1801–1953*, edited, compiled, and translated by Maxim D. Shrayer (Armonk: M.E. Sharpe, 2007) 530–531. 19–24.

[30] Erenburg, "Babii Iar" 3; Gillespie, "Babi Yar" 3.

[31] Erenburg, "Babii Iar" 13; Gillespie, "Babi Yar" 13.

[32] Lev Ozerov, "Babii Iar," *Poeziia Moskovskogo Universiteta ot Lomonosova i do...*, 3 Nov. 2007 <http://www.poesis.ru/poeti-poezia/ozerov/verses.htm#3> 2–4.

[33] Evtushenko, "Babii Iar" 4–5.

[34] Ozerov, "Babii Iar," 13–14.

[35] Evtushenko, "Babii Iar" 67–68.

[36] See Evtushenko, *Avtobiografiia* [Autobiography], (London: Flegon Press, 1964) for a detailed, though somewhat romanticized, account of how the poem came to be published and how Shostakovich became involved musically with Evtushenko's poems.

[37] Aleksei Markov, "Moi otvet," *Literatura i zhizn'*, 24 Sept. 1961, 1–2.

[38] Markov, "Moi otvet" 5.
[39] Markov, "Moi otvet" 29–31.
[40] D[mitrii] Starikov, "Ob odnom stikhotvorenii," *Literatura i zhizn'*, 27 Sept. 1961.
[41] Sheldon, "The Transformations of Babi Yar" 140.
[42] Sheldon, "The Transformations of Babi Yar" 140.
[43] Yevgeny Yevtushenko, *I Came to You, Babi Yar...*, edited by Jeffrey Longacre and Elena Morozova (Moscow: LLC Kuprianov, 2006) 6.
[44] Walter Z Laqueur et al., eds., "Khrushchev on Culture," *Encouter*, Pamphlet. No. 9, (1963) 36, 38.
[45] Laqueur, "Khrushchev on Culture" 38.
[46] "Ukrainian Mass Jewish Grave Found," *BBC News* 5 June 2007, 10 June 2007 <http://news.bbc.co.uk/2/hi/europe/6724481.stm>.
[47] "Ukraine Reburies Stalin's Victims," *BBC News* 27 Oct. 2007, 28 Oct. 2007 <http://news.bbc.co.uk/2/hi/europe/7065913.stm>.
[48] Evgenii Evtushenko, "Kamni—v Bulgakova," *Shestidesantnik: memuarnaia proza* (Moscow: Zebra E, 2006) 427–428.
[49] "Vandals Paint Swastikas, Extremist Symbols on Jewish Graves in Southern Hungary," *International Herald Tribune* 4 Feb. 2008, 20 Feb. 2008 <http://www.iht.com/articles/ap/2008/02/04/europe/EU-GEN-Hungary-Jewish-Graves.php>.

10
Converging Lines in Learning Languages, Literacies and Learner Theory: Renewed Perspective, or still a Vanishing Point?

Peter Liddell

Abstract

As we edge closer to understanding how language is processed by adult learners, how the process can be modeled in and enhanced by the computer, and how, ideally, adult learners can improve the experience and the results of learning languages, the literature reflects mixed perspectives.

In a sense, adult second language acquisition has suffered consistently and over time from the mismatch between theory and practice, program goals and learner expectations, SLA tools and their methodological context. This paper will examine some of the past misalliances as a backdrop to focusing on recent signs of converging interests in learning theories and views of language learning and its institutional role. Milestones to be emphasized include the insights gained through the study of working memory and recent studies of the place of intercultural language learning vis à vis the traditional Language, Literature, Culture Studies curriculum.

Introduction

This paper was originally invited to be a retrospective of the several decades that I have spent learning, teaching, and pondering the acquisition of foreign languages (Digital Stream plenary, 2006).

Rather less personal than that, it attempts to identify patterns of the various methods and assistive technologies in vogue in that period and that have preceded, and still now influence more recent trends. The change of focus from the 'object' to be learned, i.e. the other language, to the 'subject', i.e. the learner, has probably been the most significant shift of those years. That owes much to our improving knowledge of how the brain processes new information such as another language. And finally, the technologies assisting language learning are beginning to enable us to extend and externalize those processes — to emulate the processing of new languages, for example.

The Tradition of Institutionalized Language Learning — Language as Grammar

The Renaissance belief that understanding Antiquity was best achieved by understanding its exemplary creative works has pervaded western educational culture, particularly our study of philology, almost unbroken, for six centuries. The more specific interest in literature began around 1400, when the demand-driven 'media-revolution' (paper milling, Gutenberg, even reading glasses) began to make relatively cheaper, more easily reproduceable texts more generally accessible, beyond the repressive control of a dominant religion. Thanks to the new media, the public's intellectual interest shifted from the plastic arts of Antiquity to the written forms of their cultures (hence also to learning their languages). This, in turn, resulted in a rapid growth of the institutions, e.g. 'grammar' schools, universities, libraries, to foster their study.[1] What is most relevant for this discussion is the 'learning model' that we inherited from those times. It was elitist, centralist, and concerned with a canon of 'high' culture. Increasingly, the learner went to the resources, not vice-versa, and public 'proof' of learning was accredited by the institutions that owned the resources, and was not determined by practical usage or individual need or ability.

Beginning in the 19th century, perhaps most obviously in German-speaking states, languages and the related goal of understanding 'high' literature became a primary topic of humanistic research, and simultaneously intensified the structured approach to their study. Historical linguistics, as pioneered by the Grimms for example, set out to define and analyze languages and their relationships according to linguistic principles. As with the natural sciences, the approach was unitary—seeking the 'Ur-form' of the subject-matter—in their case, the 'Ur-language', through comparison of its recorded and reconstructed offspring.

The German situation in the industrial era is also typical of other industrialized nations, for similar reasons. In the last quarter of the 19th century, the unitary emphasis of the early years flourished, as universal education and bureaucratic standards were introduced throughout Prussia (1875 ff.). Despite the contemporary interest in dialect variance (another German contribution to linguistics), Prussian-German public policy insisted on defining and observing one standard 'national' form of the language—Duden for orthography, Siebs for pronunciation. Language teaching followed suit, by treating the target language normatively, as a single series of structures that were absolute—variation was equivalent to deviation. Those of us who still learned languages by the grammar-translation method in the mid-20th century are familiar with the legacy of that era—structured, linguistic norms, practised as paradigms (chanting verb tenses, writing out charts of adjective and noun endings), or through parsing sentences, translation, dictation, recitation, in absolute adherence to the rules of grammar—*the* language, abstracted into one unbending set of rules, best exemplified in *belles-lettres*.

The audio-lingual method, when it arrived in the late 1950s, was intended to create more balance by emphasizing the spoken language. In reality, it offered little fundamental change in principle. 'Speech', in the form of tape-recorded collations of unconnected sentences for practice, was certainly introduced on a large scale. Language labs for audiotapes became the vogue, since few students had their own recorders, and because stimulus-response and pattern-drilling were common features of that technology and of the 'live' class. This innovation further reinforced a centralized model of learning, entrenched in an institution, with a normative subject matter as the focus of learning. ALM did not reflect actual usage in speech so much as spoken examples of grammar rules. Kern and Warschauer are quite generous in their assessment of the ALM research focus: "Although audiolingual research focused on spoken, rather than written language skills, it shared two principal assumptions with the grammar–translation method: that language teaching syllabi should be organized by *linguistic* categories, and that the *sentence* was the primary unit of analysis and practice".[2] I beg to disagree. The "spoken... language skills" of ALM distorted authentic speech because they were defined by grammatically and phonetically "correct" model dialogues and pattern-drills, couched in complete but isolated individual sentences, and drawn from an anodyne, largely synthetic world with little or no intrinsically interesting, authentic context. Based on the theories of behaviourism, they focused on the end—object (*the* language), rather than the means—subject (the learners).

Although subservient to the prevailing academic interest in reading the artifacts of 'high' culture, grammar-translation and ALM were not well suited for other users of languages. The two 'methods' were an easy target for popular criticism too, simply because they emphasized the gap between written forms and real speech situations. Comedians such as the Monty Python troupe (e.g. *"The Hungarian Phrasebook Sketch"*[3]) or Father Guido, in his "*Five-Minute University*" Spanish course[4,] pilloried the shortcomings of transformations and model dialogues. A second criticism was that subordinating meaning (e.g. cultural context) to structure reinforced stereotypes, because those methods were not primarily concerned with the language in context, only with the language as a static, highly structured object, expressed through what was deemed to be 'typical'. Byram and Risager define the unitary norms of ALM and other "failed panaceas"[5] up to that point as adhering to a 19th century "national paradigm", whose exclusive focus was "the national standard norm of native speaker usage", to be taught by native or near-native speakers, in the target language, using examples from "the majority culture in "standard" or "typical" forms.[6]

Institutional obstacles to language learning

Two further aspects of language learning that represent mismatched means and ends, and reinforced the monistic influence of the methodology were curriculum and technology. As entrenched entities of institutionalized learning, they have been in some respects less flexible than any other aspect of language learning. Methods may change, but the setting (the program and the assistive facilities) has been less adaptable--until recently.

i. Technology mismatched with pedagogy
Many of the technologies we use so avidly in our efforts to immerse our students in other languages and cultures were invented for very different purposes—mostly for entertainment or information storage—the wire-recorder of 100 years ago, the tape-recorder, the VCR, the desktop computer, TV, ipods, PDAs etc. etc. (The only machine of this kind that I am aware of that was *specifically* developed for language teaching was the Level 3 video-disk player by Sony—the interactive laser-disk of the late 1980s/1990s.)

This equipment was co-opted by languages instructors for much less entertaining purposes—e.g. in the 1980s, for playing 'authentic' videos—to enhance the meaningful input by reenacting how to find a student room in Paris or Freiburg, or to show stereotypical scenes of life in the 'average' home. The mismatch between such 're-purposed' technologies and language-learning theory first became most obvious after ALM waned, but its expensive language labs survived. While the language classroom was loud with the communicative emphasis of the 1980s and 90s, the CALL computer was silently reliving the drill and practice workbooks of ALM and cognitive–constructivism. Drill and practice at an eternally patient machine, it was argued, allowed more class-time for live interaction. J.D.Bolter might call this "re-mediation"—the representation of one medium in another—but the new medium was far from reaching its potential, the minimizing of obvious 'mediation'.[7] We need much better knowledge of cognitive processes before we can approximate them technologically.

In general, then, it has been typical of our profession that we have consistently looked to new technologies that were not specifically intended to do so, to bring learners of other languages closer to those languages and their culture. We have done this in an institutionalized setting that has traditionally had quite different priorities (the study of high culture, for example, or the privileging of theory over practice); and we have done it without consistent reference to Second Language Acquisition theory.

ii. Curriculum mismatches means and ends

Beneath the practice of language-learning, and the assistive technologies we have used for it, there lies a deeper problem. The most glaring and least tractable fundamental issue facing the philology departments of western educational instititions is, according to recent publications, the continued separation of form from content—language instruction from literary and cultural studies—through the insistence on the 'acquisition' of language as an object in itself.[8] Granting instructors territorial rights to individual courses in the name of academic freedom only exacerbates the problem.[9] Where once there was general agreement about language-learning as the means to better knowledge of others' cultural achievements, now there is an artificial separation of language courses (the former 'means') and literary and cultural studies (the traditional 'ends'), and no strongly cohesive program goals in most cases. Swaffar and Arens argue extensively that the solution lies in freeing the curriculum from its proclaimed goal of 'literacy' in the traditional (Renaissance) sense of educating a culturally literate, 'well-read' member of society, and instead educating through multiple literacies, in a 'holistic' curriculum.[10] In such a carefully sequenced, multiliterate curriculum, there would be no artificial division of means and ends. The underlying, holistic principle is that in adults both are forms of processing knowledge about and in the language and culture to be studied. "The holistic curriculum building towards a learner's literacy in aspects of language and culture favors the abilities of adult learners, whose known cognitive processes underlie both comprehension and language production."[11] That passage also hints at a further premise of their argument: that a holistic curriculum relies on the individual's continually constructing meaning using all of the forms of literacy—linguistic, rhetorical, cultural, social, and technical.

From 'object' to 'subject'—the learner in better focus

The thematic metaphors of my title refer among others to the mismatches between the subjects, the learners, and the objects, the languages being learned. The subtitle also implies that this may be undergoing real improvement. Although deriving from psycholinguistics and social theory, the two approaches to be considered in the following section can be seen as opening the doors towards applying cognitive theory to create a better match between learner and learning. Both are associated with the 1970s and 1980s, but have their echoes still, in contemporary textbooks.

Cognitive-constructivist and Sociocognitive approaches

The main legacy of the cognitive-constructivist approach for the purpose of this argument is that it shifted focus away from a normative, rule-based language-as-objective-structure towards language-as-performance (particularly in writing). Hence, it eventually put greater emphasis on the context, and thence on the learner and the complexities of the cognitive processes involved in learning. Through these earlier innovations, we came to understand that as learners constructed a sense of the systems and structures of the new language, they should be encouraged to experiment, at the obvious risk of making grammatical errors. Terms like 'interlanguage', 'pidgin', and 'authentic, meaningful input' became valuable to understanding the "individual, psycholinguistic process" of language-learning.[12] The odd thing was that much of this focus on constructing an awareness of the underlying systems of a language did not at first put much emphasis on production/output, by the student—the most extreme example being the 'Total Physical Response' approach (Terrell, Asher, based on Kraschen).

The Socio-cognitive approach was based on Vygotsky's ideas of cognitive development being a result of social interaction and socially stimulated learning. Terms like 'appropriateness' (Hymes, 1971), 'relevance' (Halliday, 1978), and 'strategies' (Canale & Swain, 1980) emphasize the social, negotiative context within which learning takes place.[13] This approach, with its stepped, socially pragmatic learning process, was particularly important in Europe in the 1980s, as labour-mobility and greater political cohesion headed the EU agenda.[14] Through this approach ('communicative competence'), the learner is seen not only as an individual employing psycholinguistic strategies, but one who is firmly embedded in a community, with its own requirements for cognitive strategies like collaboration, problem-solving, experimentation.

Language Learning and Working Memory

If the learning-theory innovations of the 1970s and 1980s can be considered as shifting the focus towards the learner as an individual in a socially conditioned context, then the next step is quite logical—understanding and extrapolating learning theories from how individual learners process new information (in this case, new languages and cultures).

Swaffar and Arens' argument for a holistic curriculum begins by discussing some aspects of the skill-based language-teaching methods deriving from cognitive-constructivist theory in the 1970s, and still in common use in contemporary textbooks. Traditionally, such courses begin with simple spoken exchanges (self-identification, greeting and identifying others). Overall, these courses tend to mix practice of the four language skills quite freely. Cognitive science, however suggests otherwise:

> "[s]peaking and listening occur within real-world constraints [that are] different from those of reading and writing. Since oral responses offer little time for reflection, speaking involves simultaneous use of macro– and micromemory (the knowledge both of general frameworks and of immediate sequences in interaction). Hence speaking & listening are, cognitively speaking, immediacy tasks that restrict the learner's ability to use prior knowledge and cognitive processes."[15]

Reading and writing, by contrast, allow time for reflection and rehearsal:

> "[c]ognitively, then, these are recursive tasks.... In consequence, from the standpoint of cognitive processing, it is a mismatch to equate receptive skills (listening and reading) with productive ones (speaking and writing)." (ibid.)

The conclusion to be drawn from such an argument is that the four language-learning skills of recent tradition are not acquired equally, and the more we learn about cognitive processing, the better we can structure our syllabus. That is one of the main thrusts of a more recent survey by D. Hoven.[16] For example, in discussing the effects of new media in language learning, Hoven tackles one of the shibboleths of traditional language teaching—repetition: "[w]orking memory, cognitive load, and familiarity with the field also play critical roles in determining the usefulness of information preserved in different modes. As Kalyuga (2000,170) found, 'concurrent duplication of the same information using different modes of presentation increases the risk of overloading working memory capacity and might have a negative effect on learning.'".[17]

Working memory (much of Swaffar and Arens' "macro- and micromemory" above) clearly limits the learning process in very strict ways. In 1974, Alan Baddeley, a leading expert on Working Memory over the past 30 years, co-authored with G.J. Hitch a definition that has been refined over the years, but is still generally accepted. Working memory, by that definition, consists of two slave systems, the visuospatial sketchpad and the phonological loop, and a manager, the central executive function.[18]

Visuospatial ↔   ↔ Central →   → Phonological
Sketchpad ↔   ↔ Executive ←   ← Loop

Of these systems, the phonological loop is of primary interest for language-learning, because of the way in which information must be transformed in working memory into auditory information.

As suggested earlier (Swaffar/Arens, Hoven), the traditional, discrete four-skill approach to language learning is often taught in ways that are contrary to how the brain processes information. Regardless of the source (but not regardless of the context—immediate-responsive or pausative-reflective), the brain processes new information in the same way. "The human brain's language functions are innately auditory." [The two parts of our brain that handle syntactic processing (Broca's area), and semantic processing (Wernicke's area)] can't handle visual data (words as 'seen'). The brain always re-encodes the language which we receive visually into auditory form before working with it."[19] Baddeley provides clinical evidence of this in describing an experiment involving patients memorizing written sequences of different groups of letters or one-syllable words (visual input only). The least memorable, most confusing letter- or word-groups proved to be those with similar sounds, if spoken (e.g. T,B,G,C,D). He concludes: "if a subject is shown a sequence of letters for immediate recall, then despite their visual presentation, subjects will subvocalize them, and hence their retention will depend crucially on their acoustic or phonological characteristics." (Baddeley, loc. cit.)

However, cognitive research has shown that the phonological loop is very limited; in adults, it can only ever hold about 2 seconds of speech, or about 7 items. [This 7-item capacity grows gradually during childhood—up to the 7 or so maximum.][20]

The only way we can focus on a sequence of words (called a 'digital span') longer than 2 seconds is by recycling it back through the phonological loop, through a process of 'subvocal rehearsal,' via the executive function (note arrows in diagram above). The trouble is, that that recycling prevents other new information from entering the loop, so new information becomes mere 'noise', a distraction, and we lose the thread. As Swaffar and Arens contend, exercises designed to improve speaking skills that involve much new information (including new language forms) are fraught with cognitive obstacles. Despite that, in a traditional language-class conversation, all too often "[s]peakers must forge ahead or lose their platform for communication."[21] If they want to start paying attention again (or continue learning!), they have to pass on the acquired new information quickly into longer-term memory. Naturally, the more familiar they are with the information entering the auditory loop, the quicker they can process it out of there.

Conclusion: Technology as extended working memory

Up to this point I have presented some evidence of the discrepancy between the potential purpose and the practice of language-teaching, and signs of increased awareness of means to overcome that discrepancy by paying closer attention to cognitive processes. Cognitive theory can clearly offer new insights into the learning process, just as it is recognized that the process itself is subject to compromise by fragmented curricula, which are frequently operating within a too heavily institutionalized environment.

The underlying premise of this paper is that the teaching and learning of languages (to adults, in this case) is fundamental to humanistic education, not, as has been seen in the past 5 decades, or even 5 centuries, a subsidiary service to 'higher learning'. This argument applies also to the technologies we use in that process, which is my final point.

A major topic of recent learning theory—particularly language-learning theory—has been so-called 'multiliteracies'. This is not the place to rehearse in any great detail the arguments put forward by, for example, the New London Group (2000). Briefly, their premise is that the pedagogy of 'literacy' has traditionally focused on language only—language which is usually taken from examples of a single, national form of language. That, according to their argument, assumes that a single, discernible, correct form can be defined, and it usually spawns a more or less authoritarian form of pedagogy.[22] They argue that, by contrast, modern media, population mobility, reduced significance of 'place', a less monistic acceptance of language usage, and the multiplicity of communications options all demand a new "multiliterate" pedagogy (p.6).[23] In essence, they are arguing for less institutionally constrained, and less narrowly defined criteria for literacy than our post-renaissance traditions have allowed.

Definitions vary, but multiliteracy may be summarized for this purpose in Selber's terms as functional, critical, and rhetorical literacy.[24] 'Functional' refers to the ability to use the media of information and communication effectively; 'critical' involves the ability to reflect on that use by oneself and others; and 'rhetorical', the most productive and creative literacy, involves the appropriate expression of ideas. These principles underlie, for example, the curriculum posited by Swaffar/Arens, as does the principle of applying cognitive theory more rigorously to the pedagogy.

The argument for a multiliterate, holistic curriculum begs the question of 'how'. If the institutional setting is too restrictive for the most part (learner goes to resources), and the program of learning too disparate (curriculum unfocused, not cohesive), then attention turns to the environment of learning—physically and intellectually, the 'place' and the disciplinary program.

The one line of my argument about mismatched means and ends which was left suspended earlier was the question of the role of technology in fostering better learning. Arguments vary about the effectiveness of traditional CALL, and proponents of the convergent or 'remediated' technologies, particularly of Network-based Learning, set great store by their more promising abilities to address individual learner's needs and modern pedagogical principles more effectively (for example, Kern and Warschauer (2000) cited earlier). These and many others argue why multiliteracies *must* inform the new Foreign Language Curriculum.

There is a well-substantiated argument (Bolter and Grusin, 2001, for example) that implies that language technologies always have reflected human capabilities, but that computers have accelerated the process and reawakened the awareness that all learning takes place through language. An example of this argument is Lancashire's article, which I cited earlier. He argues that knowing more about how we process language is essential to understanding the capacity of cybernetics to extend our human abilities. He points out that the word 'cybernetics' was coined by Norbert Wiener (1894–1964) from the Greek word for a steers-man [*kubernetes*], to describe what he called a theory of messages among life forms and the machines that humans devise.[25] [Katherine Hayles used this theory in "How we became Posthuman" (1999).]

The argument goes that if all messages ("cybertexts") are governed (or "steered") by the same rules, then all the artifacts we devise to process language must in some way be modeled on human working memory—in effect, they are externalized versions of mechanisms and processes which our brains need in order to acquire and use knowledge. Marshall McLuhan made similar arguments in the Prologue to *The Gutenberg Galaxy* (1962), in saying that media are extensions of human senses, bodies and minds. In Lancashire's words: "All language technologies, whether the medieval scriptorium, the Renaissance printing house, word-processing software and hardware, and even artificial intelligence, are literally McLuhanesque 'extensions of man'. They build on working memory and radically enhance it to help us wield cybernetic control over our texts."[26] Furthermore, "[c]ybertextuality explains digital technologies as tools that regulate utterances by externalizing working memory as a locus for the recursive cybernetic cycle."[27]

The implication of this is that computers—in our case, for learning (about) other languages and cultures—have the potential not simply to mediate, to convey culture and encourage learning as familiarizing and exploration, but also to emulate, to extend the processes by which we learn. To the extent that we can achieve that, then the 'lines' of my title will truly begin to converge.

Notes

[1] P. von Polenz, *Deutsche Sprachgeschichte vom Spätmittelalter bis zur Gegenwart*. (Berlin, New York: Walter de Gruyter, 1991) 114–153.

[2] M. Warschauer & R. Kern, eds., *Network-based language teaching: Concepts and practice*. (New York: Cambridge University Press, 2000) 3.

[3] Readily accessible via Google - e.g.: http://www.youtube.com/watch?v=G6D1YI-41ao (accessed June 12 2008).

[4] Text-only version available at: http://www.templaruniversity.com/guido.html (accessed June 12 2008).

[5] M. Byram, and K. Risager, *Language Teachers, Politics, Cultures*. (Clevedon, UK: Multilingual Matters, 1999) 3.

[6] Byram/Risager, 156–7.

[7] J.D. Bolter and R. Grusin, *Remediation: Understanding New Media*. (Cambridge, Mass.: MIT Press, 2001) 5 *et passim*.

[8] J. Swaffar and K. Arens, *Remapping the Foreign Languages Curriculum: An Approach through Multiple Literacies*. (New York: MLA, 2005) 7–8 *et passim*.

[9] Swaffar/Arens, 22–23.

[10] Swaffar/Arens, esp. in Ch. 3, 57–77.

[11] Swaffar/Arens, 32–33.

[12] Warschauer/Kern, 4.

[13] Overview cited from Warschauer/Kern, 4–5.

[14] J.A. Van Ek, *Objectives for Foreign Language Learning*. (Strasbourg: Council of Europe, 1986).

[15] Swaffar/Arens, 32.

[16] D. Hoven, "Communicating and Interacting: An Exploration of the Changing Roles of Media in CALL/CMC." *CALICO Journal*, vol.23, No.2, 2006. 233–256.

[17] Hoven, 240.

[18] A. Baddeley, "Working memory and language: an overview." *Journal of Communication Disorders*, 36 (2003) 189–208. Graphic on p. 191.

[19] I. Lancashire, "Cybertextuality", *TEXT Technology*, No. 2 (2004) 9.

[20] Lancashire, 8.

[21] Swaffar/Arens, 32

[22] B. Cope, B. and M. Kalantzis, eds., *Multiliteracies: Literacy Learning and the Design of Social Futures*. (London and New York: Routledge, 2000) 5.

[23] Cope/Kalantzis, 6.
[24] S.A. Selber, *Multiliteracies for a Digital Age*. (Carbondale: Southern Illinois University Press, 2004).
[25] Lancashire, 9–10.
[26] Lancashire, 10.
[27] Lancashire, 15.

11
ДРАМАТИЧЕСКОЕ ПРИСУТСТВИЕ В ПОВЕСТИ Л.Н. ТОЛСТОГО *"СМЕРТЬ ИВАНА ИЛЬИЧА"*

Andrew A. Donskov

На элемент драматического в прозе Толстого внимание исследователей обращено давно.[1] Театр как искусство условное часто казался писателю грубой имитацией жизни, и потому в его романах тема театра нередко становилась синонимом фальши. Вместе с тем театральные эпизоды и в «Войне и мире», и в «Анне Карениной», и в «Воскресении» неизменно появляются в наиболее напряженных местах повествования, становясь важными структурными узлами. Именно сила воздействия театра на человеческую душу обусловила самую тесную взаимосвязь размышлений Толстого над эстетическими проблемами драмы со стержневой идеей его наследия — идеей единения людей.

Замысел повести «Смерть Ивана Ильича» относится к лету 1881 года. Завершается работа 25 марта 1886 года. Ее самый активный и напряженный период приходится на январь–февраль этого года. В это же время Толстой отдает много сил драматической обработке легенды об Аггее и переложению для народного театра рассказа «Как чертенок краюшку выкупал». Тогда же, 13 февраля 1886 года, Толстой дает согласие актеру П.А. Денисенко на переделку народных рассказов в «драматическую форму» и говорит о своем желании «попытаться написать... прямо в этой форме».[2] Обработка легенды закончена не была.[3] Написаны 9 картин и начата 10-я. Переложение для народного театра состоялось. Под заглавием

«Первый винокур, или Как чертенок краюшку заслужил» пьеса была опубликована в издательстве «Посредник» и в том же 1886 году поставлена на сцене народного театра Фарфорового завода в селе Александровском под Петербургом.

Этот достаточно сильный драматический аспект творческих устремлений Толстого начала 1886 года находится в русле тех размышлений об искусстве, которые проявились в его «Письме к Н.А. Александрову» (1882). Одна из «болевых» тем «Письма…» — тема театра. Она обобщенно связывается Толстым прежде всего с именем Сары Бернар, поскольку ее недавние гастроли (конец 1881 года) в России, собиравшие огромное число зрителей в Одессе, Киеве, Москве и Петербурге,[4] стали поводом многочисленных рецензий и статей, поднимавших так либо иначе вопросы о задачах драматического искусства, о критериях ценности драматического представления, о духовном уровне исполнителя и зрителя.[5] Мнения критиков об игре Сары Бернар резко разделились, но большинство из них отмечало преобладание в игре французской актрисы технического мастерства над талантом. Зрительные залы были всегда переполнены. Но отношение зрителей (особенно московских) к спектаклям Сары Бернар в этот первый приезд ее в Россию было во многом недоуменным и прохладным, что отмечалось разными рецензентами. Эти гастроли послужили даже поводом для водевиля «Сара Бернар, или Бельэтаж № 2». Его автором был М. Лентовский, основатель театра оперетты в саду «Эрмитаж», иронично описавший и тщеславие актрисы, и преклонение перед ней части зрительного зала.

Куплеты Лентовского высмеивают похотливую натуру дельцов, подчеркивают нехватку смирения у людей, показывают нелепость пристрастия знати ко всему французскому и желание низших рангом подняться по социальной лестнице. Трагизм состоит в том, что эти люди избрали себе фальшивых идолов и преклоняются перед теми, кто заслуживает порицания. Считая главным в игре Сары Бернар желание поразить, удивить и произвести эффект, Лентовский более критичен по отношению к боготворящей ее публике, как это можно увидеть в следующих строках из его пьесы:

«ДРАМАТИЧЕСКОЕ ПРИСУТСТВИЕ»

Вот битком набита зала
На спектакль у Бернар,
Но из публики не мало
И таких найдется бар:
Знает толк в сигаре,
В сцене ж ничего...
Привлекает к Саре
Мода лишь его.

Муж, который терпеть не может Сару Бернар, вынужден выслушивать разглагольствования своей жены об актрисе и о решимости любой ценой увидеть ее:

Скажу тебе я откровенно:
Желаю видеть непременно
Фру-фру, Готье и Лекуврер.
Коль я не буду в бельэтаже
Одевши модный туалет...
Ах, страшно мне подумать даже,
Что скажет свет, что скажет свет?

Будучи практически уверенным, что Толстой не видел игры Бернар ни в 1892, ни в 1908 годах, можно с определенностью предположить, что он посещал ее спектакль в Москве в 1881 году. Толстой переехал в Москву осенью 1881 года (в повести Иван Ильич переехал в Москву в 1880-м), и поскольку мы знаем, что его жена Софья Андреевна смотрела спектакль с Бернар, вполне возможно, что Толстой тоже видел ее во время первых гастролей, открывшихся в Большом театре 26 ноября 1881 года. Хотя Толстой не оставил подобно Чехову отдельных заметок об актрисе, его высказывания о ней, встречающиеся в нескольких его произведениях, говорят о неодобрении им как самой актрисы, так и заблуждающейся публики, сделавшей из нее кумира. Изображение Сары Бернар подтверждает первоначальное впечатление, что она была введена в «Смерть Ивана Ильича» автором сознательно.[6]

Активность подступа к пересмотру эстетики театра в «Письме к Н.А. Александрову», открывающем цикл статей

Толстого об искусстве, достаточно ощутима: «Что добро в искусстве? И как провести черту не туманную, а строго определенную <между> развратом и добром в этой деятельности? <…> Нам уж нельзя говорить того, что говаривали эстетики: „Всякое наслаждение искусством возвышает душу, поэтому идите смотреть Сару Бернар и слушать Саразати. Прямой пользы это не принесет, но это возвысит вашу душу". Нам нельзя говорить этого, потому что мы знаем, что если Рубини и Бернар возвысят нашу душу… мы знаем, что значит такое возвышение. Это значит похоть и зло» (30, 212).

Вопрос о критериях ценности драматического представления оказывается в прямой связи с действенностью его нравственного начала. Способность пробить окно, просвет в область нравственного мира—вот основное требование Толстого к театральному представлению. И с этой точки зрения объектом внимания писателя становится зритель с его пониманием нравственного.

Конкретное событие января 1882 года—активное участие Толстого в переписи населения в Москве—столкнуло его с огромным числом людей—реальных или возможных зрителей недавно отшумевших гастролей Сары Бернар. Во второй главе трактата «Так что же нам делать?» (начат на грани января–февраля 1882 года) такой зритель—каждый, с кем встречается Толстой в тщетных поисках содействия делом и деньгами московской нищете. Симптоматично при этом, что в толстовский анализ этих встреч вторгается тема гастролей Сары Бернар: «…ни один из обещавших… свое содействие деньгами, ни один сам не определил суммы… и ни один не дал денег. Я отмечаю это потому, что когда люди дают деньги на то, чего сами желают, то, обыкновенно, торопятся дать деньги. На ложу Сары Бернар сейчас дают деньги в руки, чтобы закрепить дело» (25, 193–194).

Одновременно Толстой обращает внимание читателя и на другое: реальные и возможные зрители Сары Бернар в своей повседневной жизни исполняют актерские функции, подменяя истинное мнимым. Вот, в частности, описание мнимой благотворительности, представшее перед читателем, словно с подмостков сцены: «В последнем доме, в котором я был в этот день вечером, я случайно застал общество. <...> В большой гостиной, за двумя столами и лампами, сидели одетые в дорогие наряды и с дорогими украшениями дамы и девицы и одевали маленьких кукол; несколько молодых людей были тут же, около дам. Куклы, сработанные этими дамами, должны были быть разыграны в лотерею для бедных. Вид этой гостиной и людей, собравшихся в ней, очень неприятно поразил меня» (25, 194).

С иной формой «драматического присутствия» в публицистическом тексте мы сталкиваемся в трактате «О жизни», начатом в период работы над «Властью тьмы» (1886). Девятнадцатая глава трактата строится как полемический диалог двух типов сознания — заблудшего и разумного. Представления обоих оппонентов о человеке и мире развернуты и аргументированы. Вступление в диалог каждого из них сопровождается авторскими ремарками: «говорит разумное сознание», «отвечает возмущенное заблудшее сознание», «говорит заблудшее сознание» и т. д. (26, 371–373). Заблудшее сознание защищает общепринятые (привычные и удобные) представления об истине. Разумное сознание разрушает их. Вовлекаемый в сферу полемики читатель не может не соотнести мотивировок каждого из оппонентов. Что же касается итогов этого соотнесения, они, прежде всего, в рождении читательского размышления как начале всякого пути от существующего к должному.

И само заблудшее сознание, и развернутые авторские комментарии к его попыткам отстоять «инерцию жизни» в последних главах трактата, как в равной степени и разрушающие «инерцию жизни» аргументы сознания разумного, самым тесным образом связаны с эстетической реальностью повести «Смерть Ивана Ильича».[7]

Одним из основных структурных мотивов повести является сопоставление прошлого с настоящим, мотив «тогда» — «теперь». Граница, разделяющая «тогда» и «теперь», — случайное падение с лестницы Ивана Ильича при драпировке гардин: «... лучшие минуты приятной жизни казались теперь совсем не тем, чем казались они тогда. <...> Все казавшиеся тогда радости теперь на глазах его таяли и превращались во что-то ничтожное и часто гадкое» (26, 106). Умирающий Иван Ильич постоянно возвращается к этой границе: «И правда, что здесь, на этой гардине, я, как на штурме, потерял жизнь. Неужели? Как ужасно и как глупо! Это не может быть! Не может быть, но есть» (26, 95).

В словаре В. Даля указано несколько значений понятия гардина.[8] Одно из них — занавес. А именно занавес разделяет по традиции акты драматического представления, сменяющие друг друга.

Период жизни Ивана Ильича до этого «штурма» — это, по сути дела, первый акт драмы, в котором раскрывается путь жизни (один из его вариантов), отстаиваемый заблудшим сознанием: исполнение роли чиновника для особых поручений, позднее — судебного следователя, товарища прокурора, прокурора; разделение людей, зависевших от его произвола, на свидетелей и обвиняемых; выступления с публичными речами, неизменно приносившими успех; разделение человеческого и служебного; постоянство подражания общепринятому («приятному и приличному» — 26, 80).

«Ролевое» начало личности Ивана Ильича проявляется и в своей непосредственно актерской функции: рассказывая жене о падении с лестницы, герой «в лицах представил, как он полетел и испугал обойщика» (26, 80). Этот пассаж отнюдь не единственное свидетельство его актерских пристрастий. Размышляя о путях сближения дочери с молодым Петрищевым, Иван Ильич строит планы постановки домашнего спектакля. Театральными подмостками для этого спектакля должна была стать гостиная нового московского дома, все детали обустройства которой тщательно продумываются героем: «Засыпая, он представлял себе залу, какою она будет. Глядя на гостиную, еще неоконченную, он уже видел камин, экран, этажерку и эти стульчики разбросанные, эти блюды и тарелки по стенам и бронзы, когда они все станут по местам. <...> В заседаниях у него бывали минуты рассеянности: он задумывался о том, какие карнизы на гардины, прямые или подобранные. Он так был занят этим, что сам часто возился, переставлял даже мебель, и сам перевешивал гардины» (26, 79). В один из моментов обустройства этой гостиной и опускается занавес, отделяющий долгий период безраздельной власти сознания заблудшего от краткого, но активнейшего по своим духовным извлечениям временного отрезка, суть которого — в дискредитации и разрушении позиций сознания заблудшего сознанием разумным.

С чего начинается этот процесс? Он начинается с изменения роли героя. Из судьи Иван Ильич превращается в подсудимого, из актера — в зрителя. Но это изменение его амплуа отнюдь не сходно с теми переходами от роли исполнителя (актера) к роли зрителя (и наоборот), с которыми читатель встречается в трактате «Так что же нам делать?». С позиций судьи («тогда») Иван Ильич не воспринимал общепринятые поведенческие установки как ролевые, с позиций подсудимого («теперь») именно это начало в ежедневном самовыявлении человека с болезненной настойчивостью высвечивается герою «ходом мысли», «ходом воспоминаний», «внутренним голосом». Вот первое посещение героем врача: «Все было, как он ожидал; все было так, как всегда делается. И ожидание, и важность напускная, докторская, ему знакомая, та самая, которую он знал в себе в суде, и постукиванье, и выслушиванье, и вопросы, требующие определенные вперед и очевидно ненужные ответы, и значительный вид... Все было точно так же, как в суде. Как он в суде делал вид над подсудимыми, так точно над ним знаменитый доктор делал тоже вид» (26, 83–84).

Спектакль в декорированной гостиной не состоялся. Но состоялся другой — в комнате умирающего Ивана Ильича.

Восьмая, ключевая глава повести построена по аналогии с драматическим представлением. В ней соблюдено единство места, времени и действия. Основные события главы — четыре визита к больному, комната которого превращается, по сути дела, в театральные подмостки. О первом посетителе — «докторе обыкновенном» — извещает звонок (внешний знак спектакля). Уже первый визит превращается в театральное зрелище: служебная маска, надетая доктором раз навсегда, прослушивания и простукивания, совершавшиеся сотни раз. Ролевая (актерская) функция второго посетителя — жены — подчеркивается авторской ремаркой: «Ее отношение к нему и его болезни все то же. Как доктор выработал себе отношение к больным, которое он не мог уже снять, так она выработала одно отношение к нему — то, что он не делает чего-то того, что нужно, и сам виноват… и не могла уже снять этого отношения к нему» (26, 102). Третий посетитель — «доктор знаменитый» — механически дублирует все сделанное «доктором обыкновенным». Наконец, четвертый визит — семейный. Внешние знаки спектакля здесь особенно настойчивы: «… вошла Прасковья Федоровна… <…> Вошла дочь… <…> Вошел Федор Петрович… <…> …вполз и гимназистик… Все сели… <…> Федор Петрович взглянул на Ивана Ильича и замолк. Другие взглянули и замолкли. <…> Все встали, простились и ушли» (26, 103–105). У постели больного их собирает предстоящее посещение театра.

Ложа на спектакль Сары Бернар была взята давно. На этом сам герой настоял еще «тогда», объясняя свое желание необходимостью для детей «воспитательного эстетического наслаждения» (26, 103). «Теперь», когда вопрос о жизни и смерти стал для него единственным «реальным вопросом», герой становится зрителем другого спектакля. Появление каждого из посетителей воспринимается им как выход на сцену очередного актера в тщательно продуманном костюме: «…вошла Прасковья Федоровна… с толстыми, подтянутыми грудями и с следами пудры на лице. <…> ее наряд оскорбил его»; «Вошла дочь, разодетая, с обнаженным молодым телом, тем телом, которое так заставляло страдать его. А она его выставляла»; «Вошел и Федор Петрович во фраке, завитой à la Capoul с длинной жилистой шеей, обложенной плотно белым воротничком, с огромной белой грудью и обтянутыми сильными ляжками в узких черных штанах, с одной натянутой белой перчаткой на руке и с клаком» (26, 103–104).

Все участники четвертого визита остаются наедине с читателем: автор-повествователь практически перестает быть посредником между ними.[9] Читатель становится непосредственным зрителем происходящего на его глазах столкновения двух типов сознания — заблудшего и начавшего активно пробуждаться. В этом столкновении открытый полемический диалог еще отсутствует. Он впереди, в трактате «О жизни». Хотя подспудно именно внутренним его присутствием и объясняется гнет общего молчания, ослабевающий порою лишь призрачно: пререкания матери и дочери о потерянном бинокле, их спор о лучшей роли Сары Бернар, упоминание пьесы «Адриенна Лекуврер», разговор уходящих в театр об «изяществе и реальности» (26, 104) игры французской актрисы.

Введение этой сцены с походом в театр является одним из значимых моментов в повести. Ирония ее состоит в том, что это была инициатива самого умирающего. Чтобы еще глубже прочувствовать эту ситуацию, необходимо вспомнить, что Толстой вообще не любил театра и сравнивал сценическую фальшь с фальшивыми мотивами зрителей. Он не мог сказать ничего положительного о Саре Бернар. Ни одна русская пьеса не донесла бы так остро мысль автора, как эта, где все иностранное: сама пьеса «Адриенна Лекуврер»[10], игравшаяся на французском языке, актеры, место действия, костюмы, декорации. Более тонким является тот момент, что сценарий, написанный Э. Скрибом и Э. Легуве, основывался на истории жизни и деятельности реальной актрисы Адриенны Лекуврер.

Другими словами, семья Ивана Ильича (по ироничному стечению обстоятельств — в соответствии с его же желанием) идет в театр, не зная, насколько на самом деле хороша игра Сары Бернар (он и сам никогда ее не видел), но с нескрываемым теперь осуждением и новоприобретенным знанием того, что же является реальным. В то время, как он лежит при смерти, они идут смотреть иностранную актрису, играющую главную роль в пьесе о жизни и карьере другой иностранной актрисы. Неудивительно, что Ивану Ильичу все это представляется одиозным, и когда они уходят, он посылает за Герасимом — единственным светлым персонажем во всей истории.

Понятие «реальность», неожиданно высвеченное автором-повествователем в словесном арсенале сознания заблудшего, ставит перед читателем проблему самоопределения между общепринятым (понимание реального окружением героя) и должным (понимание реального, в котором утверждается герой). Острота этой проблемы тем более ощутима, что сам читатель в недавнем прошлом был зрителем на спектаклях Сары Бернар (вероятность этого достаточно велика) и в силу этого становится фактически участником последнего визита к умирающему.

Стремительный рост диалогизированности внутренних монологов героя в последующих главах повести делает проблему самоопределения для читателя все более значимой и побуждает его к полемическому диалогу с сознанием заблудшим.

This is an expanded version of the article previously published in *Russkaia literatura* no. 3 (1993).

Notes

[1] См. об этом: И. Вишневская, «Театр в прозе Толстого», *В мире Толстого* (Москва, 1978) 351–385; Л. М. Лотман, «Эстетические принципы драматургии Толстого», *Л.Н. Толстой и русская литературно-общественная мысль* (Ленинград, 1979) 239–242; Н. Г. Михновец, *Взаимодействие повествовательных и драматических начал в творчестве Л.Н. Толстого 80-х годов*. Автореф. канд. дисс. (Ленинград, 1990) и др. В общеэстетическом плане проблема драматизации повествовательного текста поставлена в кн.: Joseph Warren Beach. *The Twentieth Century Novel* (New York, 1943) 146–148, 157–162.

[2] Л. Н. Толстой, *Полное собрание сочинений в 90 томах* (Москва-Ленинград, 1934). т. 63, 328. Далее ссылки на это издание в тексте (указывается том и страница).

[3] О причинах этого смотрите: Л. Д. Опульская, *Л.Н. Толстой. Материалы к биографии с 1886 по 1892 год* (Москва, 1979) 28–29.

[4] См об этом: Н. Леонтьевский, «Три приезда Сары Бернар в Россию», *Театр* №2 (1970) 142–143. Гастроли Сары Бернар в Москве в Большом театре продолжались с 26 ноября по 7 декабря 1881 года. Московские зрители увидели «Даму с камелиями» А. Дюма, «Адриенну Лекуврер» Э. Скриба и Э. Легуве, «Фру-Фру» Мельяка и Галеви (см. об этом в комментариях к фельетону А.П. Чехова «Опять о Саре Бернар» в кн.: А. П. Чехов, *Полное собрание сочинений и писем в 30 томах*. (Москва, 1979) т. 16. 397, 401.

[5] С большой полнотой отзывы о первых гастролях Сары Бернар в России представлены в комментариях к фельетонам А.П. Чехова «Сара Бернар», «Опять о Саре Бернар» в книге А. П. Чехов, Полн. собр. соч. и писем: В 30 т. Соч. Т. 16. С. 392–394, 397–400. См. об этом: Donskov, Andrew. "A note on Tolstoj, Sarah Bernhardt, and the Death of Ivan Il'ich" in *Studia Phraseologica et alia*. (München, Verlag Otto Sagner, 1992). 67–79.

⁶ См. об этом: Andrew Donskov, *Mixail Lentovskiy and the Russian theatre* (Michigan, 1985) 169–215.

⁷ «Первичность» эстетического уяснения идей в творческой практике Толстого и «вторичность» их логического оформления были впервые показаны Е.Н. Куприяновой (на материале «Анны Карениной» и «Исповеди»). Смотрите Е. Н. Куприянова, *Эстетика Л.Н. Толстого* (Москва-Ленинград, 1966) 249–252.

⁸ В. Даль, *Толковый словарь живого великорусского языка в 4 томах* (Москва, 1978) т. 1. 344.

⁹ Смотрите Михновец 5.

¹⁰ Основной темой пьесы является любовь Адриенны к Морису де Саксу—сыну польского короля—в то время, как двигателем сюжета служит ревность принцессы де Буиллон (бывшей любовницы графа де Сакса). Адриенна Лекуврер (1672–1730) была блестящей актрисой в Комеди Франсез, выступавшей до самой своей преждевременной смерти в ведущих ролях пьес Расина, Корнеля и Вольтера. Вольтер («La Mort de Mlle Lecouvreur» и «Harangue», *Oeuvres de Voltaire* (Paris: Chez Lefèvre, 1833) vol. 12, 29–31 и vol. 37, 95–95) отзывался о ней как об актрисе, которая, можно сказать, изобрела искусство коммуникации сердцем—как раз то качество, которое, по мнению некоторых критиков и зрителей, отсутствовало в преимущественно техническом исполнении Сары Бернар. Ходили неподтвержденные, но упорные слухи, что Адриенна была отравлена ревнивой принцессой. Скриб использовал эту версию ранней смерти Адриенны как основу для своей пьесы; он особо акцентировал сцену смерти, где Бернар (которая просто обожала такие сцены), по отзывам критиков, часто переигрывала. Смотрите Л. Н. Толстой, *Полное собрание сочинений*, т. 26. 679–691.

About the Authors

Angelika Arend was born and educated in Germany. Upon completion, in 1968, of a *Staatsexamen* in English and Russian Language and Literature at the Universität Köln, she left Germany and worked as a High-School teacher of German in Llanelli (Wales) and London (England). In 1971 she emigrated to Canada and resumed her academic studies in the field of German Language and Literature. She received a Master's degree from Carleton University in 1977, and a Doctorate from Oxford University in 1983. In that same year, she was offered a position as Assistant Professor of German at the University of Victoria, where she climbed the academic ladder to Full Professor and retired in June 2007. She is the author of 4 scholarly books and numerous articles in the field of German and German-Canadian literature. She has also published 5 volumes of poetry and one book of prose fiction. As a trained singer, she has conducted German-singing choirs for 20 years. Her website can be found at www.angelika-arend.com.

Andrew A. Donskov, a Fellow of the Royal Society of Canada, is a Distinguished University Professor and Director of the Slavic Research Group at the University of Ottawa. Before coming to Ottawa in 1981, he taught at the University of Waterloo and the University of Victoria. The recipient of two Pushkin medals from the Russian government for his research and many publications (as author and editor) on Tolstoy, he is the only scholar from outside Russia to be appointed to the Editorial Board of the new 100-volume edition of Tolstoy's works currently being released by the Russian Academy of Sciences. In 1992 he was elected a Full Member of the Petrovskaia Academy of Arts & Sciences (*Petri Primi Academia Scientiarum et Artium*) in St. Petersburg. Dr. Donskov is currently writing a critical study of *My life* — an extensive autobiographical work by Leo Tolstoy's wife of 48 years, Sofia Andreevna Tolstaya; he is also supervising its translation and publication in English.

Peter Gölz is Associate Professor and Chair of the Department of Germanic and Slavic Studies at the University of Victoria. He has published in the areas of German literature and film, and German as a Second Language. His recent research interests have focused on horror studies, in particular vampires on film, and he is presently working on a study of the three Nosferatus in Murnau, Herzog, and Merhige. Dr. Gölz is also President of the Canadian Association of University Teachers of German, and founder and President of HyperEdvantage Language Series.

Želimir Bob Juričić is Professor Emeritus in the Department of Germanic and Slavic Studies at the University of Victoria. The author of five books and many scholarly articles, Dr. Juričić has taught for over thirty years at UBC, Lester Pearson College of the Pacific, and the University of Victoria in the field of Russian and Croatian languages, literatures, and cultures.

Peter Liddell is Professor Emeritus of German, University of Victoria. His research interests have centred on second language acquisition, particularly computer assisted language learning, and computers in higher education. He was founding Academic Director of the University's Humanities Computing and Media Centre (1986-2007), a centre supporting research and teaching in language learning and digital humanities.

Born and raised in Moscow region, Russia, **Julia Rochtchina** graduated from the M.V. Lomonosov Moscow State University and got her PhD in Russian Studies from the same university. Her specialty is Russian as a Foreign Language. Julia moved to Canada together with her husband in 2001. Since 2002 she has been teaching Russian at UVic. She takes a special interest in Russian national culture, contemporary Russian, language learning and information technology. She has published articles on contemporary Russian morphology and developed an online tutorial www.russianforeveryone.com.
Amy Safarik received her MA in Russian from the University of

Waterloo. Her thesis, "A Literature of Conscience: Yevtushenko's Post-Stalin Poetry," focuses on the political and cultural significance of Yevtushenko's poetry of the Thaw period. Her current research interests include Soviet prison camp literature and memoirs.

Megan Swift is an Assistant Professor in the Department of Germanic and Slavic Studies at the University of Victoria. She is a specialist in modernist Russian literature and the cultural mythology of St. Petersburg. Her scholarly articles on these topics have appeared in peer-reviewed journals in Canada, Europe and Australia.

Helga Thorson is an Associate Professor in the Department of Germanic and Slavic Studies at the University of Victoria. Her teaching and research interests include foreign language writing processes, late nineteenth- and early twentieth-century German and Austrian literature, German colonialism, history of medicine, Holocaust studies, and women's literature. Her dissertation, *Re-Negotiating Borders: Responses of German and Austrian Middle-Class Women Writers to Medical Discourses on Sex, Gender, and Sexuality at the Turn of the Century*, was awarded the first annual Women in German dissertation prize.

Regan Naomi Treewater is a PhD candidate in the Modern Languages and Cultural Studies Department at the University of Alberta. She received her BA in Russian from the University of Victoria where she took every class she could taught by Dr. Galichenko. Regan studied at Saint Petersburg State University in Russia for six months before completing her MA at the University of Waterloo. Her primary research deals with Jewish culture in Eastern Europe, as well as Russian immigration to Israel. She hopes to become a professor of Russian studies.

Serhy Yekelchyk is an Associate Professor in the Department of Germanic and Slavic Studies at the University of Victoria. He is a specialist in the history of culture in Stalin-era Ukraine and is the author of *Stalin's Empire of Memory: Russian-Ukrainian Relations in the Soviet Historical Imagination* (University of Toronto Press, 2004), as well as the award-winning *Ukraine: Birth of a Modern Nation* (Oxford University Press, 2007).

www.ingramcontent.com/pod-product-compliance
Lightning Source LLC
Chambersburg PA
CBHW020758160426
43192CB00006B/364